Police as Problem Solvers

Police as Problem Solvers

SECOND EDITION

**HOW FRONTLINE WORKERS
CAN PROMOTE ORGANIZATIONAL
AND COMMUNITY CHANGE**

Hans Toch and J. Douglas Grant

American Psychological Association • Washington, DC

Published by
American Psychological Association
750 First Street, NE
Washington, DC 20002
www.apa.org

To order	In the U.K., Europe, Africa, and the
APA Order Department	Middle East, copies may be ordered
P.O. Box 92984	from
Washington, DC 20090-2984	American Psychological Association
Tel: (800) 374-2721	3 Henrietta Street
Direct: (202) 336-5510	Covent Garden, London
Fax: (202) 336-5502	WC2E 8LU England
TDD/TTY: (202) 336-6123	
Online: www.apa.org/books/	
E-mail: order@apa.org	

Typeset in Palatino by World Composition Services, Inc., Sterling, VA

Printer: Edwards Brothers, Ann Arbor, MI
Cover Designer: Berg Design, Albany, NY
Project Manager: Debbie Hardin, Carlsbad, CA

The opinions and statements published are the responsibility of the authors, and such opinions and statements do not necessarily represent the policies of the American Psychological Association.

Library of Congress Cataloging-in-Publication Data

Toch, Hans
    Police as problem solvers : how frontline workers can promote organizational and community change / Hans Toch and J. Douglas Grant.—2nd ed.
        p. cm.
    Includes index.
    ISBN 1-59147-150-8
    1. Police. 2. Problem solving. 3. Police social work. 4. Police—United states. I. Title.

HV7921.T636   2005
362—dc22   2004006035

British Library Cataloguing-in-Publication Data
A CIP record is available from the British Library.

Printed in the United States of America
Second edition

Contents

Foreword

This is an important volume. In it, Hans Toch describes the evolution of police thinking and strategies, offering examples and insights about what works and what does not. As Toch points out, the scholarly work that for the past quarter century has been cited most frequently as the greatest single influence among those who think about this subject has been Herman Goldstein's "Improving Policing: A Problem-Oriented Approach" (1979).

The major contributions of Goldstein's piece have been two-fold. The first is its successful argument that police needed to begin measuring their performance by reference to outcomes, rather than purely by statistical measures of activity. We should, Goldstein urged, assess the effectiveness of police strategies related to street crime in terms of whether the streets are safe, for example, rather than simply in terms of the number of arrests and other police enforcement actions.

The second is that it has pulled together in a single cogent argument the disparate trains of thought and logic underlying the efforts of many reform-oriented scholars and practitioners who, dissatisfied with policing as it was, were engaged in what in retrospect looks an awful lot like problem-oriented policing approaches. Goldstein identified principles for systematic problem solving in policing and made it possible to generalize and replicate what was already happening in an ad hoc fashion. Certainly, as readers will discover in this volume, the problem-oriented policing label applies to the late 1960s and early 1970s work of Hans Toch, J. D. Grant, and R. T. Galvin in Oakland. As I look back on the great reforms in the New York City Police Department initiated during 1970 to 1973 under Commissioner Patrick V. Murphy, it is clear that they also were applications of the approach to which Goldstein later gave a name. As Toch and his colleagues did in Oakland, Murphy identified the sources of many of the New York Police Department's problems and, instead of perpetuating them by responding to them in the same tired old ways, addressed them by eliminating or mitigating their causes.[1]

Thus, Goldstein's thinking may be seen to emerge from several independent strains. In concert with the earlier work of Toch and others, it points to a major road mark in police thinking rather than a turn to a totally new direction. One school of thought that has followed from Goldstein's work has come to be known as "broken-windows policing," after a 1982 *Atlantic Monthly* article written by James Q. Wilson and George L. Kelling. Wilson and Kelling argued that the best way to keep streets free of major crime was for the police to pay careful attention to minor law violations and indications of decay and neglect. In doing so, Wilson and Kelling posited, the police would keep streets and other public places from a downward slide in which they were abandoned by the law-abiding and left to the law violators. When this happened, according to Wilson and Kelling, places that had formerly been merely displeasing would become crime-ridden. At any police conference or gathering of police scholars, one can pick up on the great influence of this school of thought as terms such as *zero-tolerance* and *quality of life* are used to discuss the latest police initiatives in some town or other.[2]

---

[1] For years, the New York Police Department had been plagued with the problem of corruption in enforcement of gambling laws and regulatory ordinances, such as construction codes and blue laws that required many businesses to be closed on Sundays. Instead of responding to this solely by tracking down and making examples of corrupt cops, Murphy also changed the ways in which these laws could be enforced, greatly limiting officers' discretion.

[2] New York is one city frequently associated with the term *zero tolerance*. None of my New York Police Department colleagues, however, can recall using this phrase to describe the department's philosophies or operations. Indeed, most New York police officials consciously avoid it because they recognize that it is an impossible standard and, more important, because of its negative connotations. Instead, in scanning the literature, one finds that it is most often used pejoratively, by authors who classify all of the New York Police Department's recent strategic innovations under this broad heading and who then go on to express doubts that it has produced the results attributed to these strategies by New York City officials (see, e.g., Bowling, 1999; Dixon & Coffin, 1999; Greene, 1999; Marshall, 1999; McArdle & Erzen, 2001).

A second presumed offshoot of Goldstein's work is *community policing*, which some apparently believe to be incompatible with the aggressive types of policing espoused by Wilson and Kelling and their adherents. I have always been puzzled about why this should be so. Indeed, when I began to study for police promotional examinations back in the 1960s, I picked up on a theme that ran through all the literature in the exam bibliographies and that proved to be a great guide to answering multiple-choice questions:

- ☐ There is no such thing as a police problem.
- ☐ Instead, there are only community problems that the police are paid to assist the community in solving.
- ☐ As a consequence, there is no problem that the police can solve alone.
- ☐ Instead, the solutions to the problems the police are paid to confront can be found only by working with the community, through both formal and informal relationships.

The moral for test-taking purposes was that any answer choice suggesting that the police could solve a problem on its own was likely to be incorrect and that any answer choice suggesting that problems were best solved by police–community cooperation was likely to be correct. More important, for day-to-day operational matters, this theme suggested that the best and most effective cops were those who worked to build relationships with citizens all across their beats and sectors. It also meant that the best and most successful commanders were those who were smart enough to become trusted and credible community figures.

Thus, I have always been a bit confused about precisely what the phrase *community policing* has meant and why it is different from what I was taught as a rookie 40 years ago by the older cops I most admired. I am also puzzled about why *community policing* and *broken windows* are so frequently regarded as incompatible. Indeed, I do not believe that broken-windows policing can even be effective unless officers apply it in close cooperation with the community. When they do so, they practice a high form of problem-oriented policing. When they do not, they simply apply their own standards to the quality-of-life conditions that are at the core of broken-windows policing and serve only to alienate much of the public.

Police history has moved fast in the past generation. Indeed, it is even fair to say that modern policing has its roots only in the wave of protest and external and internal examination that began in the 1960s. Before that, policing was, by and large, a seat-of-the-pants operation devoid of any real theoretical underpinning or empirical basis. Only since the 1960s have phrases such as *administrative rule-making, accountability, directed patrol, proactive policing, differential response, representativeness,* and *diversity in the ranks* become part of the language of policing. Since the 1960s, things have evolved quickly so that, however accurate a snapshot may represent reality at a point in time, events and evolution quickly may date it.

One term that has become a subject of discussion only in the past decade is *Compstat,* the process developed by the New York City Police Department in the early 1990s. The initiation of this process was a revolutionary change in analysis of crime and other conditions demanding police attention and—most important—in the immediacy with which it held commanders accountable for anticipating and responding to them. In its first few years, both the process and the individuals who ran it have been described as highly volatile. Over the past couple of years, however, I have been a regular attendee at Compstat, and it appears to me that both the process and the participants have evolved and matured. The focus on numbers remains, but the data for which commanders are called to account now include measures such as the number of citizens' complaints received by officers and the percentage of officers who appear to record no measurable indications that they even showed up for work.

All is not sweetness and light, however, and there remains in Compstat an element of challenge and confrontation. To me, however, the degree of confrontation seems no greater than what I have seen in academic meetings and doctoral dissertation defenses at which scholars are asked tough questions about the issues they have tackled and their methods for addressing them. Certainly, I have never witnessed any attack on a Compstat participant's integrity or good faith, a statement I cannot make about my experiences in academic meetings and conferences.

Nor, to my knowledge, has any official recently been demoted for performing poorly at Compstat. Instead, the reverse seems to be true. Those who have excelled at devising strategies and at explaining why they do what they do have moved rapidly up the ranks and now run Compstat's operations.

This is not to say that recent visitors to Compstat have not been surprised by what they have seen. There may be three reasons for this. First, I suspect that many visitors have been taken aback because, perhaps excepting those who report directly to elected officials, it has been rare that police officials have been asked tough questions about the ways in which they deploy their resources. It certainly is not rare for police managers to challenge officers about what they have done or failed to do, but many observers seem surprised—or even affronted—that the New York Police Department challenges its commanders in the same way. Second, many visitors may have a view of police middle management that does not apply to New York City. The precinct commanders who undergo questioning at Compstat are a group of 76, whose commands include nearly 20,000 officers serving a population of more than 8 million. On average, therefore, each of these officials oversees a force of about 260 (that costs about $30 million), which is charged to provide policing services to a community of more than 100,000 citizens. In most places, these would be considered top executive responsibilities rather than middle-management duties, so that some might argue it is appropriate to put tough questions to such officials. Third, it also is useful to take into account the setting of Compstat: It is New York City, where what natives regard as candor and directness has long been interpreted by others as rudeness.

But the most interesting aspect of Compstat is that, whether alone or, more realistically, in conjunction with other, largely empirically derived strategies, it seems to have worked. For several years now, crime rates in New York City have declined precipitously and regularly show up at the bottom of the FBI's annual rosters of big cities. For the first six months of 2003, for example, New York's index crime rate ranked 194th—between Ann Arbor, Michigan, and Orange, California—among the 210 reporting cities with populations greater than 100,000. Maybe "rudeness" within the ranks has desirable results on the streets:

To be particularly direct and candid, maybe some of the police officials who reject Compstat because it offends their sensibilities would be well advised to look again at whether the benefits of putting police commanders on the spot include reduced crime and more civil streets.

Clearly, therefore, I disagree with Toch's assessment of Compstat. That does not make him wrong and me right. Instead, I think that we have looked at that particular elephant not only from different perspectives but also at different times. As I have learned in the 33 years since I first became Toch's student in graduate school, his perspectives and analyses always are intellectually challenging, profound, and practical. This book is no exception: It is likely that no reader will agree with everything Toch has to say, but every reader will come away with something to think about and with an appreciation for one of the great contributors to police scholarship and practice.

James J. Fyfe, PhD
John Jay College of Criminal Justice,
City University of New York
and
Deputy Commissioner, Training,
New York City Police Department

Preface

This book is about an innovative approach that lets members of progressive organizations function as applied scientists and problem solvers. This means that in such organizations work becomes more mindful. Decisions can be made based on inventories of information and analysis of data—couched tentatively, to be sure, subject to ratification through additional study. At the working level, planning and action can become linked, and the organization thereby becomes problem-oriented rather than crisis-reactive.

It is ironic that this problem-oriented approach has evolved most explicitly and self-consciously in policing. We tend to think of police in terms of brawn rather than brains, and we may conceive of police officers as spending time wrestling with suspects and engaged in hot pursuits of fleeing felons. Police are perceived as the embodiment of blind reactivity, and yet an applied social-scientific focus on work has sprung up and taken root within the ranks of police.

It is of course possible that the very reactivity of police work has invited a focus on proactivity and study of work-related problems. Highly educated white-collar workers (e.g., in education and health-related professions) are already presumed to operate in this fashion, taking actions based on analyses of relevant information.

In thinking along these lines, we undersell the nature of police work. We forget that the challenges facing policing are especially serious and complex, creating incentives for review and reform. Police plausibly gravitated to problem solving because they have problems to address. It is the police who deal most consistently and immediately with the varied and disruptive symptoms of societal problems.

It is therefore not really surprising that a profession often categorized as a muscle-bound blue-collar occupation has obliterated the distinction between everyday work and academia, dramatizing the continuity of knowledge acquisition and application. It is police officers themselves who may find this most surprising. They certainly do not think of themselves as social scientists and will warmly agree with observers who see them ill-prepared for research endeavors. For that matter, police officers do not think of themselves as social workers, social reformers, or change agents, although they are accorded these roles and are strategically positioned to exercise them.

In the face of such considerations, problem-oriented policing has been disseminated rapidly and institutionalized, not only in this country but also abroad, and serves as an encouraging example of self-generated organizational reform by emphasizing the development of rank-and-file employees and exemplifying applied social science in action. Police are thus accomplishing what organization-development gurus can only dream about.

These gurus are, however, able to support the police, and do so with increasing frequency, by facilitating problem-solving meetings, conducting training sessions, and running evaluation studies. Help is often provided by academic researchers who review problem-related literature and render technical assistance to research efforts by officers. The latter contribution is illustrated in the chapters that follow.

As befits a publication of the American Psychological Association, this is a person-centered book, which views the problem-oriented movement from the trenches, where battles—not wars—are waged. In this book I am concerned with what an erstwhile police colleague fondly dubbed the "nitty gritty" and what others have called the "human equation." The core of my interest and that of my colleagues is thus the experience of being problem-oriented and how one engenders this experience. Coincidentally, our concern happens to fit a philosophical approach fashionable in management circles that values thinking and planning of frontline workers as a vehicle for achieving quality productivity. The jobs of such frontline personnel are deemed to be expanded, and this book focuses on this expansion of the job.

Outsiders have long been obsessed with the need to "control" the police and to keep officers from abusing their power. The same goal can be accomplished through reforms in which the stress is on behavioral self-assessment and self-management.

We see professional judgment exercised in any profession when individuals are trusted to think about what they do after studying the results of their own efforts in the context of the best available information. Workers, including police officers, can do a more responsible job by making the most informed decisions possible, and from experience it is clear that police can find reflecting about the way they conduct their business meaningful and enhancing.

This book is addressed to those interested in the process of organizational change in settings in which a problem-oriented focus may be relevant. I am interested, therefore, in making the process of problem-oriented activity come alive and in conveying some sense of what such activity means to those who engage in its exercise.

An experiment I have reported in some detail in this book is an exercise in problem-oriented reform conducted before the term was invented. A second project represents an extension of the approach, as it is currently understood.

This book was born in 1991 from an earlier edition of the same name, and there have been other carryovers beyond the title. Three of five detailed case-study chapters in the book have been retained; five other chapters reappear in revised or amended form. The rest of the book is new, but in the process of creation, I have tried to remain faithful to the perspective of the original. A compelling reason for doing this was to ensure that the book continue to reflect the thinking of the late J. Douglas Grant, whose friendship and contribution I miss. Doug Grant was a charismatic psychologist who provided the inspiration for the first version of *Police as Problem Solvers*. I hope this second edition of the book can serve as a memorial to his work.

Acknowledgments

This volume is a revised version of a book by the same name, and I am grateful to Kluwer Academic/Plenum Publishers for declaring the original out of stock and releasing it for republication. In the following, I am indebted for permission to reprint excerpts from their works to the American Sociological Association and Egon Bittner (1967) for text used from "The Police on Skid Row: A Study in Peace Keeping," published in *American Sociological Review*, and to the Police Executive Research Forum and John Eck for excerpts from Eck and Spelman, *Solving Problems: Problem-Oriented Policing in Newport News* (1987).

Parts of chapter 8 of this book have been adapted (with permission) from J. D. Grant, J. Grant, and H. Toch, "Police–Citizen Conflicts and Decisions to Arrest," in V. J. Konecni and E. B. Ebbesen (Eds.), *The Criminal Justice System: A Social–Psychological Analysis* (1982). Other portions of chapter 8 and chapters 6 and 7 are drawn from H. Toch, J. D. Grant, and R. T. Galvin, *Agents of Change: A Study in Police Reform* (1975). Chapter 2 was largely derived from an article titled "The Democratization of Policing in the U.S., 1895–1973," in *Police Forum* (Toch, 1997), and is adapted with permission courtesy of the Academy of Criminal Justice Sciences.

The work described in chapters 6 thorough 8 was supported under a training grant (MH 12068) from the Center for Studies in Crime and Delinquency of the National Institute of Mental Health. The project dealt with in chapter 9 was underwritten by a grant (93-IJ-CX-K013) from the National Institute of Justice. My colleagues and I are inestimably in debt to the enlightened administrators of two police departments (the New York State Police and the Police of the City of Oakland, California) who served as our hosts, and most of all to the problem-oriented officers in these departments who became our friends and colleagues.

I am as usual beholden to the merry crew at the American Psychological Association (APA Books), and of course to Mary

Lynn Skutley and Judy Nemes. Debbie Hardin kept the project on track. Among those who helped along the way are my colleagues Robert Worden and Piyusha Singh. My wise and meticulous peer reviewer—much more than a mere peer—was John Eck. He will know how much he contributed to this book. Finally, I can never repay my debt to Karen Silinsky, who is a virtuoso at translating scribbles into computer printouts.

Police as Problem Solvers

1

The Idea of
Problem-Oriented Policing

Problem-oriented policing was officially born in April 1979, as a phrase in the subtitle of an essay. The author of the article, Herman Goldstein, was a redoubtable academic, but his essay was the kind of prescription scholars often advance with no expectation of impact. If Goldstein's concept took hold, it was because it was immensely timely and made sense to many students of policing and administrators of police departments.

Goldstein started with some history: He noted that police chiefs had for decades tried to shape up casually run police organizations in the name of "professionalization." The ideal officer had been seen by the chiefs as clean-cut, educated, corruption-free, quick to obey orders, and technically up to date. The department in which such an officer worked was presumed to look well managed, busy, and efficient.[1] By the same token, there was little concern with whether any of this well-oiled competence translated into tangible benefits for the communities that the police ostensibly served. The goal of the administrators was seemingly to improve means for the achievement of unexamined end results.

Goldstein (1979) implied that the disjuncture between enhanced means and neglected ends became obvious with attainment of efficiency. It was one thing for a sloppy and inefficient organization to not accomplish much and quite another for a model enterprise to do similarly badly. Awareness of limited impact was also painful in such instances because of assumptions that had been made and taken for granted, which new research findings could cast in doubt.

A case in point pertains to the practice of randomized, motorized patrolling, which takes up most of the time many police officers spend at work. The practice was first instituted—as were many others—to take advantage of technological advances.

Before 1920, police officers walked through neighborhoods on (flat)foot, getting to know residents and settings in which they lived and worked.[2] The advent of the automobile and telephone made it possible to place officers in cars, contacting them when they were needed and directing them to the sites of complaints.[3] Dispersal of motorized units placed any unit in rough proximity to any call, thus ensuring rapid response, and even (on well-publicized occasions) to a sensational arrest. The motorized officers cruised the streets between calls, hoping for a complaint that would direct them to a "good bust." A consequence of this avocation, which was at first disregarded, was that "by staying in their cars, patrol officers lost contact with the residents of their beats who were neither offenders nor victims. Their knowledge of community problems became more and more limited" (Eck & Spelman, 1987a, p. 13).

At first, there was no reason for the officers to stay in cars between calls.[4] Randomized patrol gave them a reason. The reason was a hoped-for intimidating effect of police presence and a presumed capacity for strategic surveillance. The visibility of police cars was said to deter contemplated crime, and eyeballing by officers was presumed to pinpoint offenses in the process of being committed. Randomization was of relevance to both these goals, because malefactors would be unable to predict when a randomly cruising officer (or at times, two officers) would appear.

The shining benefits of preventive patrol looked self-evident until they were called into question by an experiment in Kansas City (Kelling, Pate, Dieckman, & Brown, 1974), which suggested that police presence might not make much difference in practice, either to citizens or offenders. In the experiment, doubling or tripling the number of police cars on patrol did not affect neighborhood crime rates or attitudes toward police. Worse, after the experimenters discontinued patrols altogether, there was no increase in crime or demand from the public for restoration of service. These findings were buttressed by other studies that showed that few serious crimes are committed where officers could physically observe them (Eck & Spelman, 1987a; Kansas City Police Department, 1980; Skogan & Antunes, 1979).

A related question pertained to what the public regards as good police work. Goldstein felt that the criteria the public uses have to do with the outcome of police services the consumers expected. He wrote the following:

> Those concerned about battered wives, for example, could not care less whether the police who respond to such calls operate with one or two officers in a car, whether the officers are short or tall, or whether they have a college education. Their attention is on what the police do for the battered wife. (1979, p. 240)

Goldstein's point was that citizens are not impressed by efficiency of operation but by effectiveness of response. What the citizens want is police activity that addresses the concerns they are experiencing and ameliorates the difficulties they have called to the attention of police.

Police have no problems with reforms that can make the public happy, although they object to the way reforming is sometimes done.[5] The officers know that in many reforms they tend to be seen as in need of shaping up and that they become targets, rather than participants, in change. Officers will tend to buy into innovations in which they are genuinely enlisted to help improve quality of services to the public. Officers in New York City supported an experiment, for example, that improved their skill in handling domestic disturbances (Bard, 1969). More recently, community policing (see chap. 11, this volume) has found wide acceptance in many police departments around the world.

The "End Product" of Policing

Goldstein asked what police work is supposed to accomplish. Observers who have not thought about this question do not understand it, because they equate police work with law enforcement. But to what end should the law be enforced? Would one continue to prosecute misdemeanors promiscuously if there were no visible benefit beyond keeping the police busy and jails congested with harmless violators? And how much of what police do in the course of a day is actually classifiable under the "enforcement" heading?

Goldstein's aim in reviving these questions was not only to underline the fact that police do a great deal more than fight crime but to point out that crime fighting and other services of police can be equivalently defined as problem-oriented activities, in the sense that they involve addressing issues that are brought to the police by consumers of services. Goldstein explained that

> by problems, I mean the incredibly broad range of troublesome situations that prompt citizens to turn to the police, such as street robberies, residential burglaries, battered wives, vandalism, speeding cars, runaway children, accidents, acts of terrorism, even fear. These and other similar problems are the essence of police work. They are the reason for having a police agency. (1979, p. 242)

Goldstein noted that police are unique in a number of respects. They are available 24 hours a day and they have no sharply delimited mandate that circumscribes what they do. They carry considerable authority. Police also function as last resorts and are called by citizens when no one else can help them. As a result, the challenges the police face are often overwhelming ones. Goldstein noted that

> many of the problems coming to the attention of the police become their responsibility because no other means has been found to solve them. They are the residual problems of society. It follows that expecting the police to solve or eliminate them is expecting too much. It is more realistic to aim at reducing their volume, preventing repetition, alleviating suffering, and minimizing the other adverse effects they produce. (Goldstein, 1979, p. 243)

If police must respond in some fashion to a variety of problems, including crime problems, one cannot assess the effectiveness of police work by counting the number of arrests police make, ascertaining their clearance rate, or measuring the time it takes for the average officer to answer the average call. Such a numbers-oriented accounting system "is somewhat like that of a private industry that studies the speed of its assembly line, the productivity of its employees, and the nature of its public relations program, but does not examine the quality of its product" (Goldstein, 1979, p. 243). A police quality control system would have to identify and consider the problems to which the police respond, to pose the question of how effectively these problems are solved.

Problems as Behavior Patterns

One difficulty is that police problems are usually defined in terms of a criminal code, which is a list of uninformative legalistic labels. One reason rosters of crimes are misleading is that

> they frequently mask diverse forms of behavior. Thus, for example, incidents classified under "arson" might include fires set by teenagers as a form of vandalism, fires by persons suffering severe psychological problems, fires set for the purpose of destroying evidence of a crime, fires set by persons (or their hired agents) to collect insurance, and fires set by organized criminal interests to intimidate. Each type of incident poses a radically different problem for the police. (Goldstein, 1979, p. 245)

A second difficulty is more obvious and has to do with the fact that there are many situations that require attention, although no crime has been committed. The taxonomy of offenses draws attention to alcohol offenders, for example, but not to inebriates who freeze to death if police do not pick them up. Offense-centered categories also imply that the solution to a problem is to make an arrest, and there is no provision for other activities that have to do with crime, such as the counseling of victims.

Goldstein favors subdividing behavior to which police respond into categories that involve similar people (e.g., suspects) doing things for similar reasons in similar situations. The advantage of viewing human behavior in this way is that it makes it possible to think of a response that is uniquely applicable to the behavior rather than to the statute that subsumes it. Robbery is a broad label that does not define a meaningful subset; neither does purse snatching, which is an appreciably better category. What defines a problem is a category such as "teenagers snatching the purses of elderly women waiting for buses in the downtown section of the city during the hours of early darkness" (Goldstein, 1979, p. 246). Analysis of this sort of delimited behavior helps one to search for appropriate solutions, and it might even help to consider further subdivision, such as purse snatchings by gang-affiliated and non-gang-affiliated teenagers.

Behavioral categories can reveal experienced problems that are obfuscated by being buried under formalistic labels. An example of such a problem that is cited by Goldstein is being subjected to irritating noise. Noise complaints are routinely handled by police but are distributed under offense headings that obscure the fact that noise occasions a great deal of misery, that "sleep is lost, schedules are disrupted, mental and emotional problems aggravated. Apartments become uninhabitable" (1979, p. 247). For the person whose quality of life is thus adversely affected, "improved policing would mean a more effective response to the problem of noise created by her neighbors" (1979, p. 247).

Once problems (such as "noise complaints") have been defined, information must be collected that makes sense of the problems. This information includes impressions that experienced officers have acquired by answering complaints. Street experience is in fact "an extremely rich source of information that is too often overlooked by those concerned about improving the quality of police service" (Goldstein, 1979, p. 249). Some of what the officers already do might be mitigating the problem and could be emulated by other officers.

Researching a problem in the long run, however, means gathering statistics: In the case of noise, what is the number and source of the complaints? Does noise more frequently occur in given types of locations? What types of individuals are responsible for creating noise and what do they do to produce it? How is the problem currently being responded to and to what degree are the current responses effective? Such facts permit the posing of strategic questions, which have to do with alternative ways of addressing the problem.

The solutions one considers must be grounded in the facts one has gathered, but to address a problem one must think creatively. Substantial solutions often involve cooperative endeavors between police and other service providers in which a problem is solved because the police "take the initiative, as a sort of community ombudsman, in getting others to address it" (Goldstein, 1979, p. 254). Police can in such ways help create innovative modes of service delivery that fill unmet needs. They can also inspire ordinances and regulations to provide new remedies to control resistant and persistent problems. On the other hand, less difficult problems may be solved by disseminating information or providing reassurances. Sometimes simple gadgets help: Locks on doors or street lights can reduce burglary calls in some neighborhoods.

Goldstein concluded that this sort of problem-centered approach should appeal to police. After all, "the approach calls for the police to take greater initiative in attempting to deal with problems rather than resign themselves to living with them" (p. 257).

Evolution of the Problem-Oriented Approach

Since 1979, the approach first outlined by Goldstein has taken on dimensions that have rounded out the model and to some extent supplemented it. One such refinement is in the definition of problems and nonproblems. From this definitional perspective, a non-problem-oriented approach is one that focuses on incidents. When a complaint is received, the police respond to the complaint; when a suspect has been identified, the suspect is arrested. Specific situations (incidents) are addressed, but conditions that underlie them are not addressed. If we assume that such conditions are at work, there will be more complaints and more offenses, and nothing much will have been accomplished.

The net effect can even be destructive if the unaddressed conditions get worse and the impotence of the police is thereby highlighted.

From the problem-oriented perspective, incidents are symptoms. A problem exists where a set of conditions produces a proliferation of incidents. To keep incidents from further multiplying, one must address the underlying conditions, which must be identified. To pinpoint causes or conditions, one must examine incidents for clues. Such clues are garnered by looking at the patterning of incidents. Patterning has to do with common characteristics of incidents, such as who does what to whom and under what circumstances. It also has to do with how people respond to interventions that have been tried. The pickpockets referred to earlier, for instance, may have returned to picking pockets after spending time in jail, which suggests that another approach may be needed.

To look for patterns does not mean that a police department's incident-driven business must be curtailed. Policing must always remain reactive, just as medicine must deal with irritating symptoms of diseases. But both professions must do more than cope with symptoms where knowledge permits them to do more. A pattern that can be isolated does not guarantee a cure (because not all conditions are curable), but it helps define the disease so that we can think in terms of curing it. Where police incidents group—where complaints and offenses aggregate—the question "why?" becomes easier to ask, and a problem-centered solution becomes conceivable (Eck, 2003).

Traditional policing at times approximates this definitional stance, because enforcement activities (such as stakeouts) are often targeted based on analyses of crime statistics that highlight concentrations of incidents. This approach recognizes that a problem (say, a high rate of robbery) exists, but still responds to it by assaulting its symptoms. The approach also has a second feature that is at variance with problem-oriented policing as we conceive of it, which is that analysis of the problem is done by one set of people—for example, the crime-analysis section of a police department—and the responding by another group of people who have no hand in the analysis.

In problem-oriented policing as it eventually evolved, police—rank-and-file officers—do the problem solving. It is this dramatic feature (which we shall deal with in chaps. 3 and 4) that distinguishes the approach most clearly from other approaches and makes it particularly exciting. Goldstein himself pointed out that

> by drawing on the expertise of officers and involving them in devising solutions, the problem-solving approach increases the potential for more effective police responses. It also challenges the officer's imagination and creativity, generating new enthusiasm for the job. (Goldstein, 1987, p. 17)

Timeliness of the Problem-Oriented Model

As Goldstein pointed out in his seminal article, the management focus of police has been to reduce sloppiness, inefficiency, and corruption, including political interference. To the extent to which this effort succeeded, it became an advance on sloppy, inefficient, and corrupt policing. But the enterprise also had serious liabilities, both for officers and citizens. The officers often experienced the approach as demoralizing because they felt tainted by a broad brush of accusations. The officers also knew that although their discretion was being circumscribed, they were forced to exercise it daily. They were in practice on their own (except for sporadic encounters with sergeants), which meant that their ostensibly tight supervision was a fiction.

A result of ambiguity and the perception of authoritarian management was bitterness (Toch, 2002), which contributed to the genesis of an alienated officer subculture. One sophisticated group of observers (Kelling, Wasserman, & Williams, 1988), described this process as follows:

> First, use of individual discretion has been driven underground; creativity and productive adaptations go unrecognized and unrewarded. Second, police departments often fail to tap the potential abilities of their officers. An ethos of "stay out of trouble," which has developed in many departments,

stifles officers who are otherwise resourceful and abets officers who "perch" in their positions. Finally, a police culture
has developed that maintains values that are alien to both
police departments and communities. This police culture is
characterized by suspiciousness, perceptions of great danger,
isolation from citizens, and internal solidarity (the "blue cur-
tain"). (1988, pp. 2–3)

Alienated police officers are likely to view themselves as mis-
understood and rejected; they may feel that others (particularly
in the criminal justice system) bend their efforts to undo their
work. They may feel unappreciated, mistreated, and disre-
spected. They may also have little respect for large numbers of
citizens (whom they may characterize as intrinsically incorrigi-
ble) and may have contempt for their superiors, whom they
may view as removed from police work, subject to political
manipulation, and imprisoned by minority group (or racist)
concerns.

Alienated officers may define themselves as going through
motions. Conversely, they may see themselves as engaged in a
thankless crusade, unappreciated by others, which necessitates
deceiving, prevaricating, and circumventing instructions that
circumscribe.

In the meantime, citizens become alienated for a different
reason. They are often confronted with a "full enforcement"
crime-fighting model that pretends that laws are to be enforced
to the hilt and all those who violate them are to be arrested. The
formula is in fact intrinsically unworkable, but it created pressure
on police to find violators to meet high arrest quotas. This has
meant that citizens who acquired nuisance status and minor
borderline transgressors have been more frequently arrested.
These people had reason to feel themselves discriminated
against. They mostly knew other borderline violators who had
not been arrested and could thus regard themselves as unfairly
singled out. The problem is compounded when suspects who
are arrested are Black or Hispanic and officers are predomi-
nantly White.

Proactive policing of the full-enforcement variety has thus had
serious consequences in the context of cumulating ethnic and

class grievances that colored perceptions of the police to the point where it contributed to riots, many of which started with a routine effort by the police to arrest a minor transgressor.

The public has also sensed the disjuncture between efficiency and effectiveness. As police became more efficient in deploying cars, answering calls, and reducing their response time, it became clearer that this activity in many local neighborhoods appeared to be wasted, in the sense of not accomplishing hoped-for results. The means–end issue became even more salient as task forces and street sweeps failed to deter drug trading in the neighborhoods. An ironic development (to which we shall return) was a demand for the rebirth of foot patrol, which chiefs had regarded as a Stone Age practice.

New challenges also occasioned the need for new thinking. A plethora of community problems—homelessness, the decay of inner cities, the deinstitutionalization of many mentally ill individuals—posed unfamiliar difficulties for the police and raised questions that had not been dealt with before. New difficulties joined more familiar challenges (what to do about inebriates, runaways, graffiti, public housing projects, rape victims, domestic fights, child abuse, the safety of parks and playgrounds, and so forth), which had already called for problem-centered strategic thinking in the past, and had required coordination with other parties concerned with the same problems, and caused deviations from a crime-fighting definition of the police mission.

Old Wine in a New Bottle?

The view that problem-oriented policing represents a revolution is not enthusiastically accepted by everyone. There are officers who convincingly argue (sometimes in aggrieved tones) that "problem-oriented" is simply a new label for old police wine in a more fashionable bottle.

As is usually the case with such controversies, the accusation is not true or false but hinges on matters of definition. Many police officers in the past have found themselves self-consciously responding to "problems" in their communities. They have done this with strategies containing mixes of enforcement and nonenforcement options, after careful study of (or, at least, familiarization with) facts. The similarities between such activities and problem-oriented policing ventures are real. There are also differences, however, and it may be well to consider these differences using a carefully conducted police study of the past.

The study is by Egon Bittner (1967) and centered on policing in skid rows. *Skid row* was a designation first applied to logging terminals in which serious drinking occurred, and then came to be used to describe certain deteriorated sections of cities. Wiseman, who was an expert on skid rows, pointed out that areas called skid rows had come to present an enduring and consistent set of problems that centered around homelessness, subculturally supported inebriation, and substantial deterioration of neighborhoods. She wrote that

> the descriptions of Skid Row have been remarkably stable over the 50 years: the filth and stench of the hotels, the greasy cheapness of the restaurants, the litter in the streets, the concentration of "low-type" bars, or "dives." All of these aspects are mentioned again and again in both the research and the romantic literature from the 1920's until today. . . . The social silhouette of these men has not changed to any degree—idle, ill-kempt, living hand to mouth. Even the special jargon used by the habitués of Skid Row is amazingly consistent from city to city and through time. (1970, p. 4)

Given this discouraging profile of skid rows, the policing of such neighborhoods provided a daunting challenge to officers who were assigned to work in them and had to cope with their junglelike attributes. Arresting chronic alcoholics en masse would have made the officers look ridiculous and would have served no constructive purpose. Most jails were already full of alcohol offenders (who at the time made up the bulk of jail populations), taking up space needed for clients who posed more substantial threats to society.

Bittner observed that officers on skid row saw themselves as keeping the peace in the area. "Peace keeping," wrote Bittner, "appears to be a solution to an unknown problem arrived at by unknown means" (1967, p. 701). In pursuing this solution, moreover, officers had a great deal of latitude. The officers viewed as skid row specialists exercised autonomous judgments based on their individual experience and expertise. In the words of a sergeant interviewed by Bittner, "A good man has things worked out in his own ways on his beat and he doesn't need anybody to tell him what to do" (1967, p. 715).

Bittner found that the officers felt that their "experience and practice" gave them a reservoir of "street sense" or "common sense," which allowed them to "play it by ear." This self-characterization suggests impulsive reactivity, but it means something different. Bittner explained that

> what the seasoned patrolman means, however, in saying that he "plays by ear" is that he is making his decisions while being attuned to the realities of complex situations about which he had immensely detailed knowledge. This studied aspect of peace keeping generally is not made explicit, nor is the tyro or the outsider made aware of it. (1967, p. 715)

In making their seemingly instantaneous decisions, the officers claimed to rely on cues whose significance became obvious to them because they knew what to look for. Bittner reported that

> patrolmen maintain that some of the seemingly spur-of-the-moment decisions are actually made against a background of knowledge of facts that are not readily apparent in the situations. Since experience not only contains this information but also causes it to come to mind, patrolmen claim to have developed a special sensitivity for qualities of appearances that allow an intuitive grasp of probable tendencies. In this context, little things are said to have high informational value and lead to conclusions without the intervention of explicitly reasoned chains of inferences. (1967, p. 712)

Skid row officers acquired their self-styled expertise by getting to know the denizens of their beat. "Getting to know" in this context meant "the establishment and maintenance of familiar relationships with individual members of these groups" (1967, p. 707), an endeavor to which the officers dedicated a good deal of time. For example, the rounds include entering hotels and gaining access to rooms or dormitories, often for no other purpose than asking the occupants how things are going. In all this, patrolmen address innumerable persons by name and are in turn addressed by name. The conversational style that characterizes these exchanges is casual to an extent that by non-skid-row standards might suggest intimacy. (Bittner, 1967, p. 708)

An officer who behaved in this fashion acquired a great deal of particularistic knowledge:

He is likely to know every person who manages or works in the local bars, hotels, shops, stores, and missions. Moreover, he probably knows every public and private place inside and out. Finally, he ordinarily remembers countless events of the past which he can recount by citing names, dates and places with remarkable precision. Though there are always some threads missing in the fabric of information, it is continuously woven and mended even as it is being used. New facts, however, are added to the texture, not in terms of structured categories but in terms of adjoining known realities. In other words, the content and organization of the patrolman's knowledge is primarily ideographic and only vestigially, if at all, nomothetic. (1967, pp. 707–708)

That the skid row officers' knowledge was highly detailed did not mean that the officers lacked the ability to generalize about skid row inhabitants and their outlook on life. Bittner pointed out, for example, that officers felt that on skid row

the dominant consideration governing all enterprise and association is directed at the occasion of the moment. . . . It is a matter of adventurous circumstance whether or not matters go as anticipated. . . . The places the residents occupy, the social relations they entertain, and the activities that engage them are not meaningfully connected over time. . . . Of course, everybody's life contains some sequential incongruities, but in the life of a Skid Row inhabitant, every moment is an accident. (1967, pp. 705–706)

This was not only an immensely sophisticated portrayal, but turned out to be an accurate one. Jacqueline Wiseman (1970) painstakingly reconstructed the skid rowers' perspective and characterized their psychological world in the same terms as the officers. Moreover, the officers were particularly voluble in discussing victimization on skid row, which they were dedicated to preventing. Unlike less sophisticated observers, they saw vulnerability and predatory propensities as coexistent in the same individuals and varying with situations. This view not only was plausible but represented an advance over conventional social science theory.

In addressing skid row peacekeeping problems, the officers engaged in a great deal of activity that bordered on social work, although this term was never mentioned. Bittner reported that

> patrolmen note that they frequently help people to obtain meals, lodging, employment, that they direct them to welfare and health services, and that they aid them in various other ways. Though patrolmen tend to describe such services mainly as the product of their own altruism, they also say that their colleagues who avoid them are simply doing a poor job of patrolling . . . domain of the patrolman's service activity is virtually limitless, and it is no exaggeration to say that the solution of every conceivable problem has at one time or another been attempted by a police officer. (1967, p. 709)

Skid row officers did arrest people, but they never did so as an end in itself, according to Bittner. Bittner asked one officer why he had not apprehended an intoxicated participant in a fight, and "the officer explained that this would not solve anything" (1967, p. 720). The officers did arrest some participants in disturbances to prevent escalations of violence. They also arrested some individuals "for their own good," especially when they proved helpless or self-destructive. A skid row officer explained such mercy bookings to Wiseman, indicating that

> we pick them up for their own protection—they'd die on the streets if we didn't. I think it should be unlawful to incarcerate

an alcoholic . . . but without other facilities to take care of them, it's inhuman not to incarcerate them. Some men here admit they're alive today because we picked them up and dried them out. (1970, p. 77)

Enforcement strategies are used, wrote Bittner, "as a resource to solve certain pressing practical problems in keeping the peace" (1967, p. 710). He pointed to incidents in which individuals were not arrested who could have been arrested. He reported the following:

Whenever such persons are encountered and can be induced to leave, or taken to some shelter, or remanded to someone's care, then patrolmen feel, or at least maintain, that an arrest would serve no useful purpose. That is, whenever there exist means for controlling the troublesome aspects of some person's presence in some way alternative to an arrest, such means are preferentially employed, provided, of course, that the case at hand involves only a minor offense. (Bittner, 1967, p. 710)

Before the advent of the problem-oriented policing movement, such police human service activities were often not credited by other service workers, who persisted in seeing all police officers as crime fighters rather than as partners in service delivery. This observation was first made by Cumming, Cumming, and Edell, who concluded the following from a careful study:

These others, our own studies show, prefer to recognize the policeman's professional controlling function, which they both need and often call upon. Thus, it is as an agent of control that the policeman participates in a divided labor with social workers, doctors, clergymen, lawyers and teachers in maintaining social integration. The problems he faces appear to be a failure of integration within the integrative system, so that he cannot mobilize the other agents when he needs them. (1965, p. 286)

A key difference is that today's problem-oriented officer is indeed prepared to "mobilize the other agents when he needs them" (1965, p. 286). In skid rows today, for example, the police work closely with homeless shelters, whose residents can be both troubled and troublesome. Problem-oriented teams routinely deal with shelter staff members, who have learned to rely on the officers to assist them in efforts to prevent and reduce victimization. In turn, the officers will invoke shelter staff and other service providers who offer them constructive alternatives to arresting and jailing homeless individuals, which is viewed as a last resort.

From Native Wisdom to Problem Solving

It should be clear by now that it makes no sense to ask whether skid row policing was problem-oriented or not. In one sense, the answer is affirmative, but we must add, "not quite in the way we now use the phrase." What we can next ask is how we could make skid row police officers problem-oriented officers in the current sense of the term.

The skid row paradigm is heavily intuition-based. The officers exercised inordinate skill and ingenuity but did so with limited self-awareness. The officers did evolve informal group norms about quality of work. Bittner pointed out, for example, that "patrolmen who are 'not rough enough,' or who are 'too rough,' or whose roughness is determined by personal feelings rather than situational exigencies, are judged to be poor craftsmen" (1967, p. 701). These rudiments of definition tell us what quality policing was not, as the officers saw it. But what would constitute effective problem solving?

The officers tried hard to avoid this sort of question, and the reason for their reticence is instructive. On the one hand, the officers believed there are constructive solutions for problems and that one's experience supplies them. One's experience is (instantaneously) available where it is relevant, and it suggests answers. It dictates a correct course of action to the officer who is experienced—even, paradoxically, to the rookie—but it cannot be communicated to the inexperienced. By the same token it cannot be dissected because a review would destroy it and you can always know it when you see it.

But a fly in this ointment is that officers know that not all officers are infallible. If experience is a reliable guide, how can some experienced officers be less competent than others, and react emotionally, for instance, oversentimentally, angrily, inflexibly, or harshly? If undesirable traits of undesirable officers (such as skewed law enforcement philosophy or sentiment) can neutralize the benefits of their experience, why are more beneficent traits (such as compassion) irrelevant to the deployment of experience? And if varying dispositions can dictate different actions to different officers, how can experience in general serve as an infallible guide to correct decisions? The officers sensed this inconsistency, and tried to beg it, because it meant that there must be other ways of defining the correctness of decisions than the experience of their originator.

The second issue pertains to the nature of police experience itself. The officers made rounds, asked questions, and garnered a great many facts. They assumed (as did Sergeant Friday) that the facts they collected could speak for themselves. But they intuited at some level that facts cannot speak for themselves and that some sort of analytic process is in order. The process entails more than careful storage and instantaneous retrieval, which the officers prized. When caught off guard, the officers demonstrated the capacity to theorize about the problems they encountered, but they were reluctant to credit themselves with insights, perspectives, or premises for action; articulated conceptions or preconceptions; or goals or objectives.

In their exercise of discretion, the officers elected and discarded options when they acted but acted as if they had no rationale for these options. And although the officers prized learning (which means "to profit from experience") they could not learn from each other, because they did not seriously discuss their work.

Officers who operate in this fashion have awesome knowledge but cannot fully perfect it. They can repeat mistakes (which are "experience"), assuming successes. Typical encounters are amalgamated with atypical ones. To tell the difference between typical and atypical experiences one must check one's experiences against those of others. Better still, one must seek knowledge other than experience to gain added perspective.

Street knowledge is solid knowledge, and it is unquestionably valuable. Those of us who lack it (academics who are concerned with the real world) must get it secondhand. But street knowledge has to be pooled to achieve reliability and it must be supplemented to attain validity. Only after reliability and validity are secured does experience become the sound foundation for rational decisions and problem solving.

Skid row presented many police problems, and the skid row officers addressed them. There were individual problems, such as stopping a fight or securing medical care for a person who needed it. There were larger scale problems, such as incipient riots and the proliferation of aggressive mendicants. Still other problems were composite problems calling for sophisticated solutions. Soup kitchens could be ill-attended, for example, while men went hungry for lack of knowledge or transportation.

Skid row officers solved problems mostly tactically, which is not the same as solving them strategically. The officers intervened mostly individually or in ad hoc groups. They did not team up or invoke other resources (community agencies, for instance) as partners in joint ventures. Actions were mainly patterned in the sense that officers independently pursued similar results in comparable ways.

If the officers operated today, they might benefit by perusing a roster published by the Police Executive Research Forum (no date), which is titled "The Key Elements of Problem-Oriented Policing." The officers would discover that if they followed the prescription implicit in this roster, they could more effectively ameliorate skid row problems and could do so in a more thoughtful and thought-provoking way. The roster reads in part as follows:

☐ Problems must be described precisely and accurately and broken down into specific aspects of the problem. Problems often aren't what they first appear to be.

☐ Problems must be understood in terms of the various interests at stake. Individuals and groups of people are affected in different ways by a problem and have different ideas about what should be done about the problem.

□   The way the problem is currently being handled must be understood and the limits of effectiveness must be openly acknowledged to come up with a better response.

□   Initially, any and all possible responses to a problem should be considered so as not to cut short potentially effective responses. Suggested responses should follow from what is learned during the investigation. They should not be limited to, nor rule out, the use of arrest.

□   The effectiveness of new responses must be evaluated so these results can be shared with other police officers and so the department can systemically learn what does and does not work.

Building on a Foundation

One important fact about skid row policing is that the officers were not tied to their radios, nor were they under pressure to accumulate arrests and citations. They had autonomy, which they used with self-conscious verve, both in the way they patrolled skid row (circulating through favored hot spots) and in the actions they took. The officers viewed skid row as a unique but familiar world, which had unique but familiar attributes. They did not apply preconceived categories—such as legal definitions of offenses—to incidents they encountered, nor of offenders, to people.

The enterprise in which the officers saw themselves engaged (keeping the peace) is eminently compatible with a problem-solving approach. Whereas police often prize a fraction of their activities—"playing cops and robbers"—and deemphasize the rest of their work, skid row officers saw everything they did as relevant to their mission. They boasted of Samaritan acts and of ingenious alternatives to arrests. And where the officers did arrest, it was because the offenses were serious or arrests achieved other ends, such as preventing injury or violence. The context in which an arrest takes place tends to define its purpose, which means that this context (and/or the dispositions of the offender) must be assessed before one intervenes.

Police evaluate categories of contexts—such as disputes apt to degenerate unless the parties are separated—or categories of individuals—such as men too intoxicated to take care of themselves. Such categories cannot be formulated without some preconception of causation or understanding of processes, such as the escalation of alcohol-infused conflicts. These understandings and preconceptions are in no way different from social science theory, except in the reluctance of the officers to theorize. Nor are the officers' interventions different from social science-based interventions, other than in the modesty ("we simply use street sense") with which they are characterized.

Molière once wrote of a man who became a self-styled intellectual after he discovered that he had spent his life talking prose. The officers could have a similar experience with regard to problem-oriented policing. To become more explicitly problem-oriented, the officers would have to formally define the problem solving they inchoately do and begin to do it consciously. The remainder of what is called for is simply the systematizing of the assessment and analysis process, the pooling and supplementing of knowledge, the invoking of resources, and the documenting of impact.

We will return to the distinction between types of problem solving in chapter 3, where we review seminal experiences that are recognized problem-oriented "classics." We can contrast these experiences with problem-solving efforts that do not engage officers as social scientists and explore how experiential wisdom and formal knowledge can be combined.

In chapter 4 we discuss problem-oriented policing as an example of work reform and show how this approach is congruent with what industrial psychologists know about work motivation and how to raise it. Two trends—job enrichment and industrial democracy—seem particularly applicable to interventions such as problem-oriented policing. Chapter 4 also deals with change issues, which have to do with introducing innovations such as problem-oriented experiments into organizations such as police agencies, which often resist change. Chapters 5 through 9 delineate two problem-oriented experiments from the participants' perspective. These experiments can be traced step by step, because we have attempted to keep track of what happened along the way as the process unfolded.

The so-called Oakland Project, which we detail in chapters 6 and 7, was not a conventional exercise in problem-oriented police work but a problem-oriented experiment in police reform. The officers in this project did not focus—as most problem-oriented (POP) officers do—on patterns of crime and disorder. Instead, their concern was with improving the quality of police work being done in their department. Their mission was to examine the use of unnecessary force in police–citizen encounters, which is an obdurate, seemingly insoluble problem. As it happens, this problem is also immensely topical, in that it is a continuing nightmare for police administrators and a subject of pressing interest to members of the public. And the Oakland Project eventuated in a response to this problem, which has been recognized as being sophisticated and innovative.[6] The Oakland Project has thus come to qualify as a classic, of both historical and contemporary importance.

The experiment took place before the term *problem-oriented policing* was coined, but it did have to consider defuse criticisms with which POP experts grapple today. As is the case with democratizing strategies of all kinds, POP has faced worries about the qualifications of grassroots individuals whose role is to be expanded. Such is especially the case because problem solving by definition involves research, which we associate with academic credentials. One response to this concern involves familiarizing POP officers with research methodology. A more ambitious solution is that of teaming—pairing police officers with social scientists, whose job it becomes to support and empower their work. But this prescription raises a new set of doubts, centered on the viability of police–academic partnerships. Police are justly reputed to be suspicious of outsiders. It would follow that officers could prove resistant and inhospitable to consultants trying to assist them. And would elitist academics—with their publish-or-perish concerns—in turn seriously consider problem-oriented involvements?

The narrative of the Oakland Project that we relay describes relationships forged in the course of the experiment among its teamed participants. The closeness of the cross-disciplinary links is especially noteworthy, given the controversial nature of the project's central concern. To my mind, the evidence is both conclusive and reassuring. At this late date—35 years after the inception of the project—I have a letter from one of the officers, now retired—who formed its first cohort. The closing salutation of this letter reads, "I love you, Old Friend." Such are the inestimable rewards of police–academic encounters in quality problem-oriented ventures.

The model of teaming in the Oakland Project involved total participation—closer than is customary in police–academic partnerships. A more familiar role for academics to play in such problem-oriented ventures is to provide backup and documentation. This role is illustrated in our second case study (chap. 9), which describes the research-supported activities of two teams of New York state troopers. The teams dealt with the same general subject matter (that of accidents resulting in injuries or in fatalities) but faced different problems, because traffic patterns, and resulting patterns of accidents, tend to vary from place to place. Other problems customarily addressed by the police also vary from one locality to another, which is one of many reasons why community policing and problem solving go hand in hand.

In the last chapters of this book we consider current trends—including the proliferation of a model (discussed in the foreword of this book), which was initiated by managers of the New York City police. In chapters 11 through 13 we sample experiments in community-oriented policing that have a problem-oriented focus. We also describe some interesting recent experiences with successful problem-solving activities.

Notes

1. As discussed in chapter 2, progressive reformers wanted educated officers who were versed in science and concerned with social welfare. MacNamara wrote about Vollmer–the father of the professional police movement–that

   [his] prototype police officer would be at home with the microscope or polygraph, courageous and physically capable of handling street disorders, trained in fingerprinting and photography, adept at first aid, a marksman of military bearing and skills, yet so certain of his manhood as to be able to deal humanely, effectively,

and sympathetically with lost children, beaten wives, and bereaved parents. (1977, p. 180)

Vollmer and his contemporaries envisioned "professional" management for their "professional" officers. They prized the prospect of streamlining agencies, instituting centralized reporting, and efficient chains of command. Paradoxically, they thus reinforced bureaucratization trends that stifle the initiative of officers. Walker pointed out the following:

> Bureaucratization entailed the development of formal and elaborate internal procedures (civil service, training programs, etc.) that subjected the police officer to more direct control and supervision. The control of the rank and file was in fact regarded as the great accomplishment of police reform. But this was not the same as professionalization, if by that concept we mean enhancing the independent judgment of the practitioner. The police in the 1920s, however, were not evolving in the same direction as the recognized professions. Rather, police officers were regarded as objects to be controlled and directed by chief administrators. If anything, it was the police chiefs who were professionalizing, and doing so at the expense of the rank and file. (1977, p. 136)

2. Foot patrol was preferred because of this attribute. An expert of the time (Graper, 1921/1969) pointed out that "the policeman patrolling on foot has greater opportunities of studying his post and of becoming acquainted intimately with its peculiar needs than has the man who is burdened with a horse or a bicycle. He cannot cover quite as much ground in the same time, but he can cover it more thoroughly" (p. 130). Other perceived advantages included the fact that a patrolman could sneak up on a malefactor, whereas the clatter of hoofs "gives ample warning of his approach" (pp. 131–132).

3. Graper (1921/1969) referred to the first experiment involving motorized officers. He wrote that

> a novel system of patrol has been inaugurated by Chief Vollmer in Berkeley, California, from whose police department so many progressive ideas have come during recent years. Every member of the force is required to own a gasoline driven automobile and to operate it in the course of his daily work. The men are assigned to regular posts but cover them differently every day. The policeman's automobile is equipped with policeman's implements, ropes and hooks to be of aid to the fire department and to help stalled teams and motor vehicles. For the purchase and upkeep of the automobiles the city allows each policeman $27.50 in addition to his monthly salary and furnishes gasoline and oil besides. An ingenious signal system enables the members of the force in a few minutes' time to surround any block from which trouble is reported at any time of the day. This radical departure from the ordinary methods of patrol indicates that in some cities at least, new methods are being tried

and attempts are being made to lift police service to a higher state of efficiency. Reports indicate that the system in use is giving entire satisfaction. (p. 133)

4. As recently as the 1950s, it was assumed that officers would not remain in their cars between calls but would be foot patrolmen a good portion of the time. O. W. Wilson (1952), for example, insisted that

> in some respects the distinction between foot and motorized patrol is unfortunate. All patrolmen should be thought of as being foot patrolmen and should be required to perform the usual routine patrol duties including inspectional tasks. . . . The vehicle transports the patrolman from one task to another, brings him to the scene with greater speed and less fatigue, and enables him to capture a fleeing criminal.
>
> When the patrolman with an automobile performs all the duties of a foot patrolman, he must spend a large part of his time on foot. This provides opportunity for observation and for contact with citizens and thus enables the patrolman to serve as the eyes and ears of the department. . . . The patrolman who remains in his vehicle hidden in a secluded spot when he is not driving is not providing patrol service. The officer who spends all his time driving neglects his duty to make inspections, to observe, to make himself available for public service, and to make contacts with citizens. Protection against weather and relief from fatigue by occasional periods spent in driving from one location to another are to be used with discretion. (pp. 84–85)

5. Most technical innovations in policing have given managers greater control over the behavior of subordinates, and subordinates have exercised ingenuity to evade such control. Walker (1977) pointed this out in discussing the introduction of two-way radios, which presented the problem for patrolmen of "preserving for themselves an important degree of autonomy" (p. 136). An earlier control-oriented innovation was the patrol box, which the officers had to contact at prescribed intervals. But this strategy was viewed as inadequate by supervisors because it "does not necessarily mean that patrolmen are performing their duties for they may loaf in cigar stores, barber shops, restaurants and other places between pulls of the box" (Graper, 1921/1969, p. 152).

6. For a recent endorsement of the Oakland Project's prescription, see Armacost (2004). Armacost noted that "calls for some form of collegial self-regulation by police organizations are ubiquitous in the policing literature," and concluded that "the growing interest in peer review [the Oakland Project intervention] is an implicit recognition of the reformative limits of the law" (p. 544).

2

Policing in the United States Before the Advent of the Problem-Oriented Approach

P olice reforms 100 years ago were shaped by the Progressive movement, which placed great faith in the potency of reason and wanted knowledge and science to be the engines of public policy. The emphasis on the power of knowledge implied, among other things, that if organizations are logically arranged they become more efficient and can thereby produce a better world (see chap. 4, this volume). Logical arrangements of the kind envisaged by the Progressive reformers were those arrived at by hiring the best people for carefully preclassified and circumscribed tasks—and seeing to it by means of hard-nosed, hands-on supervision that these tasks were performed. Rationality also connoted formal education: Education arguably provides knowledge, and knowledge then presumably makes one more effective.

The reformers of the 1890s were concurrently obsessed with the need for rectitude and self-discipline, for abstinence from self-gratification and hedonic abandon. This concern with profligacy, deviant behavior, and unlicensed conduct has been suspiciously viewed by some historians as a thinly disguised effort by native-born middle-class Protestants to harness an immigrant underclass, which not incidentally controlled the political machines of large American cities.

Given this political context, it comes as no surprise that no-holds-barred crime fighting came to predominate as a prized police goal through much of the period. This was not only because controlling deviants had become a salient concern but because of the desire for demonstrable efficiency. And police departments did appear efficient when crime statistics were first discovered. At later junctures. unfortunately, crime rates spun out of control;[1] the single-minded pursuit of suspected offenders was also fated to lead to excesses that invited resentments in targeted communities.

The Progressive concern with deviant behavior also extended to the behavior of police. Bruce Smith, a respected pioneer police reformer, wrote that "it requires no belabored argument to present the sorry fact that at different times and places policemen have been thieves, drunks, bullies, grafters and worse" (1960, p. 244). In the minds of the reformers, including Smith, the "police problem" (as they called it) had to do with the corrupting influences of grassroot politics.

The reformers' response was to turn police departments into feudal fiefdoms. The chiefs who governed these fiefdoms became impervious to modulating sentiments of public opinion that could have taken the edge off their inflexible enforcement policies. But the chiefs were even more unreceptive to advice or feedback from their patrolmen, because officers were presumptively lazy, untrustworthy, and corruptible. The reform chiefs and their Progressive allies were not touched by the scenario of Clancy the Cop exchanging mellifluous witticisms with fellow Irish Americans on brownstone steps or in barbershops or taverns. Such folksy transactions, to Progressive ears, sounded like compromise and collusion, or worse.[2]

Suffused with mistrust of their subordinates, the Progressive reform chiefs became uniformly caught up in the need to monitor the conduct of officers on the beat. Walker observed the following:

> Much of police history could be told in terms of a cat and mouse game between patrolmen and their supervisors. From the earliest call boxes to the modern two-way radio, administrators have sought some means of monitoring the activities of their men. Patrolmen, for their part, have been equally ingenious in their efforts to nullify and subvert the latest technological innovations. (1977, p. 13)

Police Reform by an American President

One early dedicated practitioner of authoritarian supervision was Theodore Roosevelt, who became head of the New York City police commission in 1895. Commissioner Roosevelt has been described by his biographer Jay Stuart Berman (1987) as "the archetypal Progressive" (p. xvi). Berman reported that "soon after taking office [as commissioner], Roosevelt embarked on a series of nightly inspection tours. Concealing his identity, and carrying a chart outlining the various beats and posts to which patrolmen were assigned, [he] would check to see if posts were properly covered" (pp. 56–57). Berman quoted the *Washington Star* as warning New York police officers to "be prepared for trouble whenever teeth and spectacles come out of the darkness" (p. 57).

Like many who followed in his immediate footsteps, Roosevelt conceived of the police as an armed force.

> [He] often employed military terminology in his work. He spoke of "warring against crime," of the "war against corruption," and of the "resolute warfare against every type of criminal." He repeatedly applied the qualities of a soldier to police officers—courage, bravery, discipline and valor— "qualities upon which we insisted and which we rewarded." (Berman, 1987, pp. 60–61)

Under Roosevelt, "detailed march and drill procedures were developed for regular exercises and special occasions" (Berman, 1987, p. 61). As an example of minutiae in such procedures, Berman quoted the formal instructions for police baton presentation. Officers were told to "bring the baton in front of the center of the face, hand glassing the hilt squarely with the thumb up the side, back of the hand squarely to the front, point of the thumb as high as the chin, point of baton slightly inclining forward" (1987, p. 62). There were no equivalently detailed instructions to prevent the overenthusiastic wielding of nightsticks in street encounters, which has repeatedly become a source of contention.

Roosevelt made one concession to consultative management. In drafting his manual of new rules and procedures, he instructed his revision committee to "consult with the various officers in the department, who are invited to suggest, in writing, such changes and new rules and regulations as the welfare of the department may seem to require" (Berman, 1987, p. 64). The emphasis on written suggestions presupposed that only those who felt comfortable with drafting formal memoranda needed to apply.

Like other Progressive police administrators, Roosevelt was an advocate of a selection process that highlighted intellectual as well as physical standards. A police officer, he wrote, "should not only be brave, honest and physically powerful, but also possessed of intelligence distinctly above the average" (quoted in Berman, 1987, p. 68). The written test administered to police applicants emphasized "legibility, neatness, rapidity, correctness and uniformity of formation of letters and punctuation marks" (p. 72), but also required knowledge of arithmetic, geography, history, and government. Roosevelt is said to have been "shocked at the answers given by many of the competitors" (p. 73). "It is a striking commentary," he wrote, "on the ignorance of the class of people from whom the majority of applicants come, to say that nearly two thirds of the competitors in the (written) mental examinations fail to attain the requisite 70 percent" (quoted in Berman, 1987, p. 73). A not coincidental result of Roosevelt's discriminating selection procedure was that it weeded out immigrant applicants. When Roosevelt took charge of the New York City Police Department, more than half the officers were foreign-born. Out of the last cohort hired by Roosevelt in 1897, 94% were native-born (p. 76).

The paradox in the formula was that it combined the emphasis on intelligence (and later, education) with insistence on the punctilious adherence to rules and regulations and on mindless, non-discretionary, by-the-book policing. Officers were informed that what was expected of them was "the rigid enforcement henceforth of every rule and regulation of the department" (Berman, 1987, p. 80). Supervising patrolmen were told that "we shall judge you largely by the discipline of the force under you" (p. 81).

Roosevelt predictably also felt that police should be specialized crime fighters: "All activities not associated with the repression of crime," he proclaimed, "should be assigned to other governmental and private agencies" (quoted in Berman, 1987, p. 92). Roosevelt said that "all laws should be observed: all should be executed alike" (p. 95). This full enforcement paradigm, especially as directed at alcohol consumption, eventually led to ridiculous excesses that produced a public backlash. In 1897, the Democratic candidate for mayor swept to victory under the slogan, "To Hell With Reform" (Berman, 1987, p. 120).

The Contribution of O. W. Wilson, America's Premier Police Reformer

Although Roosevelt's police career was consequently short-lived, such was not the case with O. W. Wilson, the dean of American police reformers. Wilson has been pejoratively described as "a martinet" with "a penchant for orderliness" (Bopp, 1977, p. 5). What is unquestionably true is that Wilson

> unswervingly subscribed to the notions of narrow spans of control, a rigid chain of command, the sanctity of written policy pronouncements on a wide variety of subjects, specialization of tasks, carefully controlled delegations of authority and responsibility, and the close supervision of troops in the field. (Bopp, 1977, p. 5)

For Wilson, "police officers would ultimately reach the pinnacle of professionalization by doing precisely what they were told by commanding officers" (p. 6).[3]

Wilson's book *Police Administration*, which some have called "the source of much police change as the bible of professionalism," as well as "required reading for most police promotional exams" (Sherman, 1974, p. 256) is redolent with minutiae in the specifications of officer behavior on and off the job. Police are informed that "the tops of desks and filing cabinets and the floors in the corners of offices should be kept free of papers, boxes and other material. . . . and the office staff should not put their feet on desks and other office furniture" (O. Wilson, 1950, p. 391). In conversation. the officer "must avoid back slapping, forefinger chest poking, leaning on the shoulder of someone in a group, constant hand shaking, and putting his face close to the face of the man to whom he is speaking" (p. 392). The officer also "should not lounge or lean against a support when conversing" (p. 395), and "he must avoid domestic difficulties more assiduously than the average citizen; he must not gamble; he must be unusually temperate in the use of liquor, or abstain altogether from its use" (p. 393).

Despite his penchant for detailed instructions, Wilson saw no contradiction between his preferred style of management and an unflagging emphasis on the desirability of hiring educated and intelligent officers. He once infelicitously wrote, "as with a wife, selection is much more important than training" (Bopp, 1977, p. 45). When Wilson was chief in the city of Wichita in the early 1930s, he raised the entry level test score for police candidates from 79.3 to 108.35 (Bopp, 1977, p. 45). In his redoubtable textbook, Wilson (1950) wrote that "an intelligence quotient of 112 is advisable" (p. 342), and that "experience has shown that the appointment of men with an intelligence quotient below 105 is ill-advised" (p. 343). He also postulated that "the university-trained man is better qualified than one who lacks this broadening experience," and suggested that "the increasing number who are receiving university training justifies two years of college as a preliminary requirement for candidates, with provision for lowering the standard. . . . when candidates excel in other qualities" (p. 338).

By Wilson's time the emphasis on the exclusivity of crime fighting as the police mission had become somewhat attenuated. Yet O. W. Wilson helped to set the stage for contemporary travails by asserting that "strict police attention to the illegal use of narcotics is justified because addicts create a market for peddlers, and peddlers in turn attract addicts and seek to enlarge their clientele for profit. The police should do everything in their power, by conviction and treatment, to free their communities of peddlers and addicts" (p. 184). The phrase "and treatment" in this statement is, of course, significant, because it points to an endearing admixture of Progressive themes.[4] Wilson made his own position explicit when he wrote that "limiting crime control to administering justice after the criminal act is as nonsensical as restricting fire control to fighting the blaze after it has started or limiting the control of disease after infection" (p. 198). And Wilson felt that his views were shared by other police leaders of the 1940s. He wrote the following:

> Progressive police administrators recognize a need for preventing crime by correcting conditions that induce criminality and by rehabilitating the delinquent. In determining the part which the police should play in this endeavor, it is necessary to study the causes of delinquency and the means for their elimination or correction, to inventory and evaluate community social-welfare activities directly or indirectly related to the prevention of criminality, and to discover, by analysis, delinquency-prevention tasks that the police are best suited to perform. (O. Wilson, 1950, p. 199)

The concern with crime prevention led to the creation of police juvenile divisions, which provided entry for women into the monopolistic domain of policing. Crime prevention also provided a rationale for initiating coordinated efforts in which police convoked and mobilized community agencies. Wilson suggested that

> the police should break down barriers between themselves and other community agencies having related objectives by close coordination of plans and activities. . . . The police must enlist the aid, focus the attention, and coordinate activities of every agency and group in the community whose services may assist in the accomplishment of the delinquency-prevention program, and they must follow through to assure that the activity is effectively and continuously applied to that end. (1950, pp. 200–210)

Wilson proposed that community councils and other local groups study the problems of neighborhoods in which prevention efforts were contemplated. He proposed that "programs [be] enlarged or changed in order to render services to groups or areas hitherto overlooked" (1950, p. 432) and pointed out that "people resent having opinions forced on them, whereas if they participate in the development and application of a community program, they become interested in its success" (p. 421). He also noted that "lay participation necessitates decentralization" (p. 423), and he favored democratic structures and variations in the process and content of community activities to accommodate local predilections.

One of the many ironies of police reform is that ideas such as these, which are preeminently compatible with contemporary thinking, had to await reinvention. Still other enlightened ideas advanced by Wilson may be ahead of both his time and ours, such as his dictum that "the police should direct their efforts at keeping people out of jails and prisons, so long as this may be done without jeopardy to public peace and security" (p. 206).

It is also ironic that reformers who are remembered for their command-and-control organizational prescriptions had occasional second thoughts. Wilson himself remarked that "since subordinates who share in the development of procedures usually understand and approve them, the wise leader promotes their participation at every opportunity" (1950, p. 460); and he wrote,

> The essence of leadership is the ability to obtain from each member of the force the highest quality of service that he has the capacity to render; it is not the exercise of authority through commands and threat of punishment for noncompliance. Some police chiefs erroneously assume that the strength and frequency with which commands are barked and the exclusive use by the executive of the power of decision are evidences of strong leadership. The good executive makes fewer rather than more decisions; the strong leader directs and coordinates more by inspiration and enthusiasm than by the authority of command. (p. 454)

Despite such sentiments, a hallmark of early American police departments is that they were invested in rigid chains of command. It would not be unfair to argue, in the word of Thomas Deakin, that "in the 1960s, police [officers] were the victims of the professionalism advanced by their leaders" (1988, p. 233). By the 1970s, however, the tide of management philosophy and style of police supervision was about to take a new turn. Walker pointed out that, "In effect, the new generation of reformer sought to reorient the meaning of professionalism away from its exclusive emphasis upon managerial efficiency and toward encouraging a genuinely professional ethos among front-line practitioners" (1977, p. 172).

The Community-Relations Revolution

The new-age reformers, however, had a contextual problem to solve before tackling internal structural concerns. Policing in practice meant concentrations of largely White officers in high-crime minority neighborhoods. The result was what New York Police Commissioner Patrick Murphy called stranger policing, "the occupation of conquered territory by an alien army." Commissioner Murphy wrote that "under stranger policing . . . it is permissible for officers to hide in their radio cars with windows rolled up, communicating not with the community but only with each other, the dispatchers at headquarters, and their own private thoughts" (quoted in Deakin, 1988, p. 231). The officers were also expected to "aggressively" patrol; this meant that they had to get out of their cars to stop and question resentful and disgruntled citizens. Wilson himself had warned that the officer "must remember that there is no law against making a policeman angry; that he cannot charge a man with offending him" (O. Wilson, 1950, p. 393), but escalating hostilities invited questionable arrests. Such messy arrests were often witnessed by spectators who were sympathetic to arrestees; not surprisingly, this sometimes inspired collective disturbances. A wave of urban riots erupted in the late 1960s—43 in 1966 alone. The Watts riot in Los Angeles, which broke out on August 11, 1965, was sparked by a clumsy arrest of a resistant suspect (Toch, 1992).

Burning cities provided the impetus for a rethinking of police practices. One such review was that of the President's Commission on Civil Disorders (the Kerner Commission), which concluded that a key ingredient of riots was the view of police as the embodiment of "white power, white racism and white repression" (National Advisory Commission, 1968, p. 11). More focused on policing was the 1967 President's Commission on Law Enforcement and Administration of Justice, which fielded a Task Force on the Police. The report issued by this task force pointed out that "impatience, frustration, and now violence are growing quickly in minority communities and these trends are likely to accelerate. Consequently, if the problem is not to get worse, to the serious detriment of both the police and the community, drastic and creative action is urgently needed" (President's Commission, 1967b, p. 207). The report concluded that

> since police–community relations create serious problems in cities throughout the country, such relations must be one of the principal criteria in evaluating any policy or activity on the department. Indeed, in view of the extremely serious problems and the possibility that police relations with certain segments of the community may worsen, it may often be the most important factor. (1967b, p. 206)

In line with such assumptions, the central emphasis of the report was placed on reforms designed to promote and improve police–community relations. Such reforms included the creation of community relations units, the hiring of college graduates and of more minority officers to work in minority communities, and the instituting of training programs to inculcate sensitivity to cultural differences and to improve officers' interpersonal skills.

The 1967 report also raised the possibility of creating advisory groups of citizens to assist police departments. The task force noted that "where there is a commitment to exploring basic enforcement policy questions, the citizens' advisory group or policymaking board has the advantage of involving the community in the decision-making process, thus giving a broader base than would otherwise exist for the acceptance and support of enforcement policies" (1967b, p. 34). The report cautioned that "contact with well established and organized interest groups" fell short of community involvement, because involvement presupposed the opportunity for "unorganized citizenry to make themselves heard" (p. 35). At the community level, the task force suggested that individual patrolmen meet with citizens to explore their sentiments about the way arrest discretion was exercised. For example,

> Open discussion with neighborhood residents as to what their tolerance is for noise, for drunks on the streets, or for youths congregating on hot summer nights will help to produce law enforcement which protects rather than harasses the residents and induces citizens to aid and respect, rather than harass, the police. Where police discretion is involved, an accurate reading of community sentiment is an invaluable guide to the law enforcement officer. (p. 157)

Precinct-level committees could thus be formed to "elicit citizen views of police enforcement practices in the precinct"; such views, according to the task force, "should be considered as one relevant factor as to how [enforcement] measures are used" (1967b, p. 157) and "the ideal precinct committee would act as a real participant in police policy formulation within the bounds of law and the requirements of effective crime control" (p. 158).

Such prescriptions encompass elements of what later became community policing (see chap. 11, this volume) but do so diffidently and in a limited fashion. One reason is that in 1967 the officer's role was still largely envisaged in traditional fashion. The task force members took notice of the possibility, for example, that officers might observe community problems (such as "uncollected garbage, locked playgrounds, housing code violations, consumer frauds) and could "take the initiative in reporting them to the appropriate agency" (1967b, p. 162), but they added that "active police involvement in what may be labeled 'social work' programs raises profound questions about the role of the police" (p. 162).

As an example of reticence, the task force noted that some departments had experimented with foot patrols to promote police–citizen contacts. The task force then added the following disclaimer:

> A decision to use foot patrols should be made only after careful analysis, since it is a highly expensive form of coverage, geographically restrictive in nature, and can be wasteful of manpower. [I]t provides extremely inflexible and rigid close patrol for specifically limited geographical areas. . . . Moreover, close supervision of foot patrolmen has proven very difficult. (1967b, p. 54)

Community relations as a reform strategy had retained the Progressives' emphasis on rationality. It seemed reasonable for citizens to live in harmony with each other and with the police and for police to treat citizens with cultural sensitivity. Where persuasion did not convince officers or citizens of such ends, the strategy called for more exquisitely formulated arguments. As an example, the report noted that "frequently, recruits or officers are completely indifferent or hostile to [community relations] training because they do not regard it as 'real police work' Thus, unless carefully planned, community relations training may reinforce antagonism to minority groups and community relations generally." The response by the task force was that "universities and other groups having experts from various disciplines should be encouraged to develop new techniques and curricula, to run training programs, and to evaluate them" (1967b, p. 178).

The beneficiaries of most community relations ministrations were defined as targets. The notion that officers or citizens could become participants in change affecting them had not yet appeared. By this time, however, kindred notions had surfaced in the private sector, where participatory management approaches had been gaining currency (chap. 4, this volume). The next wave of police reformers would benefit from these approaches, and some of their experiments would call into question the managerial assumptions of the Progressive paradigm.

The 1967 Task Force talked of team policing, but the issue the task force members had in mind in connection with teaming was that of miscommunication between detectives and patrolmen, which resulted from the withholding of information. The proposed remedy was to promote a modicum of collaboration by associating the officers and detectives at the precinct level.

The Advent of Participatory Policing

Team policing, as it was eventually redefined (chap. 4, this volume), became a revolutionary reconceptualization of police organizations. It vested power in autonomous groups of officers who were accorded responsibility for providing police service to a neighborhood or community. A corollary was that the groups of officers would work closely with residents in defining their self-assigned missions.

In the United States, these new ideas were quietly but subversively shaped by a few innovative police chiefs and their consultants. They acquired the status of a reform movement in 1973, when the model was endorsed by yet another task force of another commission, the National Advisory Commission on Criminal Justice Standards and Goals. In defining team policing, this task force stressed the importance of self-direction. It asked,

> What is team policing? Essentially it is assigning police responsibility for a certain area to a team of police officers. The more responsibility this team has, the greater the degree of team policing. For instance, team policing that has investigative authority is more complete than team policing that does not. Teams that have authority to tailor programs and procedures to the needs of their areas go even further. (1973, p. 154)

The period between 1967 and 1973 had experienced several other police democratization experiments, which the task force members assiduously reviewed. One pioneering department singled out by the task force was that of Kansas City, Missouri. Concurrently with the deliberations of the task force, Kansas City had conducted the study we have mentioned that showed that one could reduce or eliminate preventive patrols without incurring increases in crime or fear of crime or reducing citizen dissatisfaction (Kelling et al., 1974).

The study had been suggested by a group that was largely composed of patrolmen. Kelling and Kliesmet pointed out that the Kansas City, Missouri, police department [had] received funds to add a large number of new officers. Chief Clarence Kelley conducted a series of conversations with his top command staff to determine how to allocate these new officers. Frustrated by their prosaic suggestions, he created four task forces consisting primarily of patrol officers, and asked them to develop allocation plans. The South Patrol Division ... decided that the most serious problem was youth behavior around schools. Some of the officers wanted to use the new officers to deal with this problem. Other officers firmly believed in the deterrent value of preventive patrol and, while they agreed that something should be done about the youth problem, nonetheless wanted all the new officers to be assigned to routine preventive patrol. A vigorous debate resulted, with some officers arguing the value of preventive patrol and others arguing that it had little impact Finally, the officers decided to experiment with levels of patrol to determine the efficacy of patrol before they decided how to proceed with the youth problem. Kelling was invited by the task force to help them develop a research design. Kelley approved the ultimate recommendation of the officers that an experiment should be conducted over the objections of many commanders. Patrol officers participated in every facet of the experiment, from monitoring the experiment, to data analysis; to write-up. (1996, pp. 207–208)

There was also mention of the project we describe in chapters 5 through 8, which the task force summarized as follows:

Oakland, Calif. has been involved in a complex peer-group pressure program for nearly 1 year to identify employees who are potential disciplinary problems. Initially the program is specializing in over-aggressiveness and verbal conflict traits. Employees with these characteristics are identified by a detailed reporting system, after a predetermined number of conflict incidents. An employee and a group of peers then engage in personal discussion and critique for 2 to 8 hours. This group has no power other than to offer personal observations and advice. This meeting is not part of the disciplinary process and the information resulting from the encounter remains confidential. So far the only employee who has appeared before the group twice requested the second meeting himself, claiming he needed the groups' assistance. The program's purpose is to prevent censurable employee performance, but it does not affect subsequent disciplinary action. (National Advisory Commission, 1973, p. 494)

One feature of the intervention that was not mentioned in the task force report was the crucial fact that this experiment was also designed by a group of officers. This procedure happened to be eminently compatible with the task force recommendation that "police agencies should draw on the knowledge and experience of their own personnel at all levels when formulating policy" (National Advisory Commission, 1973, p. 26). The Task Force expanded on this point by saying,

> The most effective and sensible way to overcome employee resistance to policy defining the police role is to enlist the cooperation of officers at all levels. Their varied experience can contribute to making the policy realistic and acceptable. An officer's self-respect is enhanced when he realizes that his superiors value his opinion. (p. 35)

Elsewhere, the task force expressed this same thought, with an important addendum:

> Neither the police chief executive nor the unit commander can, alone, establish goals and objectives. All employees within the agency, particularly employees at the execution level, can contribute to the understanding of the problems. These employees have face-to-face contact with members of the community and are coping with problems in the field. They, in turn, *will understand the problems to be met only through contact and discussion of the problems with members of the community.* (National Advisory Commission, 1973, p. 50, emphasis added)

The model implicit in the last sentence envisaged shared thinking between officers and citizens. It envisaged a partnership between rank-and-file officers and rank-and-file civilians to study community problems and suggest approaches to the solution of these problems. In the words of the task force,

> Efforts to improve relations between the public and the police have been most successful when the two have joined together in common causes. When the policemen who patrol a neighborhood meet with its residents to discuss crime problems in the area and jointly to develop solutions to them, there is a fundamental exchange of understanding. (1973, p. 61)

In line with such thinking, the task force recommended the following:

> Every police agency should arrange for officers assigned to geographic policing programs to meet regularly with persons who live or work in their area to discuss the identification of crime problems and the cooperative development of solutions to these problems. (1973, p. 63)

The importance of the problem-oriented aspect of the model was anticipated by the task force when it observed,

> Often an action is not successful because an officer did not understand the problem, did not determine specifically what he wanted to accomplish by the action, or did not consider alternatives. Many times an officer must take action without time to consider the formalities of planning; but if he has been trained to plan, he will be more likely to do it properly when circumstances permit. (1973, p. 120)

Starting with an obsession with the unseemliness of grassroots politics and the corruptibility of officers, reform had evolved in two decades to a point where chiefs were asked to repose their trust in officers and citizens and charge them with the solution of problems.[5] When we consider that most organizations tend to resist most change, this transmutation had arguably placed the police profession in the forefront of those who can adapt to a rapidly changing world.

Notes

1. Crime rates have at times declined (including recently), and police departments have taken credit for local crime reductions. They tend to offer different explanations for crime increases, where such occur.

2. The tendency of American police chiefs to mistrust their subordinates were reinforced from time to time by exposés of police misconduct and by corruption scandals, which have reliably led to escalated demands for tight and pervasive supervision.

3. Kelling and Kliesmet (1996) wrote that "it is hard to exaggerate the extent to which labeling the reform agenda of the early and mid-twentieth century police leaders as 'professional' was a misnomer—indeed, it was an oxymoron" (p. 193).

4. The Progressives were invested in efforts to prevent delinquency, to ameliorate mental illness, and to rehabilitate criminal offenders. They invented probation, parole, juvenile court, and the calling of social work. The Progressives disapproved of prisons and mental hospitals, whose regimes they saw as sterile and stultifying (Rothman, 1980). The reform of prisons and police departments were at times advocated by the same groups of progressive reformers (Walker, 1977).

5. Some observers (including Walker) attribute the democratization of policing to the power of police unions. But other students note that police unions are mostly concerned with improving bread-and-butter benefits rather than with enhancing the professional role of officers. Unions also serve their members by adding to bureaucratic rules rather than by questioning their relevance (Kelling & Kliesmet, 1996).

Chapter

3

Pioneering Efforts

The accounts we have available of the first problem-oriented experiments reflect their pioneering flavor and the uncertainty this brings. These accounts, however, also provide a sense of what it means for the adventure to culminate in experienced success.

The Baltimore County COPE (Citizen-Oriented Police Enforcement) project, one of the first self-styled problem-oriented police experiments, took place in a traditionally oriented police department (a stance paraphrased by Taft [1986] as, "If you didn't bust heads or lock them up, you called social services"), which had acquired a new chief in 1977. The chief was a progressive administrator (deemed "a risk taker from the start") who was interested in engendering reform. He saw his opportunity in 1981, when he encountered strongly felt community concerns that had been sparked by violent crimes. These community concerns had prompted county executives to authorize hiring 45 new police officers for the chief to deploy as he saw fit.

The chief initially decided to organize his new officers into a patrol force to fight fear. He appointed a project team, which organized the officers into three smaller units, comprising 15 men each. The units were to patrol their areas on motorcycles (a compromise between car and foot) to "have more direct contact with citizens." They were instructed to conduct "fear surveys" and "use any means within their power to quell fear" (Taft, 1986,

p. 10). The three units had no other predefined mission and received no further guidance as to what they should do. They consequently embarked on the running of door-to-door crime fear surveys, which they said made them feel "like Fuller Brush salesmen." They also ran crime prevention meetings in their neighborhoods and complained of boredom. They proclaimed that they felt nostalgic about conventional police work, and "became frustrated by what they perceived to be severe limitations on traditional tactics being imposed from on high" (p. 12). The overt frustration level of the officers became extremely worrisome and the survival of the experiment was in doubt. At this juncture—six months into the project—the chief's advisors decided that "it seemed like an ideal time to bring in Herman Goldstein" (p. 13).

Goldstein's 1979 article (see chap. 1, this volume) was intended as a prescription for managers, not police officers. The Baltimore County officers, fortunately, did not catch on to this distinction and applied the prescription to themselves. They liked the notion of doing research, brainstorming, and preparing action plans based on research results. "We needed a light at the end of the tunnel," one of them testified, "and this was our light" (quoted in Taft, 1986, p. 14).

A pair of the more enterprising team members descended on a housing project whose residents had been noted for hostility to police. The officers conducted their surveys, compiled crime statistics, photographed potholes, and measured the borders of playgrounds. Their statistics showed that most crimes in the area occurred after dark, and the officers decided to arrange for street lights to be repaired. They used their photographs to inspire the county to do road repair. They hypothesized that youth leisure was a crime-related problem and "badgered county park and recreation officials until a dormant rehabilitation and construction project was approved for a local park" (Taft, 1986, p. 15). The chief and his staff supported each of the officers' initiatives and rewarded them with praise, and the COPE model was thus institutionalized.

Institutionalization of COPE meant that the officers had to perfect routines and procedures for studying and addressing problems in their neighborhoods. Taft reported that brainstorming sessions became longer and more spirited. "We would do action plans on a blackboard and argue about them for two days," says Off. Sam Hannigan of the central COPE unit. "We felt like we were in one of those self-improvement courses where they wouldn't let you go to the bathroom." Action plans grew thicker and more detailed. Officers grew more savvy in their negotiations with other agencies. "It got to the point where we came to expect the runaround," said Off. Blair Melvin of the central COPE unit. "We learned real quick to say, 'Let me speak with your supervisor.' " (1986, p. 17)

One of the problems tackled by COPE was an apartment complex that had been terrorized by street robberies. The officer first assigned to the project did a survey of the residents and reported to his colleagues that

he found that most of the residents were elderly women who felt particularly vulnerable to street attacks. Most were unwilling to leave their apartments after dark. Their feelings were exacerbated by the conditions of the complex: many street and building lights were broken; unkempt trees and shrubs created many hiding places; rats, stray dogs, and unrepaired structural damage all contributed to the feeling— widespread among residents—that they were trapped. (Eck & Spelman, 1987b, p. 40)

The COPE officers set out to get the senior citizens organized. Neighborhood groups and community organizations supplied technical assistance, and the apartment residents soon had their own local association. A church provided meeting facilities, a baker supplied donuts, and a printer donated printing services.

The officers also arranged for street lights to be repaired and for buildings to be inspected. After the inspectors had made unflattering reports, "the apartment manager bowed to accumulated pressures, and began to refurbish the buildings" (Eck & Spelman, 1987b, p. 41). In the wake of this flurry of actions, the string of robberies stopped and residential burglaries were sharply curtailed. Equally relevant as an outcome, "COPE provided the residents with better living conditions and a new

Community Association that can help them obtain further improvements" (p. 41).

Another problem the officers tackled was a localized skid row population (see chap. 1, this volume) of men who were involved in aggressive panhandling and who had become increasingly unpopular with area merchants. The chamber of commerce demanded police action. The officers drafted a no-nonsense panhandling statute, but "knew that even stiffer sentences would not prevent the vagrants from returning" (Taft, 1986, p. 18). In considering more enduring solutions, they turned to a model that had been devised by several police departments in the late 1960s, starting with a Vera Foundation experiment, the Bowery Project, in New York City. The most ambitious of these interventions had been instituted by the St. Louis Police Department (1970), which went into the alcoholic treatment business. The St. Louis Department set up a Detoxification and Diagnostic Evaluation Center to which police officers brought chronic alcoholics they had picked up for counseling and therapy.

In communities in which police-sponsored detoxification centers had been established, experts had designed the programs and municipal executives had implemented them. In Baltimore County, for the first time, rank-and-file officers did the spade work and the designing. They interviewed hospital officials, Salvation Army officers, welfare workers, and legal authorities and they questioned vagrants "to determine if they would use such a facility" (Taft, 1986, p. 18). They studied the services available to alcoholics and reviewed laws relating to drunkenness and vagrancy. As they did this work, they expressed incredulity ("At times we turned to each other and said, 'can you believe we are doing this?' " [p. 19]), but gained enthusiasm and considerable knowledge. When they presented their implementation steps, starting with a Task Force on the Homeless (which was instituted), they sounded convincing and authoritative.

COPE received prestigious awards, but was less successful in overcoming peer resistance. Taft observed that "often riding motorcycles and wearing leather jackets, COPE officers are considered 'glory boys' by their counterparts on patrol" (1986, p. 21). He noted that the officers were viewed as something other than "real cops" who did "real police work" (p. 21). The sticking point was that COPE was not really a crime-fighting unit. As one of the founders of COPE observed, "Let's face it: no matter what you say, people join police departments to chase criminals. It's cops and robbers. And it will be very hard to break that stereotype" (Taft, 1986, p. 29).

Patrol officer resistance of this kind has struck police experts as ironic because the experts have conceived of projects such as COPE as advancing the officers' collective interests. In the case of COPE, they saw impact "on the amount of power and responsibility that is vested in the individual officer . . . the . . . approach encourages the imagination, resourcefulness and intelligence of each officer . . . exploits the enormous amount of practical experience most officers possess" (p. 22). They also noted that projects such as COPE dilute the military hierarchy of police. As reported by Taft:

> In at least one COPE unit, commanders and line officers have established such a good working relationship that, they insist, rank has become almost superfluous. "As far as I can see, the lieutenant and the sergeant are both one of us," says Off. Sam Hannigan of the central COPE unit. "We do surveys together. We go over action plans together. You could get rid of the titles 'lieutenant' and 'sergeant' and call them 'supervisor' and 'foreman.' " Says Ernie Bures, Hannigan's sergeant, pointing to his stripes, "I don't need these anymore." (1986, pp. 23–24)

Projects such as COPE also garner esteem for the police. The citizens who came in contact with the problem-oriented officers said things like "talking to a COPE officer is like talking to a regular human being" (Taft, 1986, p. 26). A study that was done by an outside researcher showed increased citizen satisfaction in COPE precincts (16%), decreased fear (10%), fewer police calls (11%), and fewer offenses reported to the police (12%; Cordner, 1986). On the other side of the ledger, bureaucrats declared themselves ambivalent, and some of them "complained that COPE officers overstepped their bounds while tinkering with community affairs in their neighborhoods. 'It's the tail wagging the dog,' complained one. . . . The lines of authority and responsibility start getting very gray" (Taft, 1986, p. 25).

Baltimore County established four COPE units and taught problem solving in its police academy. It did not claim to have a problem-oriented police department. A police department in Newport News, Virginia, on the other hand, embarked on a direction that came closer to this objective.

The Newport News Experiment

Darrell Stephens, ex-chief of the Newport News Police Department, said that "instead of creating a special unit or function, we asked line officers and supervisors to work problem solving into their daily routine" (Eck & Spelman, 1987a, p. vi). The premise of this effort was that "problem-solving can be applied by officers throughout the agency as part of their daily work" (p. xvii), and the definition of problem orientation adopted in Newport News was that it is "an agency-wide strategy to encourage and guide all its members to engage in problem-solving" (p. 5).

Newport News started by setting up a task force "to develop and implement the problem-solving process" (Eck & Spelman, 1987a, p. 7). A task force is usually a group that represents a cross-section of an organization, which has been assembled to think through a specific topic. In the case of Newport News, the task force consisted of 11 "volunteers," ranging in rank from patrol officers to deputy chiefs (the chief sat in). The group also included a consultant from the Police Executive Research Forum, a member of the federally sponsored team that helped the police department with its project. One way in which this consulting team helped was that it located promising police experiments that the task force visited and compared. An important outcome of these reviews was that "agencies that documented program effectiveness were more convincing to Task Force members than those agencies that only provided opinions" (Eck & Spelman, 1987a, p. 7).

The task force subdivided problem solving into a four-stage process, from problem identification to assessment of solutions. The group spent most of its time on the second stage, which it defined as "analysis, or learning the problem's causes and consequences" (p. 7). They developed a detailed analysis guide, listing attributes of actors (offenders, victims, and third parties), incidents (including sequence of events and contextual factors), and responses to incidents (community and institutional responses) that they felt should be covered in a study of any problem the police might run across.

The task force next embarked on two ambitious problem-solving ventures of its own. This shift from sandbox to battlefield was partly intended as a demonstration and as an inspiration to the rest of the department's members. In the words of Eck and Spelman:

> Work on these two problems accomplished three objectives. First, the two problems provided sources of information about the "real world" of problem-solving that could be used to develop the process and guide. Second, officers working on these problems received a great deal of recognition from senior officials. The experience provided by working on these problems demonstrated that department members would be rewarded for innovative approaches. Third, the successes in addressing the two problems convinced members of the Task Force, as well as other members of the department, that problem-oriented policing could work. (1987a, p. 7)

In the first project, a patrol officer was assigned to study thefts from the parked cars of shipbuilding workers in lots that surrounded the Newport News shipyards. In preceding years, between 700 and 800 thefts annually had been reported; these thefts accounted for 10% of index crimes in Newport News. Yet, car thefts were not taken particularly seriously, because individual damage was low. Eck and Spelman reported that "when the problem was first posed for study by a member of the Task Force who had once patrolled the parking areas, the idea was met with much joking and criticism" (1987a, p. 73).

The officer the task force assigned to the project, Paul Swartz, started with offense and arrest reports covering a three-year period. He obtained a printout from the city's computer and "hand tabulated the data in literally dozens of ways, focusing on three characteristics: when the thefts were committed, where they were committed, and who (probably) committed them" (Eck & Spelman, 1987a, p. 74). One result of the officer's painstaking analysis was that he was able to pinpoint "theft-prone" areas. Using spot maps, he identified seven vulnerable lots that invited the highest break-in rates.

Next, Swartz picked the brains of fellow officers and experienced detectives who worked the area, and talked to members of the shipyard's security force. Thereafter, he "interviewed several thieves convicted and sentenced for breaking into vehicles in these parking lots. He promised the offenders that nothing said in the interviews would be used against them" (Eck & Spelman, 1987b, p. 43).

The offender interviews yielded rich information about the stealing habits of two clusters of geographically separated thieves:

> Swartz learned that drugs were a prime target of the northern thieves, but stereo equipment and car parts were also targets. They especially looked for "muscle" cars, cars with bumper stickers advertising local rock and roll radio stations, or cars with other evidence that the owner might be a marijuana smoker or cocaine user. (Thrush [an interview subject] related that a roach clip or a feather hanging from the rearview mirror, or a corner of a plastic bag sticking out of the glove compartment were dead giveaways.) Thrush confirmed that the northern thieves worked together. . . .
>
> Further interviews confirmed and extended Thrush's testimony. The southern thieves were after money, rather than drugs; as a result, they concentrated on car stereo equipment, auto parts, guns, and other goods that could be fenced easily. Although they worked independently, they did know one another. (Eck & Spelman, 1987a, p. 75)

Swartz was now armed with a mine of information, which he disseminated in the form of crime analysis bulletins and talks at patrol lineups. Within weeks, three prime suspects were arrested in the process of breaking into cars, and the theft rate in parking lots dropped. This short-term result was regarded as a testimonial to a data-based inquiry, in that the police department's response to the theft from vehicles problem [had heretofore] involved mostly traditional tactics—interception patrol, plainclothes stakeouts, and the like. But these [new] tactics were directed in nontraditional ways, through extensive analysis of police records, through the pooling of the street information known to individual officers, and through development of a new data source, the offenders themselves. As a result, patrol officers knew where and when to look, and for whom. (Eck & Spelman, 1987a, p. 76)

The results of the intervention were also assessed by studying incident rates. The analysis was sophisticated and confirmed that the experiment could be deemed successful:

Time-series analysis of 39 months of reported thefts prior to the intervention and 16 months after . . . shows that *the number of reported thefts has been reduced by more than half* since the directed patrol tactics began in April 1985. This works out to a reduction of nearly one theft per day, or nearly 450 thefts prevented as of July 1986. (Eck & Spelman, 1987a, p. 76)

However, these low incident rates would be expected to jump back (and in fact, did) with diminishment of pressure. Swartz knew that he had to consider longer term solutions and "suspected that other agencies and businesses would need to be involved if the long-run response was to be effective" (Eck & Spelman, 1987a, p. 75). His campaign yielded mixed (and, at times, amusing) results. The plant security force was willing to help, but could only do so by disseminating information. Insurance companies argued that the problem was not "serious." Swartz found the following:

Although they paid a substantial amount in claims to their clients, the amount was small relative to other claims. Moreover, it was stable, so they were able to charge high premiums for comprehensive insurance and gain a tidy profit each year. A one-year reduction in thefts would mean a windfall profit for the insurers; but this would force them to reduce premiums, and they might lose money the next year if thefts returned to their earlier levels. (1987a, pp. 75–76)

A more favorable development occurred serendipitously: The Department of City Planning—which had never heard of Officer Swartz—studied parking as part of an ambitious urban renewal effort that included a plan for multilevel garages. A police detective with his ear to the ground learned of this venture. The detective had himself assigned to the site review board. There, he became the resident expert on "crime prevention through environmental design of parking lots and other . . . buildings" (Eck & Spelman, 1987a, p. 76).

The Battle of New Briarfield

The second task force problem target was a low-income project "generally regarded as the worst housing in Newport News" (Eck & Spelman, 1987a, p. 66). This housing project had the highest burglary rate in the city, which was defined as an issue to be addressed. The police had opened an office in a vacant apartment and as a result the burglary rate dropped, but it jumped back when police moved out of their office. This failure of conventional enforcement became a challenge for the task force, which was looking for worthy problems to attack.

The task was first assigned to a detective with civilian research assistants. This team went to work and found, among other things, that idle teenagers congregated in the housing development during school hours. These young truants were reputed (by residents) to pass their self-assigned free time committing burglaries and acts of vandalism. Officers who were interviewed at this time described a more comprehensive problem, which they called the "death cycle" of apartments:

> First, a tenant moves out of the unit. Kids break in, remove anything of value, and vandalize the unit. This leaves the apartment unprotected: doors remain ajar, windows are broken. Unless the unit is quickly boarded up (and until recently, the apartment maintenance crew rarely did so), addicts and

drinkers begin to take refuge there to get high, and kids continue to play in the structure. The unit deteriorates more quickly, now that it is exposed to the elements. The combination of weather and vandalism create structural defects in the exterior walls, floors, and ceilings; over time, these defects get worse, and may spread to adjacent units. Sometimes the unsavory users intimidate the legitimate residents next door. In any case, residents of neighboring units are likely to leave. This creates opportunities for other units to be broken into, pillaged, and made uninhabitable. . . . In the end, the entire row of units becomes vacant. (Eck & Spelman, 1987a, p. 67)

The team ran a survey of residents, after they pretested questions and moved mountains to ensure a high response rate. The respondents in this survey spoke freely, and the picture they painted was bleak. They said that crime and the fear of crime had circumscribed their lives. For instance, "one young mother stated that she was so afraid of a break-in that she did not even keep food in the unit. Instead, she kept it at her mother's home and took a bus three miles whenever she had to prepare a meal" (Eck & Spelman, 1987a, p. 68). There were residents who did not go outdoors, and most adults never went out after dark.

Physical conditions were the residents' next most pressing concern. This concern was not only expressed in general terms but was documented with illustrative instances:

Some told (and showed) interviewers real horror stories: in some units, roofs or floors had caved in and the residents left to the elements for up to six weeks; a water main had recently broken, flooding parts of the complex for nearly a month before it was repaired; cold drafts blew through large cracks in numerous door and window frames. (Eck & Spelman, 1987a, p. 69)

The sense of stark disillusionment and resignation that pervaded the survey responses impressed the task force and reinforced its resolve to act. Eck and Spelman (1987a) pointed out that "prior to the survey, Task Force members were more likely to blame the residents for their plight than to sympathize with them. But after the survey the Task Force members became much more concerned about the community" (p. 71). The survey also had undergirded observations that had been made by officers about the intimate link between deterioration and criminal offenses, that "the poor and deteriorating conditions were one of the causes of the burglaries, as well as one of the consequences" (p. 69).

Officer Haddix, one of the members of the task force, "took it upon himself to improve the physical conditions at New Briarsfield" (Eck & Spelman, 1987a, p. 71). He started by persuading the reluctant manager to have all trash removed, including from a swimming pool that had become an unsightly garbage dump. He arranged for streets to be cleaned and for abandoned cars—which littered the area—to be towed. The detective who had initiated the project now became a real estate detective. With the help of brokers and other experts on the machinations of tax deduction gambits, the detective located successive partnerships that owned and milked the deteriorated complex. He filed a detailed report of his findings with the chief, who relayed the document to the heads of city agencies, inviting them to attend a meeting under police sponsorship. This meeting was unique in that it became "the first combined action by Newport News city departments on any issue of its kind" (Eck & Spelman, 1987a, p. 71). The actions of the group were strong and decisive: Owners of the development were given 30 days to bring their buildings into code compliance or have the units demolished. The Department of Housing and Urban Development (HUD) took over the complex, with the understanding that a new development was to be built. Two years later, the city bought the complex, which was finally demolished in 1989 (Police Executive Research Forum, 1989a).

A third officer, Officer Lyons, had moved into the area as a foot patrol officer and became a community organizer. He expanded a crime watch group and formed a second organization to lobby for tenant rights.

In the meantime, outcome data were collected. They showed a 35% drop in the local burglary rate, which had previously been going up. They also showed improvement in attitudes toward the police and "a great deal of cooperation from the residents" (Eck & Spelman, 1987a, p. 72). Physical changes had occurred, and the complex "remained relatively trash free since the initial police cleanup efforts" (p. 72).

Expanding the Process

Task force members undertook these problem-solving efforts and inspired other officers to join them to the extent to which their schedules permitted. Among the many projects that were initiated in this way were studies of domestic homicides, gas station drive-offs, assaults on officers, driving while intoxicated (DWI), disturbances at convenience stores, localized drug dealing, robberies in office buildings, commercial burglaries, vacant buildings, rowdiness in a skating rink, trespassing dirt bikes, and disturbances at a shopping center.

The assault project was typical of the smaller scale efforts. It was a study conducted by a sergeant in the internal affairs division, who reviewed a large sample (7 months) of police assault incident reports. The sergeant discovered one fact that was surprising: Half of the incidents had occurred in the booking room of the headquarters building. On a hunch, the sergeant visited booking rooms in other police departments and concluded that "the layout of the room needlessly put arresting officers at risk of assault" (Eck & Spelman, 1987a, p. 91). The sergeant persuaded architecture students from a local university to redesign the room, which was later renovated.

The sergeant had simultaneously discovered that some of the younger officers appeared to be assault-prone and that several of the offenders had been repeatedly involved. Based on these facts, she decided "to look at the problem from a psychological perspective, again with the help of local universities" (p. 92).

Activities such as these provided officers new and different experiences. Eck and Spelman (1987a) pointed out that Newport News police "have conducted literature reviews, interviewed prostitutes and thieves, surveyed businesses, held conferences with local public and private officials, photographed problem sites, and searched title and tax records" (p. xxiii). Most of the officers who had done such things testified that they had enjoyed the activities and prized the knowledge they acquired. They said that they found research tasks "more interesting than chasing calls for service or investigating reported crimes, especially when problem-solving periods were interspersed with periods of doing more traditional police work" (p. 93). There were some officers, on the other hand, who became "impatient with analysis of problems for which the proper responses seem[ed] obvious to them" (p. 93). In fact, "the tendency to act before analyzing," according to Eck and Spelman (1987a), "pervades the department" (p. 94). Eck and Spelman (1987a) also noted that "there have been occasional grumblings from officers not assigned to solve problems that their problem-solving comrades have not pulled their fair share of incident-driven weight" (pp. 95–96).

According to the results of a police department survey, 60% of the Newport News force (and its entire top brass) found the problem-solving approach to be personally useful. This did not mean, of course, that the process had been institutionalized. Only a third of those who were involved in projects felt that "I have received the recognition I deserve for my efforts" (Eck & Spelman, 1987a, p. 98). This fact made sense because, "although personal satisfaction from serving the public well is in itself a strong incentive, most officers rely on their fellow officers and supervisors when judging whether their efforts are worthwhile" (p. 100). A reward system for problem solving was not systematically instituted and is difficult to design. Time budgeting was another constraint, because incident-driven policing makes peremptory demands, which must take precedence. Assignments also proved too inflexible to allow all problem solvers to remain with problems until they were solved. Moreover, time pressures invite shortcuts, so that "officers often skip the analysis step and jump directly into proposing the solution" (p. 101). It is also hard to change public perceptions of the police, and "explaining problem-oriented policing may be difficult" (p. 109).

Research and Reform

The link between research and reform lies at the core of the problem-oriented approach, which assumes that underlying conditions can be illuminated and solutions can be inferred from inventories of facts. One sticking point is that of possible gaps between diagnoses and prescriptions, or between data and suggested implications for action. Social scientists and officers are well-intentioned people who want to see improvements in undesirable social conditions. Humane interventions are intrinsically worthy, but this is different from having data that document their desirability. All kids should have playgrounds, for example, and to promote the building of a playground is a noble and satisfying endeavor. But one may not have data that support the need for such a project, such as inventories of extracurricular pursuits of neglected children or observations that show playground sites (or prospective sites) to have been coopted by drug dealers. At best, data tell us that one can solve two crime-related problems (the need for constructive play activities and the dismantling of a crime site) with a combinatory intervention. No such rationale applies where a disused lot is photographed on general principle with the preexisting intent of shaming a parks department into building a playground.

A caveat applies where previous data, collected elsewhere, have led to an inference that can be invoked because it covers the situation one has encountered. Such has been proposed by advocates of the "broken windows hypothesis" (Wilson & Kelling, 1982), which holds that deterioration of a neighborhood leads to community disorganization, which very much includes high rates of crimes. This assumption justifies standard problem-oriented moves, such as cleanups, disposal of abandoned cars, new street lights, road repairs, and so forth. The approach makes more sense, however, with follow-up assessment to prove that the interventions worked. It is possible, for example, that the steps taken have locally evanescent results, which suggests that cultural norms must be addressed as physical improvements are effected. Simply doing something because it was done elsewhere does not qualify as buttressing. Conditions may be similar, but may also be in essential respects unique. Senior citizens, for instance, do not benefit from playgrounds in their neighborhood and may find them a nuisance.

In the New Briarfield housing complex project, a newly created data-based causal model was available, supplied by officers who had observed crime-deterioration links in the "death" of apartment units, buttressed by survey data that described trapped tenants and their disengagement. Subsequent police actions plausibly interrupted causal chains, involving the predicted effects of crime-infested abandoned buildings on the lives of remaining tenants. The project is a rare and sophisticated example of what the problem-oriented model looks like when all the inferential leaps can be made.

One difficulty is that the questions the typical analysis poses (who? where? how? to whom?) do not necessarily answer the question (why?) that pertains to causation. And it is additionally not obvious that if we could answer this question, we have the means to neutralize causes, which are usually long-term, obdurate, complex, and linked to other causes. Detoxification, for example, does not neutralize causes of alcoholism and has no chance of curing hard-core alcoholics. But that is not really the point. A problem-oriented approach is not designed to remedy structural problems but to make sure that one does not ignore them. And the first step to this end is to recognize that symptoms occur in groups, and have common origins. It also helps to get a feel for the human consequences of causal chains, as did the task force that reviewed the New Briarfield survey and sensed the alienation it depicted. Richer problem definition leads to more substantial responses, which can cumulatively make a difference that improves people's lives.

The best problem definition links experiential data with descriptive statistics, so that problems can be pinpointed and explored in depth. Officers may have a "feel" for a problem through close familiarity with individuals who manifest it, but may not be able to distinguish typical from atypical manifestations of the problem. Managers may know the scope of a problem in quantitative terms but may have no sense of what it means in human terms when one meets it live on the streets. Each perspective requires supplementation from the other perspective, although each may view the other as irrelevant. The problem of discordant perspectives has been described by Elizabeth Reuss-Ianni, who wrote,

> Reduced to its essentials . . . the conflict over how best to identify organizational or managerial problems and to seek

data necessary for problem solving and decision making embodies a tension between those who look to the folklore of the job and those who seek scientific or rational solutions to management problems. Each method may be valid, but each also has its limitations. The experiential empiricism of conventional folk-wisdom or "war stories" of practice provide an existential mode of problem identification, at least of the practical problems of day-to-day policing. It does not, however, provide a means of systematic data seeking or of generalizing beyond individual experience, and is consequently easily dismissed by those looking for scientific solutions. Many established police procedures and practices thereby escape serious questioning or attention. Routine data collected, including activity logs, arrest and crime coding sheets, and statistics on response time, provide standardized means of gathering information on the job. But field personnel frequently dismiss the data and the findings derived from them as irrelevant to their problems. As a result, many practitioners fail to use any research-generated data for improving practice or setting policy. (1983, pp. 18–19)

Science and Experience

Among plausible cop-outs (no puns) for an officer who is not interested in problem-oriented policing is to point out that he or she is not qualified to do social science research. Officers who make this argument are either trying to be funny or needlessly diffident, because research design and statistics are communicable skills and other assistance—computer programming, for instance—can be rented. Specialized expertise, such as knowledge about real estate or architecture in Newport News, for example, is also available in a community or at campuses.

Officers have an advantage over social scientists because they have a wealth of experiences. Firsthand experience is combinable with other data to the benefit of both. Experience helps make sense of data, whereas data ratify experiences. But combining experience and data requires translation of one information source into terms that are assimilable by the other. This means that officers cannot maintain that their experience is ineffable and that their premises must remain unexamined. They cannot advance arguments such as the following:

> It's hard to explain why I did that and why it worked. I've been here a long time, and I've learned what makes these people tick. They know me too. I know that's no answer, but if you watch a pizza baker throw dough in the air and asked him what he did to make it come down in a circle all the time, he probably couldn't tell you either. It's just something you learn over time, is all. (J. Fyfe, personal communication, 1990)

There is no way of combining knowledge, defined in this fashion, with scientific findings, because science assumes that facts must be checked, whereas the officer argues that "the unique conditions and nuances of any police field situation cannot be precisely replicated" (J. Fyfe, personal communication, 1990). This self-serving assumption is not only antithetical to science but to rational problem solving in general. If police situations are unique, they call for perpetually unique responses, and there would be no point in looking for patterns among incidents or solutions to groups of situations.

Science must in turn learn to accommodate experience. The scientist who works with police cannot tell officers, "Don't expect me to pay attention to your war stories, though I'll grant that some are entertaining, in a repulsive sort of way." Cross-fertilization of knowledge presupposes that we recognize that

1. Experiences can be pooled; if some are indeed unrepresentative, this fact emerges (and can be corrected for) when we compare experiences. If experience tells me that civilians explode when I appear on the scene, yet other officers elicit courteous responses in the same situation, this suggests that there may be reasons (such as my own behavior) for the difference between my experience and that of my colleagues. If, on the other hand, others make observations comparable to mine, this suggests that we are experiencing a reliable set of events that can be subjected to analysis.

Experiences always become data once they are recorded. The arrest report that memorializes my ineffable experience can be combined with other arrest reports. Items that may not have struck me as noteworthy (such as the age of the suspect or the presence of spectators) may emerge in tabulations as variables that help explain the outcome of my encounters.

The difference between experiences and data may be such that the former are an improvement on the latter. A questionnaire response suffers from brevity and may be biased by the question to which it responds. A narrative is richer and redolent with nuances that may illuminate a problem. Combined with the questionnaire response, the narrative aids interpretation and adds flesh to bones. One Thrush the Booster (the Newport News car thief) may be worth hundreds of arrest reports, and—more critically—helps make sense of them.

2. Experiences can be sources of hypotheses. The Newport News officers who described the "death cycle" of tenement dwellings advanced an experience-based theory, which was a richer theory than social scientists looking at statistics could have produced. This theory describes conditions that the officers had observed in revisiting the same locations over time. The theory portrayed stages corresponding to these conditions and made sense of them. We are invited to verify whether these stages occur in the same order in other housing complexes and we can ask ourselves whether the same process is at work. If a hypothesis is not experience-generated, on the other hand, it must stand the test of experience as a first check if it is to apply to real life. If I have a theory about car boosting that does not make sense to Thrush, chances are that I am wrong.

3. Doing social science can be experience. Gathering data gives one a feel for the subject one is gathering data about, which explains why it is important for officers to do research themselves, rather than

having it done for them. In doing a fear survey, the officer gets an intimate sense of the experience of fear and an enhanced appreciation of why he or she should be concerned about fear. Doing research educates and changes attitudes and is used for this purpose in problem-oriented policing. Questioning citizens in livingrooms provides officers with experiences that involve citizens as consumers of service rather than as suspects or complainants. Citizens who are surveyed have counterpart experiences, which involve officers as people who care. An equivalent benefit arises from questioning other officers, which places respondents in the role of experts, whose experiences and observations are valued. Other contacts—such as with bureaucrats—can provide officers with a sense of how citizens must feel when their needs are unattended to.

Finding Researchable Problems

A criterion for selecting entry points is to ask whether a police department faces problems that officers find puzzling and whether inferences can be drawn from research that would enhance police understanding of the problem. A second criterion would be whether enhanced understanding would help the police address the problem more sensibly or effectively.

Any police department knows of areas in which officers feel they could use greater understanding or where they respond with diminished confidence. In a review of problem areas that faced a state police department, for example, one such problem area had to do with an army base that had been opened in a remote rural setting. Officers who had dealt largely with farmers suddenly encountered a panoply of difficulties, some of which were enforcement-related and others service-related. These problems would now call for networking arrangements that could link the police force with municipal government and military authorities. Unfamiliar challenges could be illuminated by information (such as inventories of incidents and surveys of military families and area residents) help officers formulate strategies to meet these challenges.

If problem-oriented inquiry is to be perceived as relevant, it helps to start where the police feel that their experience falls short of guiding their actions. Such feelings spark a desire for knowledge, which can be attained through research. Knowledge is experienced as enhancing understanding. It also guides action and makes it more responsive and effective.

4

Organizational Change Issues

P olice departments are paramilitary organizations. This not only means that police wear uniforms and are marched to and from classes during training but that officers receive orders that pass through chains of command. These orders often presume the need to go into minute detail about what is required. They also presume that deviations from compliance are sanctionable.

These two features of police departments are not exclusive to the police but have been the lot of most workers in most organizations since the advent of the industrial revolution. They are products of a philosophy that achieved its low point with an approach called "scientific management," which was the cutting edge of management theory before World War I.

Scientific management was the brainchild of Frederick Winslow Taylor (1912/1947), who was obsessed with what he saw as inefficiency, which he attributed to personal and group-supported laziness.[1] "The natural laziness of men is serious," wrote Taylor, "but by far the greatest evil from which both workmen and employers are suffering is systematic soldiering . . . which results from a careful study on the part of the workmen of what they think will promote their best interests" (1912/1947, p. 32). Taylor charged that "so universal is soldiering for this purpose, that hardly a competent workman can be found in a large establishment . . . who does not devote a considerable part of his time to studying just how slowly he can work and still convince his employer that he is going at a good pace" (p. 33).

Taylor's proposed solution to this problem was twofold. First, he felt managers should ascertain the correct way of doing every job and next write detailed instructions about how the work was to be done. Managers should realize, he said, "that there is a best way in doing everything, and that that best way can always be formulated into certain rules; that you can get your knowledge away from the old chaotic rule-of-thumb knowledge into organized behavior" (Taylor, 1912b, p. 36). What Taylor meant by "rule-of-thumb" were the workers' own ideas about how to do their work, such as bringing their own shovels and shoveling coal in some favorite fashion.[2] With regard to shoveling, Taylor took the position that time and motion studies had prescribed a standard shovel that holds 21 pounds, and that "the most efficient method of shovelling is to put your right arm down on your right hip, hold your shovel on your left leg, and when you shovel into the pile throw the weight of your body into the shovel" (p. 40).

Taylor called for the creation of a managerial class that would plan and direct the workers' activities in as detailed a fashion as possible. In his own factory, he wrote, "it meant the building of a large, elaborate labor office where three college men worked, besides their clerks and assistants, planning the work for each of these workmen at least one day in advance" (Taylor, 1912a/ 1947, p. 39). The point that mattered to Taylor was that workers were not to think about their work, which was the prerogative of managers. In testimony before a congressional committee, he argued,

> It is next to impossible for the workman to develop a science. There are many workmen who are intellectually just as capable of developing a science, who have plenty of brains, and are just as capable of developing a science as those on the managing side. But the science of doing work of any kind cannot be developed by the workman. The development of the science of doing any kind of work always required the work of two men, one man who actually does the work which is to be studied and another man who observes closely the

first man while he works and studies the time problems
and the motion problems connected with this work. (Taylor,
1912b, p. 235)

The Human Relations School

Taylor was not only an autocrat but an industrial engineer for
whom technology was the guts of productivity, with the human
element almost subservient. If Taylor were alive today and running a police department, his main interest would be in using
information technology to define the best targets for enforcement
activities and to ensure that police officers and their supervisors
address these targets. We discuss a well-publicized example of
this approach (the so-called Compstat strategy) in chapter 10.

The risks of a purely technology-centered approach were recognized as early as the late 1920s, and the critique gave rise to
a perspective called the human relations school of management.
This school was first headquartered at Harvard University and
identified with a psychologist named Elton Mayo. The data on
which the approach was based derived from a set of experiments
referred to as the Hawthorne experiments, after the factory in
which they took place. These experiments started with a study
by engineers who sought to determine optimum illumination
levels for fast output. Their findings did not make sense (production seemed to go up irrespective of lighting conditions), and a
group of workers was assembled to explore the phenomenon.
These workers experienced a variety of working arrangements,
but seemed to find all of these irrelevant compared with their
supervision (benevolent) and their fellow workers (congenial).
The research participants in the experiment—which was known
as the relay assembly test room—also made decisions about their
work, but the importance of this fact was not discovered until
decades later.

Many textbooks have discussed the experiment as showing
what happens when beneficent attention is paid to individuals
in social interventions. The argument goes that when one attends
to people who are accustomed to being part of a crowd by placing
them on a stage (figuratively speaking), they will expend effort,

try to please, and demonstrate high morale. This result—the so-called Hawthorne effect—is supposed to make any experiment work for a short period of time. Once the novelty wears off, however (the "honeymoon period" ends), the impact on participants is expected to dissipate.

The Hawthorne experiments included an observational study—the bank wiring room—in which it was noted that workers sabotaged efforts to make them work harder. The juxtaposition of contrasting experiences (with relay assembly and bank wiring workers) suggested to the researchers (Roethlisberger & Dickson, 1961) the following:

> Much collaboration exists at an informal level, and it sometimes facilitates the functioning of the formal organization. On the other hand, sometimes the informal organization develops in opposition to the formal organization. The important consideration is, therefore, the relation that exists between formal and informal organizations. (p. 559)

There were groups of workers who were hell-bent on producing and others who followed Taylor's stereotype by limiting production, and it seemed hard to account for the difference. The experimenters concluded that engineers (like Taylor) did not hold the answer:

> From the Relay Assembly Test Room experiment [observers] could argue that the company can do almost anything it wants in the nature of technical changes without any perceptible effect on the output of the workers. From the Bank Wiring Observation Room they could argue equally convincingly that the company can introduce hardly any changes without meeting a pronounced opposition to them from the workers. (Roethlisberger & Dickson, 1961, p. 560)

To the experimenters, the answer seemed to lie in the social arrangements involving workers and fellow workers and workers and supervisors. A group that felt respected, supported, and appreciated would in this view work hard. A group that felt affronted by demands of authoritarian managers and engineers—particularly if these demands disrupted group process—would retaliate by lowering production. Technological changes would be resisted because "they frequently result in the social dislocation of individuals and groups and disrupt the interpersonal relations which tend to give these individuals and groups their feelings of security and integrity" (p. 579).

Few episodes better illustrate this point than the rage that once surrounded the controversy about the use of one-person versus two-person patrol cars, after early studies had suggested to police chiefs that two-person cars might be less cost-effective and not appreciably safer than one-person cars. Whatever the merits of the studies, following their lead undersold the importance of riding partners to officers, which has been described as rivaling the intimacy of marriage.[3]

Police students—Reuss-Ianni, among others—contend that police chiefs have often ignored the social world of precincts, thereby earning the average officer's enmity. Reuss-Ianni wrote the following:

> Management cop culture seeks to maximize the bureaucratic benefits of efficient organization, rational decision making, cost-effective procedures, and objective accountability at all levels of policing. As in all classical bureaucracies, the model proposed by management culture would do away with the organic and non-rational bounds among people as the basis for organization and decision making, substituting a consistent system of abstract rules and departmental operations and applying these rules to particular cases. (1983, p. 6)

Reuss-Ianni saw the process as a vicious cycle in which interventions that violate the informal (street officer) culture produce additional resistance to change. Of police managers, Reuss-Ianni wrote:

> Specifically, they have a "gut feeling" that informal social systems in the precinct are important, but have no clear understanding of what makes the informal social networks so critical to policing, nor how they operate. As administrators attempt to develop new programs aimed at reducing the discrepancy between "downtown" and the police officer's precinct subculture they seem compelled to somehow force

these new programs into the existing formal structure of the department. That structure eventually corrupts the function, frustrates the administrator and usually increases the officers' alienation and cynicism. (1983, p. 18)

Change resistance takes the form of self-defined stress, in which administrators, and their actions, are defined as the stressors (Toch, 2002). According to Reuss-Ianni, the result is conflict within police organizations:

This conflict isolates the precinct functionally, if not structurally, from headquarters. The isolation produces disaffection, strong stress reactions, increasing attrition of personnel, and growing problems of integrity. This in turn reinforces street cop culture resistance to attempts by headquarters managers to introduce organizational change. (1983, p. 4)

Early in the sequence of Hawthorne studies, personal interviews with workers were conducted for research and management training, and they were later continued as an end in themselves. Some 21,000 employees were interviewed, and these workers experienced the sessions as a testimonial to the company's interest in them, in contrast to the usual experience of anonymity, which they deplored. Workers expressed strong feelings about work-related conditions to the interviewers and talked about their personal problems, which seemingly benefited from being talked about.

The lessons that were derived from all this had to do with the need for a kinder, gentler work environment and for warm and considerate supervisors. The human relations school felt that workers must be decently paid but that this was not enough. They concluded that workers need security, congenial fellow workers, and warm and understanding bosses who listen with empathy and care and treat workers as individuals.

Climbing Maslow's Hierarchy

Human relations was an advance over Taylorism because it assumed that workers could be loyal to their employers and did not have to be bullied into working. In fact, a premise of human relationists was that shaping the production process without considering the workers' perspective was counterproductive in that it invited resentment and resistance.

Human relations, however, less obviously agreed with some of Taylor's assumptions. It supported the view that people had to be seduced to produce and that production was the goal of managers but not workers. Most modern developments in work and organizational reform—including problem-oriented police experiments—derive from the demise of this long-standing assumption.

The key figure in the reframing of managerial perspectives—at least in the United States—was a psychologist named Abraham Maslow. Maslow is known for depicting motivation as a stage-by-stage hierarchy in which higher needs emerge as lower needs are satisfied. In Maslow's words:

> Man is a wanting animal and rarely reaches a state of complete satisfaction except for a short time. As one desire is satisfied, another pops up to take its place. When this is satisfied, still another comes into the foreground, etc. It is a characteristic of the human being throughout his whole life that he is practically always desiring something. (Maslow, 1954, p. 69)

As work settings have progressed, with management moving from Taylor to Mayo (with a little help from labor unions), this successfully disposed of rock-bottom physiological needs (by increasing pay), safety or security needs (by affording retirement benefits), and social needs (human relations). This meant that managers were now faced with the next higher set of needs, which Maslow called esteem needs. These were needs that focused on self-esteem or self-respect and on appreciation from others. The former (self-esteem) needs, according to Maslow (1954), include "the desire for achievement, for adequacy, for mastery and competence, for confidence in the face of the world, and for independence and freedom"; the latter esteem needs comprise "the desire for reputation or prestige (defining it as respect or esteem from other people), status, dominance, recognition, attention, importance or appreciation" (p. 90).

Once the two sets of esteem-related needs come to the fore, managers have the option of trying to satisfy these needs or of ignoring them, which is tantamount to squelching them. Maslow wrote the following:

> Satisfaction of the self-esteem need leads to feelings of self-confidence, worth, strength, capability, and adequacy, of being useful and necessary in the world. But thwarting of these needs produces feelings of inferiority, of weakness, and of helplessness. These feelings in turn give rise to either basic discouragement or else compensatory or neurotic trends. (1954, p. 91)

Maslow also implied that if managers could satisfy their workers' esteem needs, they would find that many of the workers might be happy, but some would not be. In Maslow's hierarchy, after esteem needs are met, "We may still often (if not always) expect that a new discontent and restlessness will soon develop, unless the individual is doing what he is fitted for" (1954, p. 91). The restlessness Maslow referred to has to do with the highest human need (self-actualization), which is "the desire to become more and more what one is, to become everything that one is capable of becoming" (p. 42).

Maslow's views about motivation were influential because they seemed to make sense. Less obviously, they raised questions many felt had to be raised about assumptions that had come down to us from Taylor in supervisory approaches that substituted carrots for Taylor's sticks. Incentives (whether positive or negative), had been deemed necessary because one assumed that work is a chore for most people, who want security, structure—and possibly congeniality—at work (McGregor, 1960). In Maslow's scheme, this view describes workers who are motivated by lower order needs. Higher needs (esteem, self-actualization), however, define a person who needs work that gives him or her a sense of accomplishment or an opportunity to grow. Maslow suggested to managers that if such needs (esteem, actualization) were not met, workers would become frustrated. A more immediate implication related to styles of management. Security-centered workers were assumed to need direction, guidance, and structure, but people governed by higher needs were deemed to prize autonomy and self-direction. Lower-need-motivated workers would have to be provided with rewards while higher-need-motivated workers would have to be afforded self-rewarding opportunities. They would have to be let loose to show what they could do, so that they could do their best. In the words of Douglas McGregor:

> Management cannot provide a man with self-respect, or with the respect of his fellows, or with the satisfaction of needs for self-fulfillment. We can create conditions such that he is encouraged and enabled to seek such satisfactions for himself, or we can thwart him by failing to create those conditions. (McGregor, 1960, p. 92)

A different way of making the point about managerial style is to say that traditional management practices were congruent with needs of workers who were dependent children, or childlike adults. If we assume that workers are not children, this means that under traditional management, "formal organizations are willing to pay high wages and provide adequate seniority if mature adults will, for eight hours a day, behave in a less mature manner" (Argyris, 1957, p. 18).

The depth of feelings that workers such as police have about their managers has fascinated students of organizations, including Mayo and McGregor. McGregor observed that adults who are treated like children can be expected to react childishly when they feel insecure. He wrote that "the adult subordinate's dependence upon his superiors actually awakens certain emotions and attitudes which were part of his childhood relationship with his parents, and which apparently have long since been outgrown" (1944, p. 56). Irrationality in work settings was most blatantly invited by Taylorism, which prescribed treating adult workers as if they were lazy and misbehaving children.

Enriching Jobs

Some implications of Maslow's perspective have been clarified by Herzberg, who was another well-known psychologist. Herzberg asked engineers and accountants (and later, others) to recall memorable situations (critical incidents) that illustrated high points and low points of their work lives. In classifying the situations that were mentioned, Herzberg discovered that rewarding occasions invariably had to do with the work itself. By contrast, dissatisfying situations had to do with contextual factors, such as company policy and administration, supervision, salary, interpersonal relations, and working conditions (Herzberg, 1966).

Herzberg referred to this second set of conditions as "dissatisfiers." He also called them "hygiene factors," because he felt that their absence could spell an unhealthy work environment. In Herzberg's view, hygiene factors must be present in all work situations, but they can never inspire workers to work harder or better, except for short periods of time.

Satisfying experiences (motivators) pointed to factors that could make people work harder and better. He specifically mentioned five factors: opportunities for achievement, recognition, interesting or meaningful work, responsibility, and advancement. These commodities are of the kind that are available in the job, and not in the context of the job, although recognition and advancement must be externally supplied. All motivators respond to higher needs, which implies that these needs are alive because lower needs (hygiene factors) have been met. Motivators also continue to engage higher needs, because they promote growth and stimulate further development.

The prescription that followed from Herzberg's research is called "job enrichment," which simply means that jobs should be designed to enhance the sorts of motivators identified by Herzberg—a sense of accomplishment and recognition for one's achievement, work the person finds interesting and meaningful, greater responsibility, and the opportunity for personal growth and advancement. There are several other listings of job attributes, but they are variations on Herzberg's themes. Hackman and Oldham (1976, 1980), for instance, suggested that jobs should offer skill variety, task identity (the chance to complete a whole piece of work), task significance (importance or impact on the lives of others), autonomy, and feedback (information about how well one has done). A diagnostic "task identity" question, for instance, would read as follows:

> To what extent does the job involve doing a "whole" and identifiable piece of work? That is, is the job a complete piece of work that has an obvious beginning and end? Or is it only a small part of the overall piece of work, which is finished by other people or by automatic machines? (Hackman & Oldham, 1980, p. 298)

A parallel task significance question reads as follows:

> In general, how significant or important is the job? That is, are the results of the person's work likely to significantly affect the lives or well-being of other people? (Hackman & Oldham, 1980, p. 299)

If one applies this type of prescription to policing, it is obvious that jobs in traditional police departments vary in the extent to which they can supply enriching commodities. Task identity, for instance, may be available to detectives but not to patrol officers. Patrol officers may be expected to feed information they have gathered to detectives, who get credit for solving cases based on such information. Detectives would tend to maximize task identity by concentrating on cases that can be solved. Task significance seems built into police work, but officers often feel that they are in fact accomplishing little, because citizens are indifferent and the criminal justice system undoes their work. As for feedback, complaints such as "you are damned if you do and damned if you don't" suggest that officers get no sense that anyone knows when they do good work.

Enriched jobs are designed to inspire quality efforts, because rewards derive from using skills to best effect, to accomplish something that matters. The excitement would be in doing quality work, in seeing it done, and in knowing—and having other people acknowledge—that it is done well. None of this can occur if the criterion for assessing work is the number of widgets one produces, with no indication that widgets matter or that anyone uses them.

One cannot expect an organization to have much concern for quality production if it plays a numbers game in which numbers are ends in themselves, as are arrests or citations in some police agencies. If officers are told to go forth and bring numbers, they must avoid situations that do not yield numbers and terminate "unproductive" encounters as quickly as they can. They must, of course, waste no time searching their souls about the validity, significance, or appropriateness of any arrests that help meet their quotas. This consequence has been deplored by the National Advisory Commission on Criminal Justice Standards and Goals, which has written,

> In evaluating performance, police departments rely heavily upon how many arrests officers make. Such a criterion, standing alone, is inappropriate as a measure of success in crime control unless factors such as the quality of the arrest or the ultimate disposition of the case are considered. Such a solitary standard may also distort measurement of the quality of policing on an individual level by ignoring such essential variables as an officer's use of discretion or his reputation for fairness and responsiveness to citizens. In no instance should the number of arrests be used as the only measure of an officer's productivity. (1973, p. 151)

What Maslow and Herzberg imply is that workers (officers) can be motivated to produce if they are afforded opportunities to take pride in doing quality work the organization (the police department) values. This presupposes that the organization is willing and able to show that it approves of the skilled exercise of ingenuity and initiative.

Who Does the Thinking and Planning?

Taylor held the intransigent view that managers must think and plan, whereas workers must work and be subservient. He reinforced a time-honored caste system by hiring college graduates (middle-class individuals) to do the thinking and planning. This arrangement perpetuated a tradition typified by the military, where officers have always been upper-crust individuals, and those who have to unquestioningly obey their orders have been untutored sons and daughters of farmers and laborers. Police organizations have become exceptions to a rule in which caste membership occurs through lateral entry and is correlated with class and educational backgrounds of managers and workers. Although in some countries police managers are invariably university graduates (lawyers, for example) who are laterally appointed, such is rarely the case in the United States. A chief may be imported by a police department but he or she will usually have started as a patrol officer in some other department and worked his or her way through the ranks.

Because in police departments managers tend to be promoted rank-and-file workers, it is ironic that the precedent to which they subscribe is a "paramilitary" one, which sharpens the distinction between order givers and order takers. This fact has become doubly ironic because castelike organizations, such as factories, had taken a lead in democratizing decision making, whereas police organizations had remained relatively undemocratic. The American version of organizational democracy started out as the quality of work life (QWL) movement. The QWL concept was born in the automobile industry, where it was first pioneered at the General Motors plant at Tarrytown (Guest, 1979) and at Harman International—an automotive supply factory—in Bolivar, Tennessee (Duckles, Duckles, & Maccoby, 1977). These pioneering ventures were different from each other, but both involved shop-floor groups that met and made proposals for innovations or reforms. These proposals were approved by labor–management committees and often called for continued worker participation in their implementation.

We have pointed out (in chap. 2) that in policing, democratization was a notion first introduced by virtue of the fact that the President's Commission on Law Enforcement and the Administration of Justice (1967a, 1967b) favored the enactment of experiments in team policing. One of the goals of team policing—highlighted by John Angell (1971)—became that of promoting "a flexible, participatory, science-based structure" for neighborhood police work (p. 194). Angell (one of the founders of this model of team policing) felt that a constraint that faces most patrol officers is that they "tend to become nursemaids to the specialized officers such as investigators, and juvenile and traffic officers"; patrol officers must also deal with "their inability to affect their own working conditions (and the) continued utilization of classic autocratic managerial techniques by traditional managers" (pp. 192–193).

Angell's concept of a team was that of an autonomous group of officers charged with policing a localized community with input from citizens of the neighborhood. Angell's assumption was that "no procedural guidelines will be imposed on these teams by administrators in the organization" (1971, p. 196). He also argued that officers should elect their leaders (coordinators) and rotate leadership among themselves. Team goals would be set in group meetings with citizen participation, and officers would assess each other's performance. Teams could ask for technical assistance—for instance, from investigators—but they would not be obligated to do so.

Team policing had a checkered history and rarely lived up to Angell's prescription. Some experiments, however, took the notion of officer participation seriously, even at implementation. Sherman, Milton, and Kelly described the planning stage of one experiment (that of Holyoke, Massachusetts) in which 25 of 30 randomly selected officers volunteered for participation:

> In Holyoke, after the team members were selected, the outside consultants made it clear that the patrol officers, not the consultants, were responsible for developing the experiment. The consultants limited their own role to suggesting options and furnishing specific information. In this case, planning became training. . . . Subcommittees of patrol officers were formed on such matters as uniforms, equipment, how to perform an investigation, and the rules and procedures for the team. Once the officers were convinced that the program was their own, they took the initiative. They made some quick decisions on equipment by contacting vendors directly. The decision to wear blazers was reached after the uniform subcommittee had arranged for fashion-show presentations.

Another subcommittee developed a new team policy and procedures manual, which spelled out its policymaking process and the functions of the team chairman and various committees. (1973, p. 64)

Another team experiment (in Los Angeles) started with a retreat at a location "selected for its atmosphere of calm and meditation" (Sherman et al., 1973, p. 47). Roommates were paired across ranks, and open discourse prevailed in all deliberations:

> The most critical and uncomfortable session was the opening one. Captain Vernon . . . announced that during the seminar all ranks would be ignored and that any person who addressed another by rank would be fined ten cents. Dinner seating arrangements were changed at each meal to break up the old cliques (traffic, investigators, etc.) and to prevent new ones from forming. The officers were advised that each could interrupt any discussion by shouting "process" when he felt that the discussion was straying from the point. Everyone would then vote on whether the shouter's point was well taken and whether they should get back to fundamentals or continue in the same direction. Together the members of the new team decided that they would work three watches, with overlap; that they would have six marked police cars and four unmarked cars; that no team cars would be sent out of the area except in an emergency; that the traffic officers would continue to take a primary interest in traffic but would function more as generalists; and that investigators would be deployed by area. (Sherman et al., 1973, p. 48)

Such beginnings are auspicious but no guarantors of success. An individual taken out of an autocratic organization and given a taste of democracy cannot be reinjected with expectations of having become a convert. The unlikelihood increases where power arrangements in the organization are left inviolate and where some individuals are democratized and others are not. Sherman pointed out that police middle managers left out of team policing became skilled at sabotaging incipient experiments. For example,

In Detroit the Beat Commander project was announced at roll calls with such prefatory remarks as "listen to this shit!"

In Dayton such language was equally shrill and damaging. Shortly after the team policing program was announced, the captains circulated rumors that it was a communist conspiracy, manipulated via federal funding to get the police to cease law enforcement. Team patrolmen complained that the captains would tell the director of police what a great idea the team program was, then turn around and tell their men that the program would destroy the department. (1975, p. 368)

The remedy used by some departments to counteract resistance was to include all key players (even those not directly involved) in the thinking and planning:

Kansas City, Missouri is one successful precedent for involving midmanagers, and all other levels, in a comprehensive planning process to improve the department. A task force of two patrolmen, two sergeants, two captains (there are no lieutenants there), and a major was established in each patrol division in order to identify community and organizational problems and develop programs to solve them. A constant effort was made to communicate with all other officers in the divisions, soliciting their suggestions and reactions to preliminary plans. (Sherman, 1975, pp. 376–377)

Sherman noted that "it may be possible to expand the power of each level simultaneously with benefits to the entire organization" (1975, p. 372). He also pointed out that power can be supportive as well as controlling (a fact opponents of discretionary policing often ignore) and that people in authority can be invoked to lend assistance rather than to give orders. In democratized organizations, "the followers (patrol officers) must do more leading of themselves, and the leaders must lead in new and different ways" (p. 373). Sherman also concluded that "only if policemen at all levels can feel that this is 'our' way of doing things, rather than the boss's pet project, will democratization of any sort have a chance" (p. 377).

Total Quality Management

A contemporary version of organizational democracy that has been applied to policing is called Total Quality Management (TQM). The allusion to quality has to do with the goal of the intervention, which is to involve organizational members in a continuing and continuous effort to improve the quality of their products or services.

The movement has had a somewhat strange history. It was instituted with American help in postwar Japan, but was reimported into the United States because of a concern about America's inability to compete with Japanese industry. The concern was with quality decrements resulting from an emphasis on high numerical output. This concern was most strongly felt in organizations that felt upstaged by their Japanese competitors. Later, the movement spread from the private to the public sector, with TQM becoming fashionable at state, municipal, and federal levels (Carr & Litman, 1990).

Some of the pioneering figures in the TQM movement who were most influential were statisticians and industrial engineers who conducted training exercises in which they highlighted techniques that teams of workers in any organization could use to assess the reliability and the accuracy of the work in which they were engaged. The focus was on improvements that could be effected in production processes and procedures. The ultimate criterion was defined as customer satisfaction—especially in human service organizations in which other quality indexes were hard to come by.

TQM shared attributes with earlier work reform approaches, such as the emphasis on team structure and nonauthoritarian supervision. Top managers in TQM organizations, however, were accorded a goal-defining or systemic leadership role, starting with the promulgation of a consequential mission statement. TQM also emphasized the gathering of data, with each member of the organization becoming a student of information relating to his or her level of activity. Assessments of quantifiable output measures, however, were to be avoided as presumptively intimidating and therefore counterproductive.

In policing, the most noteworthy TQM experiment took place in Madison, Wisconsin. The history of this project has been recorded, both by the chief of police who initiated the experiment and by the evaluators who studied it (Couper & Lobitz, 1991; Wycoff & Skogan, 1993). The chronology is in some respects overwhelming, because it covers accounts relating to overlapping committees, councils, and task forces concerned with studying specific problems and making recommendations for action to the chief.

The most salient feature of the Madison experiment was an experimental police district (EPD), sponsored by the city as a model TQM project. The EPD was an open-ended venture that included one sixth of the department's personnel and one sixth of its resources. It was an operation that had been planned carefully by its prospective participants and had been designed to run in a nonhierarchical, egalitarian fashion, reminiscent of police teams. EPD members met in groups at work to define problems and plan their activities. They ran surveys of residents to help them with their planning and to gauge customer satisfaction. The officers were also themselves surveyed by the evaluators, who were interested in their level of morale and job satisfaction. The surveys confirmed that the EPD officers had placed great emphasis on quality, which the evaluators called "value added service." They explained,

> Basically, this means going the extra distance to do a good job: spending more time at calls for service; making follow-up visits or calls to problem addresses; analyzing calls for service to identify problems and proactively contacting those involved to seek a solution; and, in general, taking more time to understand the problems and concerns of citizens. (Wycoff & Skogan, 1993, p. 29)

The EPD group's supervisors supported the focus on quality service through the study of data. The evaluators noted that "the lieutenant and the captain . . . are leaders in problem-solving. They accomplish this, in part, by collecting and presenting crime statistics, accident statistics, information on repeat calls for service, results of surveys given to citizens and EPD personnel, and information they receive from neighborhood groups and alderpersons" (Wycoff & Skogan, 1993, p. 30).

The evaluators concluded their review by observing that, "Surely, the most dramatic finding in this project is that . . . it is possible to change a traditional, control-oriented police organization into one in which employees become members of work teams and participants in decision-making processes" (Wycoff & Skogan, 1993, p. 84). The evaluators added, however, that the model combined its stress on participatory problem-solving with an emphasis on the importance of quality-centered leadership. They pointed out the following:

> The Madison process of change should not be misunderstood as an employee movement that did not require a strong leader. Although the goal of the change is participatory management and information flow that moves from the bottom to the top of the organization, that is not how the change in Madison occurred. It was not a response to a demand from the bottom. It was a response to the vision a strong leader— a strong leader who had employment security. . . . In fact, we have seen a tremendous amount of change in American policing during the last twenty years, and for the most part it has been initiated by leaders who had to prepare others in the organization to accept and carry the torch when it had to be passed. (Wycoff & Skogan, 1993, pp. 87–88)

The Police Officer as a Problem Solver

Although officers use considerable discretion, the context in which they work usually deemphasizes it. New officers are enjoined to "play it by the book," and the "book"—a more or less hefty departmental manual—is a compendium of mandates that cannot anticipate the situations officers encounter on their beats. The President's Commission on Law Enforcement observed in this regard:

> What such manuals almost never discuss are the hard choices policemen must make every day: whether or not to break up a sidewalk gathering, whether or not to intervene in a domestic

dispute, whether or not to silence a street-corner speaker, whether or not to stop and frisk, whether or not to arrest. Yet these decisions are the heart of police work. How they are made determines to a large degree the safety of the community, the attitude of the public toward the police and the substance of court rulings on police procedures. (1967a, p. 103)

The context of policing is a strange paradox in that there is much talk that police are a "profession," a claim that is undergirded by selective recruitment and training. But recruitment and training are insufficiently tied to outcomes (embodied in quality productivity), which would benefit from selection and training. To ignore the process whereby police quality productivity can be achieved is tantamount to labeling a surgeon a professional because he has gone to a good medical school—never mind what he does or does not do in the operating room.

The emphasis on intuition and street sense (chap. 1) may be a way for officers to say, "We exercise discretion as professionals in a sub rosa, unsupported fashion." And because officers generally do not discuss why they do what they do (unless they write police procedural novels), they substitute intuition for rationale. Theirs becomes a profession based on art rather than on systematic knowledge.

The paradox in all this is that it defeats the ostensible point of the system. Managers are presumed to control the officers' behavior, but officers make hunch-based judgments, which are unconstrainable because they are inaccessible. Rational judgments by professionals, by contrast, can be held to criteria such as congruence with agreed on facts and conformity to standards, and can be examined for premises on which they are based. Supervisors can monitor such exercises of discretion but cannot affect hunch-based actions, except for disastrous errors in judgment, when it is usually too late.

In problem-oriented organizations, dangers that are inherent in expanded discretion can be reduced because problem solving is reviewable. Inappropriate definitions of problems and solutions can be addressed. Where misplaced enthusiasm leads to bias or exercises of unfettered zeal, one can credit the ingenuity of the officers and encourage them to seek alternative solutions. One can make the logic (of decisions) explicit and achieve closer congruence between organizational and individual goals.

The Officer as "Intrapreneur"

Problem-solving officers escape the constraints that Taylor placed on workers, and such officers do a job Taylor reserved for managers. They study work-related situations and make decisions based on systematic inquiry. What they enact can be applicable to future situations of the same kind. They can set precedents, such as in initiating new services, which expand the purview of their organizations. Problem-solving officers may not only learn from what they do, but they can teach others. They can also originate and implement interventions that may be institutionalized and emulated.

In a foreword to a report about Baltimore County's COPE (Citizen-Oriented Police Enforcement) units, police Chief Behan wrote that "the COPE units answer the 'means over ends' challenge by making police officers real 'intrapreneurs'—giving them wide latitude to go beyond the well-trod path of standard procedures, and to try innovative approaches they think will work" (Taft, 1986, p. 4). *Intrapreneur* is a term that has been used for privileged oases in which constraints that fetter members of an organization are suspended to encourage innovation and initiative. The favored intrapreneur is the creative person in an otherwise bureaucratic setting who is allowed to do what he or she thinks best. His or her situation is one that combines self-actualizing enrichment with autonomy. It is the apex and the culmination of work reform.

The model unfortunately has a downside for the rest of the organization. The intrapreneur (such as the slightly eccentric scientist who comes and goes as he or she pleases) is surrounded by nonintrapreneurs who cannot do what the intrapreneur can do.

If we take work reform experts seriously, we need to move on a broad front. This means that the average officers' intelligence must be respected, their ingenuity valued, and their professional judgment trusted. A department where this happens can multiply opportunities, supports, and rewards for problem solving. It can do so across the board, while delegating a few officers now and then to pool their knowledge and thinking to address challenges that face the police collectively. A department that operates in this way would have harnessed its officers to subserve organizational goals while the officers pursued their own goals, which would have to do with being good cops. They would do this because they want to do it, which is what motivation is all about.

Notes

1. Observers influenced by Taylor saw police as innately lazy and corruption-prone. Walker (1977) noted that "if one were to believe a 1915 investigation of the Chicago police, patrolmen spent most of their time in saloons" (p. 10).
2. Davis (1975) echoes Taylor's concerns. One of his arguments for departmental rules in policing is that "the quality of enforcement policy will be improved because the preparation of rules will lead to appropriate investigations and studies by qualified personnel, including specialists with suitable professional training. No longer will it be made primarily by the offhand guesswork of patrolmen" (Davis, 1975, p. 113).
3. The controversy predates the advent of the police car. Graper (1921/1969) mentioned that "when regular patrol service was first established it was customary to assign men to patrol in pairs. This policy was followed because it was deemed unsafe for one policeman to patrol alone" (p. 131). The one-person versus two-person patrol-car controversy was intensely waged following World War II. O. W. Wilson (1952) complained at the time that "in order to enjoy the companionship of a brother officer during routine patrol and the comfort of his presence in hazardous situations, some patrolmen are eager to prove that one-man patrol-car operation is unduly hazardous" (p. 85). Wilson saw sociability as leading to inefficiency and corruption. He wrote that "the officer patrolling alone . . . is more likely to give his undivided attention to police duties. The presence of a second officer results in time spent in non-police activities; two officers are more likely than one officer to be involved in small delinquencies and infraction of the rules" (p. 83).

5

The Oakland Project

O nce a problem-oriented experiment has its foot in the door, how does it work? How are problem definitions arrived at? How do policemen ask scientific questions? How do they collect data and mesh these (if they can) with experience? How do they face tedious chores of analysis and inference? How do they deal with conflict, such as challenge to habits and to norms of their groups? How do they work through ideas for change? How do they sell such ideas to superiors? To peers? To bureaucrats? To targets of programs?

In answering these sorts of questions, nuances matter. Thoughts and feelings must be captured to convey a sense of the process as it unfolds for participants. One wants to know how it feels to sit down the first day and ask oneself, "Why are we here?" And it helps to know how one continues to live with— as one officer put it—the "dim light at the end of a long, long tunnel." There are also transitions such as between the end of one process (a solution that makes sense) and the beginning of another (a program that works). The problem-oriented experience is unbelievably rich and it helps to have it available in the words of those who have lived it.

This chapter and those that follow present an account of problem-oriented activity that preserves details, flavor, and authenticity. The participants in the activity agreed to have the process memorialized. They recorded high points of sessions, summaries of achievements, and reactions to experiences as they unfolded. The officers in the project also taped conversations with key players in settings in which they worked. Such process research shows respect for social science and faith in lessons one can convey to those who follow in one's footsteps.

The Oakland Police Department

The story we convey took place in an agency (the Oakland Police Department in California) that had a tradition of hospitality to research. This fact was a mixed blessing because there had been "hit-and-run" exercises that had left officer participants feeling exploited. The experiment we detail is therefore an example of renewed trust, and one in which officers risked new disillusionment. The spur was that the officers wanted to make a contribution to policing, although the odds seemed discouraging.

The Oakland police cover a metropolitan area of 75 square miles, and in the 1960s deployed close to 700 uniformed personnel and a patrol force of 400. The city of Oakland had approximately 360,000 inhabitants and was "a city of contrasts and a variety of cultures" (Muir, 1977, p. 7).

Oakland was then and is now a study in contrasts, and the hills overshadowing its deteriorated core contain many affluent homes. But Oakland itself is poor: Most of the streets the officers patrol are slum streets—some teem with life and others present shells of buildings and seedy, ugly commercial sites. Minority enclaves are concentrated in sterile housing developments and small, crowded homes. They range across the spectrum, from Black and Hispanic to Asian, American Indian, and Eskimo.

Many of the city's problems have been fruits of poverty, discrimination, urban decay, and political turbulence. Antiwar activists in 1967 had held massive demonstrations against army induction. A riot had ensued and the police had intervened, "formed a wedge and moved into the demonstrators, swinging billy clubs" (J. Wilson, 1968, p. 199). Many young people were hospitalized as a result, and the police department was blamed. Other criticisms followed bloody battles with the Black Panthers, in which fatalities occurred on both sides.[1] The Panthers had made Oakland their headquarters and centered their efforts for years on a war against the police. They served food to children, then taught them to sing, "There is a pig upon the hill. If you don't kill him, the Panthers will." They distributed a free coloring book to children. Kids could color "a black man shooting a pig-faced policeman as a young girl looks on. The caption: 'Black Brothers Protect Black Children' " (*Time*, 1969). The Panthers shadowed police officers and taunted the officers mercilessly as they conducted their business. Their rallies (monitored by the police) threatened extermination of Oakland officers.

Such developments had ramifications beyond escalating the hatreds they engendered. J. Wilson (1968) estimated that more than 38% of Black citizens had "formal involvement" with the police in a typical year. Every Black person interviewed in a survey conducted by J. Wilson at the time charged that he or she had been harassed by the police (p. 191).

The police department had responded to the problem by inviting minority group involvement. It had encouraged complaints against officers (including anonymous complaints) and processed these quickly and punctiliously under supervision of the chief. The strategy discomfited officers but did not reassure citizens. J. Wilson reported that

> in Oakland almost every patrolman interviewed was bitter about the fact that the internal affairs section "harassed" them, investigated them, and disciplined them, often, they claimed, unfairly and over minor issues. But also in Oakland, the [Black citizens] refused to believe that internal affairs was doing anything at all. (1968, p. 187)

Monitoring of officer behavior had become routine in the Oakland department, which was noted for its straight-laced integrity and lack of penny-ante corruption. Officers took pains to observe rules and kept close records of their actions. The officers' punctilious adherence to rules was illustrated by J. Wilson, who told the following story:

> In Oakland, the police parking lot is across the street from headquarters. The direct route to take to and from the

building is to cross in the middle of the block. Routinely, interviewers watching the shifts change saw officers leave the building, walk to the corner, wait for the light, cross, and walk back to their cars. "Once or twice, maybe, I'll dash across the street," a patrolman told an interviewer, "but you get used to not jaywalking, and that's the way it is all the time." (1968, p. 180)

In Oakland, officers were nationally recruited, generously compensated, and rigorously trained. Their training included emphasis on minority group relations, but was also heavily legalistic, because the Oakland philosophy was one that highlighted full and fair enforcement of law, emphasizing formal dispositions, including arrests. Oakland since 1950 had been an arrest-driven police department, and the productivity of officers was defined in terms of the number of arrests they made. Arrests and citations were seen as responses to crime and ways of preventing crime. "The more traffic tickets you issue," wrote J. Wilson (1968), "the better the chance of catching a real criminal; if you catch a real criminal, you make yourself look good; thus rewarded, you have even greater incentive to make more car stops" (p. 182). Most officers in Oakland prided themselves on being tough and enforcement-oriented. Muir wrote that

> history was handed down within the department. For example, in the scuttlebutt of the locker room, incoming rookies would be regaled with the stories of the free-for-alls between the department and the [Hells Angels], a notorious motorcycle gang. . . . Those stories abounded with powerful images and homilies; thus, the realities of history transformed themselves into lessons for today. (1977, p. 9)

The new Oakland chief of police at the time is a central figure in our story. He had been reared in the department's legalistic tradition but came to question its premises. Muir described the chief's perspective and the way his troops stereotyped him in the locker room. Muir's account is perceptive and worth quoting in full. He wrote that a constant topic of conversation in the ranks was the chief. His policies and his personality aroused strong feelings. He evoked hatred and respect, and often from the same men. Whenever the officers spoke well of him, they admired the undoubted clarity of his mind. They referred to [what they saw as] his philosophy as "progressive." He tolerated no brutality, no illegality, and no graft among his men. He imposed the strictest controls on the use of firearms. He publicly applauded the due process revolution effected by the United States Supreme Court, and he took steps to explain to all his men how to adhere to the new restrictions on interrogations and searches and why adherence was a good thing.

When his men spoke bitterly of him, as a general rule they referred to his personal quirks and particularly to the unnecessary humiliations he inflicted on them, in his public disparagements and private scoldings of them. Because of his personality, he was not a popular chief. Under his tutelage, his men were often sullen, full of animosity, and increasingly resentful of his brittle, acerbic, and denigrative style.

But no man among the officers I met doubted that he had turned the philosophy of the department upside down, from a legalistic, arrest-prone, evenhandedly repressive department in which a policeman's arrests (as quantified on his weekly "activity sheet") were the unchallenged measure of his worth, to a service-oriented one, where too many arrests were treated as a signal of police ineptitude and where anything novel was assumed to be better than the old police methods. (Muir, 1977, p. 10)

Muir noted that the chief's personality was unfairly characterized by officers, who resented his subversion of the enforcement-oriented culture of the Oakland police and his emphasis on service activities. The chief—Charles Gain—himself has written that

there is a growing awareness of the need to improve our abilities in coping with people problems. . . . We have, then, discovered that a series of order maintenance activities which have grudgingly been performed in the past are important to our mission and that they should receive new recognition. They should be, and in some cases are now, given equal

importance with crime prevention and control because of
their frequency and significance to our clientele—the citizens
we serve. (Gain, 1972, pp. 5–6)

The goals of Chief Gain's administration included:

1. stress on the observance of suspect rights;
2. increased attention to police–community relations;
3. deemphasis of public-order crimes;
4. introduction of new and improved service modalities;
5. stress on "quality (as opposed to quantity) enforcement"; and
6. reduction of police–citizen conflict.

The chief valued evenhandedness, but not in the sense of
evenhandedly arresting offenders in borderline crime situations,
which invited resentment and promoted conflict with citizens.
It is with respect to this area of concern that the chief encouraged
research and innovation.

From Research to Reform

The authors of this book and a colleague (Ray Galvin) began
our association with the Oakland police in connection with a
study we were conducting in California of recurrently violent
offenders. At this time (the mid-1960s) the department's planning
and research unit was reviewing police–citizen confrontations,
and the review suggested—as did studies elsewhere–that specific
officers experienced the lion's share of problems. Although these
officers were generally found to be productive, other officers
were similarly productive without appearing to invite conflicts.
Obvious questions arose about what the attributes of the problem
officers were and the manner in which they incurred their difficulties. A study seemed in order, and the chief asked us if we
would undertake it as an extension of our own research.

We consequently interviewed a number of Oakland officers
and incorporated our impressions in a book titled *Violent Men*
(Toch, 1969, 1992). In this book we described patterns of violent

behavior, which consisted of commonalities among violent involvement of the same individual over time. This approach led us to a typology of violence-prone men based on themes that seemed to characterize their violence. We also looked at encounters that involved two violence-prone protagonists, such as a problem police officer and a violent offender.

In interviewing Oakland officers, we found our research participants eloquent and forthcoming. We also heard self-analytical insights in the side comments the officers made while they told us about their experiences. Some of the officers were concerned about their involvements, which had led to unfriendly inquiries and had endangered their careers.

We discussed our interviews with the chief, who shared our impressions of the officers. The chief thought it would be desirable to save such officers, if an intervention might make this possible. The chief also wanted a vehicle that could address the larger organizational problem, which had to do with high rates of police–citizen conflicts. His assumption (which we shared) was that this problem included our participants but transcended their conflict-inducing activities.

The idea we evolved was in some ways unprecedented. We envisaged a part-time unit of patrol officers, called the Violence Prevention Unit. This group would be charged with studying police–citizen violence and devising interventions that could address the problem. To start off, such a unit could be created with our involvement if we obtained the needed government sponsorship.

The next step carried risk: We proposed to eventually staff the unit with violence-experienced officers, including former participants of our study. We would begin with seven officers, some of whom would have histories of violent involvements. Later, these officers would work with other officers, who would all be violence-experienced. Matched subjects would make up a comparison group whose behavior we would study.

The officers in the unit would have a free hand in setting their own agenda, with the understanding that they would do some research. This would hold most particularly for the first group, which would define the problem with which the second generation (of three groups) would have to deal. The first group would be entitled to make proposals, and the other groups would be obligated to make them. This was premised on the assumption that the first seven officers would have their hands full preparing to run the second phase of the project, which would relegate us to the sidelines.

The intervention we devised is problem-oriented in that groups of officers were to be charged with studying a problem and ameliorating it. But the project was different and unique in that many of our officers had a hand in producing the problem they were charged with addressing. Every problem-oriented effort aims at products, but to varying degrees, one must also care about what it can do for participants. In Oakland, in particular, we hoped that our problem-oriented groups would become learning experiences and vehicles of personal change. We hoped that officers could satisfy their esteem needs by contributing to organizational reform and that their approach to policing might become commensurately enlightened.

As we have noted, Oakland, at the time of our intervention, had been a notorious enclave of arrest-driven legalism. It was touted in textbooks as espousing a control-centered philosophy, of the sort that problem-oriented policing was invented (10 years later) to address. Our project was part of an effort by the chief to counteract this philosophy and to enact serious reform.

Our selection procedure for project participants involved serious risk. No one expected that this approach would be easy. But at the least, the chief, and those of us who ran the project, could not be accused of having stacked the decks to document the potential of rank-and-file involvement and the possibility of turning a police department around.

Inception of the Program

In late June 1969, three of us (Grant, Galvin, and Toch) conducted group interviews designed to select the first seven members of our Violence Prevention Unit. Approximately 80 officers were interviewed. These were drawn from four sources: (a) officers who had been included in our own violence study in 1966 to 1967; (b) officers drawn from high-incidence lists of "resisting arrest"; (c) officers recommended by their superiors as "good officers"; and (d) officers suggested by peers as promising group members.

What we wanted was to locate individuals with violence-related experience, who were held in high regard by other officers. The latter attribute was essential to us. Candidates were chosen by rating the quantity and quality of their contribution to the interview situation. Those who were listened to with respect were invited to participate. All who were asked agreed to join.[2]

The seven officers who were included in this first group ranged in age from 26 to 41, with a mean age of 31. Their time with the department varied from 1½ to 18 years, with a mean tenure of 6 years. Three had been participants in our study (one took up a whole chapter of our book); four were secured through other sources. All were male.

The arrangements that we had worked out meant that each officer remained on his beat three days a week and worked on the project two consecutive working days. During these two days the group met from 4:00 p.m. to midnight. The last half hour of each meeting was reserved for tape-recorded statements.

During the summer of 1969, the group met for 11 weeks—a total of 176 hours of meeting time. The group continued on a less ambitious schedule between mid-September and June of 1970. As a rule, the group put in eight hours every two weeks, except for more intensive planning sessions in December and April. In the summer of 1970, the seven officers conducted the second phase of the project.

We first describe (in chap. 6) the 1969 summer session. Our subsequent review takes us from the inception of ideas to some results of implementation.[3] Although we have changed the names of participants, the reader may get some sense of our officers as persons and their progress in the groups.

Notes

1. With regard to police violence, Bobby Seale (a one-time Black Panther) has reminisced that "they (the police) wounded 60-odd of us, we wounded 32

of them. I think the reason we killed less and wounded less was because they had . . . more equipment" (quoted in Barclay, 1989). Huey Newton has said that the Panthers' stance toward the police was influenced by Malcolm X. The derivative view "that blacks ought to defend themselves with arms when attacked by the police became one of the original points in the program of the Black Panthers" (quoted in Hevesy, 1989). Newton was involved in the killing of Oakland police officer John Frey on October 28, 1967, in one of several gun battles.

2. The second-generation members of the project (chaps. 7 and 8) were randomly selected—through multiple coin tossing—from officers who had accumulated high violent-incident rates. These participants were neither self-selected nor picked because they had special skills and interests. It is difficult to argue that the project could have benefited from a Hawthorne effect, given that officers remained involved over a period of years.

3. The eventual discontinuance of the products of the project was a painful step for the department to take, and one that it took reluctantly. Skolnick and Bayley reported the following:

> As the department had to cut manpower by more than 100 between 1972 and 1979, virtually all of Gain's innovative programs were cut from the departmental budget. Gain's successor, George Hart, says that the "critical incidents" program [sic] was perhaps the most valuable of those cut. "But," he explains, "we couldn't afford it. The peer review panels usually occurred on days off, and the union required that we pay each panel member time and a half. I figured that each panel cost about $3,000. We simply couldn't afford to continue this worthwhile program." . . . "It's true," he says somewhat ruefully, "we don't have a lot of programs. But it's tough to have innovative programs during a period of economic austerity." (1986, pp. 151–152)

The Oakland police began to experience violence problems almost as soon as the interventions were discontinued. Skolnick and Bayley (1986) noted that "the worst year for the department, the absolute low, was 1979, when nine black males, including a fifteen-year old, were gunned down and killed by Oakland police" (p. 155). A large assembly was held in the wake of this incident, and "the Mayor wisely recessed the meeting as the anger and resentment reached a really frightening pitch" (p. 155).

The problem to which our intervention was addressed has repeatedly resurfaced. The department's administration, according to Skolnick and Bayley (1986), "would like nothing better than to develop a predictive device to ferret out problem cops, potential users of excessive force" (p. 156). This is still on the drawing board, with the department committed to "the acquisition of software and computer hardware to create an improved early warning system." The move is one of 52 tasks required of the department in an agreement signed on January 22, 2003, resulting from a lawsuit that alleged that "four Oakland police officers, known as 'The Riders,' engaged in false arrests, planting of evidence, excessive use of force, lying in police reports, and other misconduct" (Police Assessment Resource Center, 2003, p. 1). The officers have been fired.

6

Defining a Problem:
First-Generation Change Agents

Two groups of relative strangers—seven officers and three civilians—convened at 4:00 p.m. on an early summer Wednesday in the Oakland police headquarters building. One of the civilians gave a succinct welcoming speech outlining the violence-reduction project. He promised the officers that we would not tell them what to do but that we would provide resources and help. He acknowledged that the group could face some tough assignments, some tense moments, and understandable problems of trust, but he assured the officers that if they stuck with it, they might learn a great deal from their involvement.

After this statement, the group began at once to consider entry points into its subject. As a start, the men listed types of encounters and incidents likely to produce conflict. They then selected one category—the family dispute—for closer examination. As a first exercise, they considered "cues" available to the officers as they entered a family fight, which could warn them of impending trouble. The officers also speculated about ways their department could affect their response to such cues. Among the contexts they listed as making a possible difference were recruit training, dispatching, and communication.

During the course of this first session, several officers took a lead in urging more systematic inquiry. One of the officers, for example, requested statistics on the relative prevalence of arrests for resisting arrest:[1]

I think we should know almost percentage-wise what amount of 148s [resisting-arrest arrests] occur in family beefs, when they occur in car stops, walking stops. Do young-looking policemen have more? Do recruits just out of the academy have more? What type of policeman has the most 148s? And then, if we can put our finger right on a specific problem, maybe come up with some reason as to why they're happening, and maybe a solution.

Another officer complained about a rush to draw conclusions and called for more concern for reliability in the content analysis of street incidents the group had been discussing:

When we went through a couple of incidents, we went immediately to an analysis; I would have preferred to have more incidents on the floor so you could draw them together rather than trying to do an individual analysis. We didn't want to move to the analysis of the incidents as quickly as we did. We would have preferred to have the information out and then do the analysis so you have more possibilities to draw from.

One group member even advanced the suggestion of a research project; someone had mentioned role-playing and he asked whether one could tape-record calls, to permit a step-by-step review by the group:

Officer: You mentioned the actor-type thing where you go through these emotions of the typical family scene. Why couldn't we go to these things and have the officer tape it, rather than try to act the thing out?

Staff member (*encouragingly*): That might be extremely useful.

Second staff member: Are you suggesting a hidden tape?

Officer: Hidden, naturally, from the people involved. And it would give us that point of view. I'll admit the officer will perhaps not present it in the same light he would without this. But by the same token, it would give you an idea of the things that do present themselves and develop a pattern.

Officer 2:   We certainly would get the citizen's side of it.

Staff: We've got seven officers at this table, some of whom will be responding to that kind of call.

Officer 3:   We'd look kind of obvious carrying a tape. . . .

Officer: No, just like small things. Just like your transceiver. It wouldn't make any difference, and then you could see how each different officer handles. . . .

This idea was not pursued during the session, but was revived, discussed, and implemented at a later date. This also held true of other ideas raised during the first sessions.

Trust problems did arise, as expected, but they were mostly low-key and usually were handled with overtones of humor. The following exchange is fairly typical:

Officer: Well, I'd like to be called Sam from now on. Because every time he refers to Mills he's using my first name, and I'm the one that's going to get the ax.

Staff: May we have it for the record that Joe is Sam.

Officer: One thing that I heard several times tonight, and I'd like, of course, to express my opinion, was I think there's some doubt on the part of you gentlemen, not the officers, but the gentlemen who are conducting this program, as to our honesty, because of the trust we might place in whatever's going on. And I think that you're going to have as complete cooperation as possible. I don't think there's going to be any problems withholding information, not wanting to say something because you're afraid of what could happen. Going on to one of the points that Hiram made. . . .

Officer: The name is Genevieve.

A staff member who handled the first group summary paraphrased several spirited remarks made by the officers during the session. One of these quotes sparked the following interchange:

Officer: The summarizer mentioned, "If violence was to occur, hit first," which was kind of general. And I'll clarify that very briefly, because it doesn't sound good on the tape, first of all. Secondly, we were speaking of a specific incident at the time, and the general conversation, at this particular time in the conference, was that if you happen on an individual that was outwardly going to become violent, we were in fact in position where it would not behoove us to lose. And that if this were to occur, if in fact violence were to occur, and were to be leveled on us, that it would be much to our advantage to level it first in coping with the situation. So I'll leave that.

Officer 2:   How are you going to put it, "The officer should be in the position to take appropriate action"?

Officer 3:   I thought what you were saying was that the best defense is a good offense?

Group members did show some reserve in relation to other officers—often producing an illusion of harmony and unanimity. One of the men noted the following in the summary:

I think there was some reticence on the part of the group to challenge each other. I saw people who obviously didn't agree with the other guy sort of let it go, and I don't think there's anything wrong with challenging each other. I mean, we're all trying to find areas here. I think if we test each other, we'll move a little bit forward and have a little better possibility of getting to these points . . . if somebody doesn't agree with somebody, that's fine.

In addition to the indirectly raised issue of trust, there was resistance on the part of one group member to the emphasis on officer violence. The argument raised by this man (which he renewed in several other sessions) contained two themes: (a) police officers tend to respond to civilian contacts in standard ways and (b) civilians are responsible for any resulting violence:

Officer: The officers here are all experienced; they've been on these calls. I think it behooves us to think about that we are all one nature, that even though there are certain small things that we would tend to differ with, that we are police officers, and we are of a state of mind as police officers. We should, perhaps, get into a different plane, perhaps interviewing people who are the victims of family disturbances.

Staff: Participants?

Officer: Participants of family disturbances to find out what is going through their mind, what response, what state of mind they were in when the officer arrived on the scene. At the point where they settled down and discontinued their violent nature, what caused the discontinuation of their violent nature. And this is just scratching the surface of family disturbances here. There are many other conditions. We only discussed 10; I'm sure there are many others.

In connection with the tape-recording idea, the same officer proposed that the tapes would demonstrate that "the officer goes in and uses all these ideal responses, and still gets the militant-type response from the people; it may show that it's not entirely at the officer's discretion to prevent these things from happening."

Beyond this objection, the group voiced little concern or reluctance. They stipulated their mission, accepted the staff, and launched bravely and unhesitatingly into their assigned subject. If they harbored resistances, these remained latent. Testimonials ranged from "I enjoyed the session. I feel like I'm much better for it," to "I'm going to learn a lot up here," and "a lot of what was said up here will keep coming back to me." The program had achieved—it seemed—qualified acceptance.

Evolving a Joint Frame of Reference

The second session continued and amplified the exercises that were initiated the previous evening. The group moved to a second category of violence-prone incidents, involving crowds of juveniles. Again, personal experiences were used as a basis for discussion, and there were some disagreements among group members about the handling of calls. The analysis proved systematic, compared with that of the first session. The group produced a detailed inventory of situational cues to violence and discussed the consequences of behavioral options facing the responding officer. Drawing on language used by a staff member in his introduction, there was discussion of "games" played by officers and suspects and of component "strategies" and "moves."

It had become obvious, late in the session, that despite the lack of any formal indoctrination, the group had accepted this common language, which it used easily and comfortably. As a staff member put it:

> I think when we speak of "games" from now on in, we all will be pretty much talking about the same thing. When we speak of "cues" and "moves," we'll be talking about the same thing. It isn't just a matter of anybody using this language just to do somebody else a favor.

Several members of the group voiced their surprise as they discovered evidence of systematic differences in police conduct, including their own. One officer stated that he

> was under the impression that these are all the results of incidents, and everybody that's involved here, that is, all the policemen that are involved, have always been the same. I've had a tendency of not having any insight into how I did anything. It was revealing to me to lay it out and just to compare it with the rest of the fellows just to see where the differences were, in regard to what was suggested for me, and the differences in my attitude. Perhaps I'm all wet in my attitude, I don't know. But I never had given it any thought before, and it has been enlightening looking at myself.

The dissenting voice was that of the previous night's holdout, who reiterated that

> we have a sameness of mind and a sameness of thought; it does exist, I believe. And I don't think that it should be forcefully changed to please the staff. Not that you're inferring this, but I just thought I would bring it out that we have the same sameness of mind and thought that you do.

These views were ventilated in the context of a no-holds-barred debate, featuring open but friendly disagreements. One officer noted proudly that "tonight we exposed our souls possibly a little more, and we're willing to talk about things and take variance with each other more than we did last night." Others concurred with this assessment of the evening's climate. As another officer put it:

> I have something to say about last night, and that is that I'm very pleased with last night because it got us to where we are tonight, and I find myself somewhat disappointed that tomorrow night's not going to come until next Wednesday. The ball's rolling, and you just kind of hate to see it stop.

Coming after a 16-hour marathon, such tributes confirmed the existence of a surprisingly high level of group morale. This fact is particularly surprising because most groups with open-ended agendas are apt to start off with expressions of anxiety and demands for structure.

Facing Larger Implications

During the third session, the group received a visit from their chief, Charles Gain. The chief endorsed the violence prevention program and emphasized the uniqueness and importance of the group's work. He said, in part,

> I'd like to impress upon you the significance this project has to me and to the Oakland Police Department and policing in general. We find in policing today that so many things are occurring, and sometimes we don't know why, and too much the tendency is to do nothing about it. So that when we can identify that there are problems, and this is a problem area as you well know, to me it is absolutely essential that we explore and that we find out what is going on, why it's going on, and what can be done about it; hence the emphasis on this problem in my judgment. It's highly important; it's not something I can do at all. And there are many areas, of course, where this is true. It's something where we have to have people who are involved in the nitty-gritty, gut level, if you will, of police work. So it's highly significant to me. I think it's going to be a landmark thing for policing if it turns out the way it should; and, of course, that's totally unknown

now, I suppose, to any of us. But it will be a classic-type study, one that will surely benefit this police department and individuals in an area where day by day we are finding there are problems on that street. And there will be a spin-off and a trade-off for policing throughout the country, so it would benefit officers as regards safety of their persons, and also citizens. I think most importantly, it's something that you have to do. Again to emphasize that I can't do it. It's something that no number of experts could do from the outside. It's something that individuals who are involved in the work process themselves have to engage in, and that is a highly important part of it.

Pleased with this endorsement, and bolstered by the chief's expression of confidence, the group set to work. It proceeded to randomly review arrest reports of high-incidence officers. The result was an animated but unsystematic discussion, with little closure. One officer complained,

When we get down to going over these reports, which I thought was a waste of time—it's my opinion, of course, maybe everybody doesn't agree, and I want to hear about it. But don't believe that we had any objective or purpose in mind when we started going through these things. We didn't know really what we were looking for. I'm speaking of my-self; I should say "I"—I didn't know what I was looking for; I didn't know what to look for, and I think, in my opinion, we kind of went off on a tangent of nonrelevant analysis of the whole thing that didn't really . . . when I think about all the discussion about all these different reports, I don't think we came up with anything that was worth a damn as far as furthering our real objective in this thing. And it's because of the lack of objectivity, because of lack of purpose on my part, that I wasn't able to come up with anything. Had I known what the staff, who, I might add, has been very patient in letting us run on these things . . . had I known what really to look for, it could have well been that I would have come up with something. But I didn't think that I had any clue at all as to what to look for, and so consequently I just ran through these things and listed things that really didn't move me at all. I don't think I've gotten anywhere with this report reading.

Another officer took issue with this negative assessment and he complained of a tendency among some group members to defend every action of the officers who had filed the reports:

In going over the reports, I don't think it was a total loss for me, because there are a couple in this stack right here where I would not have done what the officers in this particular case had done. It wouldn't have been that important to me. I can't go against Joe's analysis that it was good police work. I just don't think that the end result at this point in my career—I'll put it that way—would have made the damned thing worth while to me. Everybody looks at it differently, probably everybody in this room does—the officers anyway. I just feel that it isn't worth the hassle at this stage. Ten years ago it might have been different.

The subject at issue also brought a personal reaction by one of the staff:

I must confess that I have trouble with visualizing an officer standing there watching a person who is handcuffed being beaten up. I have trouble coping with this thing, and I have a hunch that here's an area for me to work through; I don't know which way I want to go. I just have an unresolved problem here which I find myself worrying about at this stage.

This statement elicited solicitous concern from several members of the group:

Officer: [You object] from a humanitarian point of view?

Staff: Yah, I guess so. The problem is I really want to be with you guys. On the other hand, I can't reconcile myself to that kind of business.

Officer 2: I could have a solution for you after it's all over.

Staff: OK.

Officer 2: You've got 32 hours a week you can ride next to me in a patrol car.

Staff: All right, I will take you up on that.

This interchange produced an arrangement whereby one of the staff sometimes accompanied group members on patrol. This not only furnished feedback opportunities but also helped cement rapport between staff and officers.

Third-session morale was again high and discussions uninhibited. A spectrum of views (with "rightwing" and "leftwing" advocates) had begun to appear. The group had also begun to form its own identity and in-group loyalty. In discussing possible interviews with high-incidence officers, for example, there was much concern about locker-room reaction:

When we talked about the possibility of bringing officers up here and possibly showing them some report and asking them what they thought about it, and hoping that they would give some idea as to some of their problems, there are going to be officers in this department, and probably some of those that we choose, that are going to be very resentful of the fact that we've picked them out to partake in this study, or whatever you want to call it. And I'm just wondering is there some way that we can contain this resentment and prevent it from going downstairs amongst the ranks to where it would be harmful to our program? All it takes is one officer to go downstairs and say "these guys are a group of finks," or "this study is no good," and it could spread around this department like wildfire, and we'd have a real problem.

The group had coalesced despite differences, and had preliminarily come to feel that it had a distinct function. In the weeks ahead, the group was destined to struggle with the definition and scope of its aims.

The Inadequacies of the Academic Approach

At its fourth meeting, our group had reached the juncture of discontent with talk. In the session summary, one of the staff diagnosed the condition as follows:

I think if we don't [get to work through the details of our projects] the group is going to get an increasing feeling that we aren't getting anywhere, that this is too vague and sort of bull-sessionish, and it's going to be very hard to conquer this, because sort of saying that there is some vague sense of something that we are carrying away, which is knowledge, ain't going to satisfy us. There's just so long that we can say "Gee, I'm getting a new look at this," without this getting a little unconvincing in our own minds.

This statement provided the stimulus for a frank explosion among the officers. One group member, who had previously declined to comment on the sessions, proclaimed:

Officer: I'm at a point of really wondering just what the hell we're up here talking about. I think a good example is our discussion with the sergeant in the lounge before we came up today. The only thing that we could relate to this man about what we're doing, the only thing I could say was, "Well, our purpose is to see if there was some way, through research, that assaults that occur on the street, directed against police officers, can be proportionately cut down. I realize they can't be completely obliterated; it's impossible. But our purpose is to find some way, if any, of how to proportionately cut them down." Now, great, you know!

Officer 2:   The next question is "How?"

Officer: Well, honest to God, I just sit here right now; I'm tired, I was argumentative tonight. . . . I'm almost at a point of frustration, because I don't think we're getting anywhere. I don't know what to say. I don't know what we're trying to do, still . . . ! I think what the staff is doing is sitting back on their laurels, and waiting for us to come up with what they want us to come up with anyhow. Now, wouldn't it be a shortcut if you just tell us what the hell you want, so we can get into it and maybe find out something! That's all I have to say.

Despite feelings of this kind, which were shared by other officers, the group members had made progress on several fronts. For one, they had experienced an opportunity to test and revise a formal hypothesis. In reviewing incidents volunteered by one member of the group, the officers had guessed that one of the suspects involved was violence-prone. The "rap sheet" was secured, and the hunch confirmed. Later, in another incident, the civilian participant in the confrontation proved to have a record clear of assaults. This finding produced an interest among the group in additional investigation of police assaulters.

The session had also yielded a volunteer among the group for a trial interview, and he was furnished the opportunity to explore alternatives to his actions. The officer, who had struggled with the temptation to defend his behavior, commented,

> I feel that one thing that's got to be destroyed in part of us—in all of us to a great extent—is our automatic attitude of defending the officer's action. We identify very quickly with the officer; and I think we're going to have a tendency, to a great extent, to try to find reasons why the guy was right. I really don't want this totally destroyed in me, but nevertheless, I'd like to be able to have enough of it broken down so I can at least look at the problem objectively and say "Well, damn it, the guy did make a mistake."

The staff had tried throughout the session to deflect the group from the habit of evaluating (and therefore, defending) officer actions. In the context of this struggle to arrive at a nonevaluative level of discourse, the idea for a critical-incident questionnaire was born:

> I'm not going to argue with Officer Mills there about everything is good police practice, but I think George and I can agree that it would be kind of nice to find out what other officers think about what's good police practice. And I think we can do this; I think we have the imagination here among us, the way we talk, to build the instrument, to put down the incidents and the questions that relate to the incidents, so that we can find out what people think.

Prelude to Action

Early in the fifth meeting, a member of the staff listed the research possibilities that had originated with the group, and the group set to work. The members initiated four projects: (a) they collected all arrest reports by one officer and studied these for patterns; (b) they discussed a trial run with live recordings on the street; (c) they resolved to administer a critical-incident questionnaire on police interventions; and (d) they resolved to interview the civilians (Hell's Angels) involved in a publicized conflict with a group of officers.

The group expressed satisfaction with its progress and with the staff feedback that initiated it. Bill, the officer who had exploded in the previous session, asserted,

> Bill: We had a guide to follow tonight when we came to work, and I think as a result we got a few more things done, and we had a little more direction than we've had in the past.
>
> Officer 2:   We can thank the staff for that.
>
> Staff: Excuse me, but I think we can thank Bill and the comments when we left off Thursday; we had a mandate to be well organized.

A number of practical details were discussed. The group resolved to notify other officers involved in taped incidents beforehand, to obtain their consent. In the case of the critical-incident survey, the group anticipated implications of the findings. As noted by a staff member,

> I think we have laid what one could over-fancily call a conceptual base for this critical-incident survey. I'm not quite sure that we are all convinced of this being terribly worthwhile, but I think we have enough consensus here so that we can proceed. And it will be our first really formal research effort, in that this will call for the development of items, for the design of some kind of sampling procedure, for formal analysis in which we will be engaged; those of us in the group that have not done formal research before will be engaged in the kind of thing that is usually reserved for PhDs.

The pattern analysis of the officer's reports yielded a number of hypotheses, which the officers thought plausible. One of the group commented,

I think that we got a lot out of the reports tonight, at least I did. In studying a lot of reports from one particular officer, I think that you can see a pattern as to why he might be having some of the trouble that he's having out on the street. I think that it was a much better way to go about it than studying a lot of different officers' reports, and trying to get something from that. Just sticking to one man you get a much better view of it.

In this sense, the experience was a breakthrough, because for the first time the officers analyzed incidents in terms of patterns, as opposed to merits or demerits of action. One officer reiterated the following:

Maybe we ought to be getting off the kick of justifying every action that a police officer makes just because he is a police officer. We seem to be heading in that direction an awful lot. We spend an awful lot of time justifying what is done, rather than finding some of the reasons for it.

The group was pleased, but the labor of the session had none of the "honeymoon" flavor of the first meetings. A staff member summarized the phenomenon and extrapolated it by telling the group the following:

It seems to me, we worked pretty hard. This session was probably a little less fun than some. On the other hand, I think we are off the kind of note of unhappiness we were on at the end of last session. In order to get off it, we had to sacrifice some entertainment, and I had to sacrifice some correct procedure and do a lot of pushing that I don't like to see myself do. But from here on in, I think we are working, and next time we will be forced to immediately go into the business of working out our interview if we discover that we have people available. And from 8:00 on, this group is going to turn into a research group, in the sense that it will actually be out there asking questions, getting answers; then we can think about them. The next day, Thursday, we can revise our procedure and our thinking in terms of what we've found the previous day, and again we'll be busy getting information and thinking about it.

The Travails of Planning

The next session brought another stage in a cycle that repeated itself, with variations, throughout our project. The joys of untrammeled debate had been followed by a call for action that resulted in working sessions. The latter usually proved taxing. Restless interludes were followed with elation over achievement; this led to doubt over impact.

The sixth session was one that called for detailed planning, and the group showed apprehension and boredom. A staff member summarized the sequence of events:

> We started the session by going over the tape recorder and its use, and there was a lot of joking about erasing and the procedures for erasing, and a lot of reluctance to talk into the tape recorder. There was a reiteration of the doubts in reference to the recording of other officers and even of recording incidents which we got yesterday in the last session. . . . From the tape recorder we moved into the instrument, into the design of the critical-incident instrument. The group went right to work on it. They produced a whole series of incidents, although at one or two junctures they got off into collateral discussions. . . . During that discussion two of the members of the group went down to the patrol division to make their contacts, and upon their return they reported that there had been some joking about the unit's role as a fink group. . . . When that discussion of fink-type joking was initiated, the whole range of public relations problems for the unit was broached. Some members of the group made the very sensible suggestion that the members ought to make themselves available for questioning at lineups about the function of the unit. They also expressed some anxiety and interest relating to an Information Bulletin about the unit which was to be released soon.

The staff member analyzed the situation, as he saw it, for the group:

> By and large, I think we can regard today's session as being 90% a working session. It's about the first time we've actually

sat down and worked—other than, say, what happened yesterday when we looked over these reports. I was a little
afraid, because by and large I know how boring this can be.
I warned you about this last time; I warned you about this
when we started. It's, on the one hand, obviously a little
frustrating to just sit around and have a bull session, because
you get the feeling you aren't getting anywhere, and we had
this out last week. On the other hand, when you really move
to respond to this, and you start saying, "well, let's not talk
at all, and let's start working," this brings in another set of
frustrations, and you have to face those. It's going to pan
out, because as soon as we go on to the next step, we'll get
information back, and when you get information back and
you look at it, and it makes sense, and you have questions
that are answered, that's where all this frustration looks less
frustrating. But at the moment, when we're just kind of sitting
around, worrying about thinking up incidents and how to
word them, and so on, there is no immediate payoff.

The "payoff," as it happened, was relatively close at hand. In
fact, it emerged during the next session.

The Fruits of Labor

In its seventh session, the group members conducted (and analyzed) an interview with officers involved in the incident with
the Hell's Angels that had attracted the group's attention. The
officers also reviewed the first version of their critical-incident
questionnaire.

The group members emerged from the evening with the feeling
that their mission had integrity and that they could easily defend
it. As one officer put it:

There is a closer support of the staff and confidence in this
new experiment or process. (We feel) that we are in fact
moving forward toward an end product that we, I think,
find mutually agreeable. The enthusiasm we had tonight was
comparable to the first couple of times we were here. I think
this enthusiasm brought us back to the realization that we

haven't severed ourselves from the other officers, a feeling that was kind of . . . allayed tonight.

The cooperativeness of interview subjects left the officers with a feeling of potency. One group member commented,

> I don't know that my enthusiasm ever did reach a terrible low point in this project. I guess I always hoped that something was going to come out of it. But after tonight I find that, although I may not be able to express it, that somehow I've got a renewed enthusiasm that there can be some good come out of this group and that there probably will be. I'm beginning to understand more why the staff have been so cagey with us, in perhaps letting us see this for ourselves, rather than telling us maybe what we can accomplish. No question in my mind that they had a lot that they hoped we could accomplish up here, and that they could have told us what they hoped we could accomplish. If they wouldn't have an idea what could be accomplished out of this, there would have been no need for the project. After talking with these guys up here tonight, I think that maybe we all saw in that one incident, the Hell's Angels incident, that there was perhaps a very big alternative. And it renews my enthusiasm that something meaningful can come out of this.

The session also produced a research idea that was to occupy much attention at a later date. This idea arose during discussion with one of the interviewees, Officer Beam. The summarizer noted the following:

> One thing that we thought about and Beam brought it out himself was the influence that the older officer has on the new officer, the training officer on the rookie officer. And I think we should and will take a long look into this aspect. Do we need to be more selective in placing new officers?

The group tried hard to "sell" itself to its guests. In this effort, the members met with partial success. The guests did "buy" the group's credibility but not its concern with violence. The group, in turn (to maintain credibility), showed no inclination to argue the violence case, once the interviewees forcefully made their point:

> During the interview, the group took the opportunity to try to sell the four officers on the merits of the Violence Prevention Unit. They tried to sell it on the basis of it being an avenue to reach the chief—and incidentally, the interviewees voiced all kinds of strong feelings about the administration. So one of the ways the group justified its existence was by characterizing itself as an effective avenue for the expression of grievances. There was also some talk of reducing violence, but the interviewees seemed to cut this short by voicing very strongly their views that violence was a function of the situation, and that the only way to deal with violence was to have adequate weapons and physical force and competent physical specimens—and that furthermore, violence isn't really necessarily bad. I mean, "why all this concern," was the question, "with riots"? The implication being that maybe a good riot isn't so bad after all.

The informal leader of the visiting team, Officer Beam, availed himself of the group forum to make a strong proviolence statement. According to the summarizer, he

> talked almost continuously, and very volubly, and not only related two incidents in response to questions about them, but expressed himself at great length about his own philosophy with regard to interpersonal interactions, police work, and responses to violence. There was a strong pitch about the necessity to meet force with force, to instill respect, to show power, to set precedents by moving into situations forcibly—the merits of direct physical action, the merits of hardware, the need for some kind of tactical force, and so on.

Members of our group listened to this statement with seeming reverence. A staff member later confessed his trepidation, wondering whether

> Beam's pitch was so convincing that it could set us a month back. And as I was sitting here watching everybody nod their

heads and say, "Isn't that true. Shit, isn't that exactly what it's like! Isn't it really true that we gotta go out there and display force in order to get them to respect us? And isn't it true that we gotta mount a machine gun on the rear fender? Ain't it a fact that the only thing these guys understand is a show of force?" There was a kind of nagging doubt in my mind about, gee, you know, we lost everything!

Although in its analysis of the interview the group returned to previous form, the lesson remained. The pull of the locker room had been felt. In the months to come, we would experience it repeatedly. We could build a subculture, but we could not, with equal ease, insulate and defend it. Contagion runs both ways. Change agents are subject to change and to impact.

Review of Aims

The principal activity in the eighth session was identical to that of the previous day: The group interviewed officers involved in the Hell's Angels incident. This time the question of interview objectives was raised and cast a pall of gloom over the group.

The issue was posed by a staff member, who embarked on a talk about interviewing procedure early in the session:

I picked precisely the wrong moment to feed in some technical information about interviewing. The reasoning behind it was, "Well, we're now in the process of interviewing; this is the time it would make most sense—while we're doing it." In fact, it backfired because what it very plausibly sounded like was a kind of critique of what happened yesterday.

The technical information was lost on the group (in the words of one officer, "Most of it went over my head"), but the discussion did pose the question of aims and accomplishments. The group had rushed to embark on a research venture. The advertised aim (comparing police and suspect versions of an incident) had receded in favor of divergent, unverbalized ends. One of these was to sell the group; another was to explore the philosophy of special-duty officers; a third, investigative fact-finding; and a fourth, cementing group thinking. Once this became obvious, the success of the previous evening's venture was less evident. The staff summarizer noted the following:

> We did emerge, by virtue of this ambiguity of our objectives, into a kind of unhappy state where we were shouting at each other about what went wrong when in effect that is a question you can't really answer because you can't talk about what went wrong when you don't know what's going right.

Group morale was low. The officers who had been interview participants felt attacked and deprived of credit. Others demanded structure. One officer stated,

> I think it's about time we start getting down to the nitty-gritty of what we're doing, go back a little ways, bring up what we have done, and perhaps this will give us some sense of what direction we're going to go. Now we've been here two months, and we've rambled on and on and on, and we've brought up a lot of problems, and we've brought up a lot of different areas that possibly will be applicable to this survey, but it's been two months, and we need something solid and concise to go on. We've been here eight times; I'm sorry, one month, and I think now we need to get things set down in concise terms as to where we have been, and where we're going to go.

The interview the group conducted again went smoothly. It was lively, with much give and take. The exploration centered on special-duty philosophy and stimulated considerable discussion among the group. One of the officers volunteered to prepare a summary of interview content and conclusions. Another group member brought up the critical-incident survey, and the group spelled out sampling and distribution procedures.

Two Steps Forward

The next session saw a rebirth of morale. The group witnessed a significant victory in the form of a good tape. A cassette recorder had been borrowed for experimental use, and one of the officers, Bill, had produced a powerful, pointed incident involving a family fight and its resolution. Bill supplied explanatory comments and the group added to them. Several officers suggested that the discussion, added to the tape, could make a useful, self-contained training tool.

The group spent several hours with the commander of the special-duty unit whose members had been the previous week's guests. The supervisor had requested the interview under the impression that the group was interested in his unit. Although the time was tangentially invested, it proved satisfying. The interview went well, and the group was flattered by the opportunity to talk with a supervising officer. A staff member noted,

> There's no question that everybody was very much with it. Again the group gave a number of testimonials to a guest about their own conversion and insight, and so on. And even when he sort of misunderstood and sidetracked, they returned to it to make sure he got the point. I think the group was also reinforced in that they saw that they were perceived as powerful outside. The questioning today was nowhere near as irrelevant as it was last week, in the sense that most of the questions that were asked were fairly incisive and to the point, and there wasn't any of the spurious agreeing with. It could have been extremely inviting. After all, the man who was here was a lieutenant.

The group also discussed definitions of the police mission (a subject reopened by the interviews) and the chief's problems in implementing his definition. The officers resolved to take up this question with the chief when the opportunity afforded.

A Happening

The next session proved to be a high point in the group's development. In line with previous plans, the suspects' version of the Hell's Angels incident was ascertained, together with information about the motorcyclists' view of police, life, and each other.

The officers felt that the interview was eye-opening and that their guests (in particular, the Oakland chieftain of the Angels) were impressive spokespersons for their camp. One officer exclaimed, in the wake of the experience:

> I'm really at kind of a loss of words, because I'm so damned impressed with that Sonny! I can see why those guys look up to him, because, it seems to me that whatever in hell he decided to do in life, he would have been "A-1" at it. The guy makes a lot of sense. I'm very impressed with him. I'm not saying that I'm so sympathetic with the Hell's Angels that I'm seeing their side, and not the police side; that's not the case at all. The guy put forward a very frank and forthright presentation; his answers were very concise, very clear. Undoubtedly the guy lives and believes what he represents. I was very impressed with it. You know the full impact of it, I really haven't had time to think about it, and I'm sure that I will be giving a lot of thought to exactly what took place in this exchange of words in this interview.

Another group member confessed,

> You know our orientation as to what the Hell's Angels are. Before coming on the police department I heard about their big rape raids across small towns in the United States. When you first come into the department, going through rookie school, you hear various officers talk about them; nothing good is ever said. I was so surprised that a guy could sit there who is an outcast as far as society is concerned, that the guy could sit there and just speak so frankly and in such a way that everything he said, you could just hang on the word; the guy's got a hell of a way of expressing himself, and I guess the reason it is, is because it's so damned simple.

Some members of the group proposed a Hell's Angels session with recruits in the academy. One suggested a videotaped discussion. Another officer argued that veteran officers, like himself, could most benefit from group contact:

> I think it's too bad that more people couldn't have heard it besides us seven. I'm wondering if maybe the fact that it was

so spontaneous in such a unique situation. . . . if they went before a class of recruits or something I think something would be lost in it. Maybe not, but that's my opinion. I think something might be lost, and right this minute I think the most important thing isn't impressing a class of recruits, it's impressing the officer that's working the street now, like I was impressed.

The interview had gone extremely well as a technical effort. The men had spent the afternoon with a nonpolice group and had created an atmosphere of cordial openness, in which much information was obtained. A staff member characterized the session as an "impressive exercise in communication and seeing the other guy's point of view." He added,

Except for one little tense moment involving a little notice on the board, which was not meant for our guests, depicting police officers confronting eight motorcyclists with a legend such as "It's pretty lonely out there—" except for that, which they took with pretty good humor, there was really very little tension about this. An extremely free exchange. And I might say I was extremely impressed with the way we were able to question these people without being patronizing, hypocritical, or hostile. There were some questions asked that were quite sharp; the answers were frank. What we told them seemed to me to be quite frank.

A point noted by the summarizer was that, viewed as a subculture, the Hell's Angels appeared to have orientations and problems similar to those of some police officers, and particularly to the special-duty officers with whom they had clashed:

One point that we certainly got out of this, most of us got out of this, is that there are some parallels between Hell's Angel problems and police problems. That came through quite striking with points such as young Hell's Angels, young police officers; the code of brotherhood. And also we sensed, I think, that in some of the things they were describing, they could have been talking about one of the units in this department very aptly.

One officer said that in managing group problems, the Hell's Angels might, in some ways, be better socializers than their police counterparts:

> He mentioned something to me that impressed me that is diametrically opposed to how we think, how we act, and what we, in fact, do on the street. And that's when he brought up the fact that "when we see a guy out of line, we stop him, man, and kind of let him know that he's out of line." This is diametrically opposed to anything I've learned in six years, and it's opposed to what Sam has learned in all the time he's been on the force. I'm wondering if it might not be a good idea. I think that it could be done in such a way, that Bill brought up plenty of times up here, or a few times up here, that he's maybe saved somebody's ass, or maybe saved some policeman from getting the grease by very tactfully and unnoticed grabbing some guy and getting him the hell away from there. We make mistakes; I've made mistakes; everybody here has. Just like Sonny Barger said, the whole Hell's Angels group has to suffer because of one man's mistake. We have to suffer because if I get in the shit, and Sam and Bill have to come in and bail me out, they're not going to be happy if I'm wrong; then they have to ride my heat too. We brought it up, but it's something to think about.

The success of the experiment did not blind the group to the need for planning further activity. They scheduled interviews to document their case for more systematic assignment of training officers. They discussed recruit-training innovations of various kinds to improve the sophistication of young officers in the human relations area. They also talked about questionnaires.

A Rebirth of Anxiety

In their next session, the group prepared itself to meet the chief the following night. In the context of worry about the chief's reaction, the group became concerned about its effectiveness to date. Once again, Bill was the catalyst of discontent. According to the summary,

When we were talking about our discussion with the chief tomorrow night, Bill made a statement that kind of kicked off a good deal of discussion and kind of brought us back to that third or fourth session when we started saying, "Where in the heck are we going?" It seems kind of surprising that it would pop up at this time, but Bill said that if the chief asked him what we've accomplished down here, he says he wouldn't know what to tell him, and I think it probably made us all start thinking, "Well, what the heck would we tell him that we've accomplished down here?" Then it kind of gave us the idea and a little bit of worry that, "Son of a gun, have we really accomplished anything?" I know I think it kind of affected me that way to a certain extent, and I find myself wanting to charge ahead and act on a lot of proposals that have been made, a lot of ideas that I thought were kind of held in the balance.

It seemed plausible that such worries were inspired by awe of the chief, but they took the form of complaints about progress. The staff met these complaints, as in the past, by reviewing the group's work and its plans. The reminder proved reassuring:

With his [staff member's] summary of the things that we do have in the fire that have not really been pushed to the wayside, I think perhaps it kind of made us feel like, feel better about what we had accomplished up here, of what we may accomplish.

The men spent part of the session interviewing an officer who had a high incidence of conflict experiences. The interview was a model of self-study. The interviewee—a young man with some graduate school—was articulate in thinking about himself. He produced a number of observations, one of which related to the impact of training on his own development. The testimonial renewed the group's enthusiasm for its study of training-officer assignments, apparently endorsed by the interview subject:

It seemed to be in Joe's mind that the training officer will cause many lasting impressions in the new officer's method of operation on the street. Joe can see a lot of merit in properly selected and properly trained training officers. He seemed to indicate to me that he changed after four years, or during the four-year span of time, kind of by the trial and error method.

Group morale was raised by the interview and by the discussion it inspired. But the officers remained concerned about their impending talk with the chief.

An Identity Crisis

The summer was at its midpoint, and throughout, the group had struggled with its role. The members felt the group to be powerful but saw no evidence of impact; they viewed themselves as productive but could not claim any products. They felt themselves needed but had received no praise or recognition. In the context of this crisis, the chief's presence was propitious and ominous. Too much was at stake, and too little was possible. The hidden agenda of the session made demands that were unreasonable and inchoate.

In listening to the group, the chief was afforded hunches rather than data; he heard a litany of crude ideas and unformulated hopes for change. He understood that he was seeing a group in search of a mission. His assigned role was that of a creditor whose clients had prospects but little collateral. Given this scenario, the chief did the best he could. He urged the group to proceed; he shared thoughts about the department and its mission, he testified to his faith, and he expressed confidence in the officers.

The group felt deflated without knowing why. One of the staff observed the following:

> The chief responded, it seemed to me, perfectly frankly, in terms of what went on in his mind, from the vantage point of his desk, to some general questions we raised. The fact that he was doing so here, and the fact that he was putting so much effort into it, could conceivably have been seen as a positive feature; instead I think it sort of made us increasingly depressed. I don't quite understand why.

The session was contaminated by the group's depression. The group interviewed the sergeant of a special-duty unit, without knowing, or caring, why. While waiting for their guest, they listened to tapes that had been produced under unsatisfactory acoustical conditions. One incident had been recorded over and the rest was static. The experience was described as a "waste" or "minor tragedy."

The sergeant, who had requested the session, appeared in a friendly and expectant mood. The group had no questions, and the sergeant made a statement, throughout which the officers sat preoccupied. There was a long silence, which one officer broke by inquiring about the Hell's Angels incident, which had been reviewed on four previous occasions. While the sergeant covered the ground once again, the officers doodled. At length an officer inquired, pointedly, about the prevalence of violence among the sergeant's men. The interview ended and the sergeant left.

Bill, who had been one of the most obviously depressed members of the group, reviewed his role and came close to an apology:

> Bill: I don't know if I've been a disruptive influence on this group for the last couple of days. I think I have, for some reason, fiddley-fucking around with a piece of paper while Jack's trying to summarize, which isn't really very cute for a grown man.
>
> Jack: It's all right—it's all right.
>
> Bill: No, but I'll tell you what. Maybe I've let a few personal problems I happen to have lately in to sort of push this thing out of my mind, and I've lost a hell of a lot of enthusiasm for some reason, I don't know why. I don't want to. But maybe like Waterman says, if we can get down and start producing something concrete, it'll come back. And that was a real boring, shitty night, as far as I'm concerned, and practically a complete waste of time. And like I say, I don't know why.

Other members of the group were equally puzzled but thought they saw some hope. They called for project-related work, and resolved once more to move ahead.

Task Force Activity

Officer Waterman, the group's conscience, had called for small task-related work groups. He had proposed that he would have liked to

> spend some of this time instead of talking and interviewing, to go to smaller groups and sit down and get some of this stuff down on paper. I'm a paper man when it comes to projects. I would really like to pursue this training-officer thing. . . . And we've all bitched about this radio room for as long as we've been on the street; we've told our sergeant about it, sometimes we've bitched about it on the air; we've called him up on the telephone so mad and told him, the dispatcher, off over the phone because we couldn't do it over the air. Here's a chance maybe to do something about it, and I'd like to get down to the nitty-gritty. I really would.

In line with this proposal, the group divided into subgroups, and worked on the training-officer study, the idea of a radio room survey, the technical problems of tape recording, and the analysis of the questionnaire pretest.

Progress was made on each front. The critical-incident group diagnosed a communication gap within the department on the basis of supervisor–subordinate differences. They discussed special uses for the instrument, involving a number of target groups:

> It was brought out that it could be sort of found where the communication gap lies, if any, between the DC and the chief, the deputy chief to the captain to the lieutenants down to the sergeants and the patrolmen; whether or not the patrolman was reacting in a way that the sergeant wanted him to react, or in other words, differences of opinion; if these differences between particular sergeants exist and influence subordinates that work under them. And the patrolmen, just giving it to them in a straight way, and then giving it to them and having it filled out on the premise of "What do you think the chief would want you to do?" to find out if there's a lack of knowledge as far as the chief's policies are concerned. It

sounds kind of garbled. Then we brought out that it could be given to special groups, rookies that are just on the street, and Sam came up with the idea, or somebody did, that it'd be kind of interesting to find out what they'd put down on this thing. Then, of course, time on the job would have something to do with it, and the high 148s, guys that we've talked to . . . to see if their answers are a little different.

The live-taping group explored ways of editing material and devised a "sound-on-sound" technique for the processing of incidents. Waterman, whose avocation is electronics, became director of the project:

We talked a little bit about the ways of transcribing these tapes and dubbing information into them to make the critical points in the incident more meaningful. We talked about whether to do this by a stop-and-go process; in other words, play a part of the incident, then when we reach a critical point in the incident, where maybe it turns to violence, or where violence was averted, stopping the incident tape and dubbing it by voice sort of as explanation of what occurred there from, say, from what we've learned up here about the way people react. This is one way we talked about it; another way that might be meaningful was discussed as to whether or not to try the sound-on-sound technique of bringing the incident in kind of full bore, so that the whole incident can be heard, not the whole incident, but the critical points of the incident, and then kind of fading the incident into the background and bringing the narrator's voice in till it's in the foreground; in other words, when the narrator's being heard, the listener will still have the psychological effect of hearing the incident going on in the background, much like these narrative shows in TV do. I feel personally that it wouldn't be too hard to do with sound-on-sound-type equipment, and I brought up the point that I have some rather nice recorders at home where this type of thing can be carried out, and I'm perfectly willing to make a few experiments at home, not only by myself, but anybody else who wants to come over and kind of tinker around; we may try this technique. It may be more entertaining to the rookie sitting in the classroom listening to it in this manner.

The total group felt encouraged (with one caveat):

Officer: Well, I think overall for tonight, we've gotten more done just from the standpoint of deciding what we're going to do, and then getting right down to the nitty-gritty of planning it out. I saw a renewed enthusiasm from this standpoint, that we were getting down to doing something of what we're here for.

Sam: Well, I'd like to go on record as saying that I can't stand that word "NITTY-GRITTY"!

Officer: Strike "nitty-gritty."

Officer Waterman, the organizer of the subgroup procedure, predicted continued progress:

Seriously speaking, last Thursday I thought was a catastrophe. I think everybody here thought it was a catastrophe. Today I came in very sleepy, you know? I wasn't really looking forward to. . . . Now I feel we've got something that we're all going to be sinking into from here on out; at least for a couple days, the enthusiasm is going to be renewed.

But not all was auspicious. The Oakland police were facing strike possibilities, and several of the officers were worried. The officers were also in an oddly humorous mood: Bill talked of mass resignations, and someone mentioned firing the staff. In a more serious vein, the issue of locker-room reputation had again risen:

Joe brought in an incident which I think is worth mentioning. He was present in a situation in which an officer had become a little impatient with a suspect, and Joe found himself forced to exercise a little calming action. Then it developed that another officer present at the scene took it upon himself to misrepresent Joe's participation in a way which could conceivably partly reflect on Joe's membership here. Now I guess that we decided that there probably was no immediate connection between the repercussions of the incident and Joe's membership in this unit. We decided, I think, that this was probably the backwash of an interpersonal difficulty, a personality conflict. But on the other hand, it gave rise to a series of comments that have to do with the reason why Joe brought this up here; namely, that there is a question of what does our role here imply in terms of how we are seen, and what does it imply in terms of the strategy we have to follow in order to be able to do what we feel we ought to do? But I think, at an even more significant level, what it implies is that some of us, at least—and I think many of us here feel that in some way—if we haven't changed our thinking, at least we have articulated it a little more, so that what we have to cope with is not what people think of us as members of this unit, but what we have to do in order to cope with what we feel is new and different about the way we think.

Despite these ambivalences, the next session (the 14th) went smoothly. Members of two subgroups embarked on individual research assignments. One officer interviewed the commanding official of the training division while his subgroup drew up criteria for training officers. The radio room task force embarked on interviews with dispatchers and on observations of the radio room (including the monitoring of calls). The group also began to prepare a flowchart of the dispatching process.

The questionnaire group, temporarily without a specific task, spent its time reviewing the design of the entire project. In response to inquiry from one of the officers, a staff member shared the project proposal with the group and delineated the men's role as trainers in the next stage of the study. The subgroup began to discuss the procedure for selecting trainees and control groups:

One of the biggest things that we discussed in my opinion was how are we going to get these people up here, the second group which will be 17 people that are violence prone? And then we have another group that we are going to watch, that we aren't going to do anything with that are also violence-prone, for comparison. We discussed how we are going to get them up.

The entire group met briefly for status reports, declared itself satisfied, and disbanded.

Diminishing Returns

The 15th session was reserved for subgroup reports to the total group. It went badly. The bulk of the discussion turned on the need to revise some of the questionnaire items. Several hours were invested in rewording four questions, and the task was boring. An effort to add one question to the instrument, which consumed 30 minutes, proved fruitless. Bill, a member of the questionnaire task force, felt particularly despondent, in part over the redundancy involved in the group's review of subgroup work:

> But then again I feel that when we sat in here for five hours and went over these things, that we were much more aware of what we were doing and what we wanted to do and that it was just as impossible for the others to come in here and to jump right in and understand the whole picture as it would have been impossible for us to jump right in and understand their study of the radio dispatcher or the training officer, because we just didn't spend that much time talking about it.

Staff members also expressed some worry about group morale:

> But I do think in general the fact of the matter is that we need to think of some way of enlivening the situation here with some variety. I mean, we have responded to the call for complete tasks. That gets us into a lot of routine. I think maybe it's about time we swung the pendulum back pretty soon and got into something which is a little more interesting, and then got back to our tasks.

The officers had not reached a complete low but made it fairly obvious that they were bored. During the last hour, which called for the summary, the men abstained. A staff member later recorded the following:

> The group was most blatant tonight in a growing tendency to shut off the shared discussing and summarizing during the last hour of the day's session. It reached a point tonight

where it was made blatantly clear around the table that none of the officers were to contribute anything, and indeed that was almost 100% the way it worked out. The staff made the main statements that were made and only upon being called upon directly did Bill add anything to the discussion.

The session ended early, on a restless note.

The Feel of Success

The next session (the 16th) was a stormy one, but suffused with enthusiasm. Closure had been reached on several projects, and the officers were happy with their achievements. The questionnaire group had a draft of their instrument and a design for its administration. The tape group had produced an incident that inspired a stimulating analysis session. The dispatcher group presented an impressive draft report.

Controversy arose with respect to the training-officer project. Several objections were raised to the criterion list, including a demand by staff for more emphasis on human relations skill. Waterman, as spokesperson for the task force, replied heatedly. Another officer (Bill) played a conciliatory role:

> I got kind of hot last night about somebody talking about or criticizing what we had done in here on this questionnaire thing when we had spent four hours. I didn't think it was right for anyone to come in here and in five minutes kind of rip me apart. So I've got a lot of sympathy for Hank, because you guys have really worked your tails off in there apparently and really thought this thing over. You've done a lot of hard work on it and I'm appreciative of it. I think it'll work out and we certainly don't expect you to come in here and everyone to agree with everyone else.

Waterman, who had agreed to review the criterion list again, stressed the group-product aspect of the projects:

> I was somewhat offended by what occurred after I finished reading these criteria. . . . Like Bill said, this was my baby,

but in a way this whole thing is my baby, too, everything that's happened in this unit. It was a response that I didn't expect. I by any means didn't expect staff's response, and I don't think he expected mine. Anyway, I just wanted to point out that this whole field-training-officer thing is a group effort of the whole subcommittee, both phases of it so far, as the additional phases will be.

Both the negative and positive reactions showed ego involvement of officers in the projects with which they had been concerned. Each subgroup member became an advocate of his group's effort. A staff member recalled,

When we started the tape-recorded incident today, there was a lot of restlessness and a lot of kind of sighing and sitting back with a pained expression on their faces. But when they heard the results, they became quite sold, and of course it is significant that Young, whose incident it was and who was the main participant, was especially sold. He was quite anxious after the session to inquire how do we incorporate this into group training and so on. The same thing happened with these other projects. For instance, Bill, who is by no means gullible, has become extremely sold in the critical-incident study to the point of seeing all kinds of applications of it that are even vague to me. Both he and Sam have been trying to sell this instrument to the rest of the group, where at least Bill, before he became involved in tabulating the responses, was asking questions like "What the hell good is this?"

The men were generally pleased and looked forward with vociferous anticipation to early tangible products.

The Group Has a Guest

The 17th session was spent with a visiting expert, Chief Fred Ferguson of the Covena (California) police. The staff had invited the chief because of his role as innovator, particularly as the originator of ingenious training techniques. The chief's officers had participated in role-playing on the street, including a stint as jail inmates and a night as make-believe skid-row alcoholics. Chief Ferguson related these experiments, and the group listened with interest and enthusiasm. In turn, the men shared their own activities with the chief.

The group's reaction to Chief Ferguson is illustrated by comments such as the following:

> Quite possibly we should have had Chief Ferguson in here when we first started, because he is quite dynamic. He does something new and different every day. . . . We started on a project here that's never been tried before and I think it would have been helpful to us to have gotten his views early in the game.
> I feel that this man has an awful lot to offer law enforcement. Apparently, I don't know how many people around here have even heard of him. I never had until he came here. That's probably my fault. It was really a pleasure to listen to him, and it was also a pleasure to be associated with somebody of his caliber, and I'd like to thank the staff again for bringing this man here. If you've got any more like him we'd sure like to see them.

The techniques discussed by Chief Ferguson proved of considerable interest. Bill—a natural mimic—became especially taken by role playing as a training technique:

> I can see a lot more use in this role-playing as a training method now that I've talked to him and I really would like to go and see it. I think it would be an asset to the group; and like I was telling Joe—he couldn't believe it—I'd go down there on my own time and pay my own way down. I really would. I'm that interested in it.

Chief Ferguson, in turn, was impressed with the group's work and with their enthusiasm. The officers had talked about specific projects, each warmly emphasizing the work with which he was most closely associated. One officer observed,

> The interesting thing to me about this last hour, for instance, is that if we had this guy here two weeks ago, and if we had gone around the table and we had described the group to him, we would have said all kinds of things about what we were doing here, none of which was said. And it wasn't only that we have the most recent experiences in mind when we think about what we do here but also that we seem to be very involved in the projects that we are associated with. And each one of us, I think, is most strongly attached to the project that he is immediately involved in.

Chief Ferguson had planned to stay for half the session but was sufficiently impressed to spend seven hours with the men. He left with parting remarks concerning what he saw as the "power" of the group.

An Unsuccessful Exercise

The next session began with a presentation by staff of the outline for the second phase of the project. The group was almost exclusively concerned with the manner in which they would introduce the project to the stage-two trainees. As one officer put it,

> Step one would be to introduce the program to these people, to put out a sales pitch to them, to let them know that violent experiences are an asset as well as a liability, I would suppose, and that we're neither condemning nor condoning these violent-type situations. Also, that we don't want anyone fired. It was kind of agreed that this would be a very good pitch, that we felt anyone who is having these problems, if he's a good officer, he's worth saving. He's worth helping him keep his job.

One interesting sidelight evolved as a result of the previous session. Sam had declared himself incapable of role-playing and was goaded by Bill into a display of short but unplanned anger. He confessed that

> in what Bill was doing—this role-playing on a small scale— he did raise me up. For a second there he got me going a little bit, which was spontaneous. He did a very good job of it. I think there's a lot of merit in what he did and the way he did it.

Another positive event in an otherwise dreary session emerged from a tape played by one of the officers. This tape provided an excellent recording of excerpts from a session in which the officer had dissuaded a motel guest from committing suicide:

> We played Joe's recording at the Thunderbird, where he helped this fellow with the solution to his money problems and turned a real sympathetic ear to the guy, perhaps helping him to work out his emotional problems as well. At one point staff stopped the recorder and asked Joe if this is police work. I think we all agreed that it is police work. My own thoughts on this is that we go out and catch a burglar, for instance, and we take two or three hours sometimes to write up the reports and tie up the loose ends and get the evidence. I think the possibility of a man losing his life, or the fact of possibly saving a man's life is possibly worth the two hours that Joe stated he spent on this particular call.

The remainder of the session was perceived as relatively unproductive and was terminated early.

Intensive Work

The next two sessions were spent in project-related activity, partly in task forces. The group's concern in the first session was mainly with the tape project and in the second, the questionnaire results. The taping discussion was initiated by Officer Waterman, who had prepared a meticulously edited incident:

I showed up a little late for work with some tapes that I'd been working on until about 4:30—a tape I was working on. During the past couple of days I've been working on this sound-on-sound technique. Actually, what I wanted to do was to make a tape that would demonstrate the process of using sound-on-sound and keeping the incident phased down in the background so you could still hear the incident at the same time you were hearing the explanation. Much to my surprise, it came out better than I'd really expected. I came up with an almost finished product. Perhaps it needs a little bit of editing, but it turned out very well. What I did was I took two incidents that I recorded over the weekend from our little Sony portable recorder, and from that recording I made a tape in one track of one of my stereo recorders. I used the other stereo recorder; I jacked the incident from one recorder into the first track of the recorder that I was doing the composite tape on and hooked the microphone into the other track. As I went along recording the incident, at certain points I would just use the volume control on the track that had the recorded incident in it and phase it down to a low level and just speak into the microphone some explanations of what was going on at that time, some descriptive explanation.

The results were impressive. Bill described them as follows:

Although it was quite some time after the incident happened, you still got the feeling that he's like a newsman standing out where Rome is burning or some Goddam thing and he's telling you all about it.

The taping group discovered, as the evening wore on, that it had the beginning of a respectable library:

We spent the whole evening listening, first of all to this composite tape that I'd put together, and then after that we went through three cassettes that were recorded by Bill and our two Joes. We found that we had a good variety of incidents—much more than we expected from our previous experiences.

The subgroup made a determined effort to communicate its enthusiasm to the other officers and to promote more tapes. Bill argued,

> It's probably hard for the guys that are in the other room to get real enthused with this, because you haven't done any-thing with it. You've been working with training officers and radio room projects and you've been real involved in these things where we've been involved here, and it's hard in turn for us to get enthused about what you're doing. But we've really got something in these tape recordings, in these critical incidents that we're putting down on tape. It's going to be something that's going to really be a fantastic first. It's going to be a hell of a training tool. But we're going to have to have everybody's cooperation. Now I've been guilty of leaving that thing in the locker myself. But with this sound-on-sound we've got something that's really going to be good, it's really going to be worthwhile.

Bill also reasoned that the dramatic impact of the edited tapes should be a motivator among second-generation trainees:

> Another thing that just crossed my mind is that it's not only a training tool, but if we can work these things up interestingly enough, this is going to be a real good thing for involvement next summer, when we get these guys up here. Because if the tapes sound good enough and wild enough and interesting enough, they're going to want to take that goddam recorder out and do the same thing. I would.

On a more low-key note, the subgroups concerned with the dispatchers and the training-officer study reviewed outlines for their reports. They anticipated having completed drafts ready for editing at the next meeting.

During the next session the reports were written, despite the fact that some time was required for coding of the questionnaire. At the end of the session, the studies were ready for editing and presentation to the chief. The critical-incident data had been coded. The tabulations showing intradepartmental differences were summarized by the subgroup.

Stage Fright

The group began its penultimate session by scheduling task-force presentations for the next afternoon. According to the staff summarizer,

> We started off with going over our schedule with Chief Gain tomorrow and outlined a program that we'll present to him. Chronologically we'll begin at 2:30 in his conference room. The field-training study will be gone into. It's printed up in a nice form, I was really impressed with it and from what I've read of it, I think you did a real good job on it, for what that's worth. At three o'clock the training tapes will be presented to him. And at 3:30 we'll go into the questionnaire results. At four o'clock the dispatcher study will be presented. At 4:30, the chief will be down here and we're going to have a group discussion with him. We might even get into what we're going to do next summer with the chief, if we can and if he's interested.

Planning was followed by a discussion, led by the staff, of eight principles of group dynamics, as summarized by Cartwright and Zander (1968). The group considered each principle in relation to its own activities and those of prospective second-phase trainees. The discussion went well until dinnertime, but was then discontinued. Instead, the group wallowed in cynicism, pessimism, and doubt. As one officer put it,

> I will be very happy if anything comes out of this, but like I say I'm not going to jump into this thing 100% and bust my ass on it and get all worked up about it until I see that there is going to be some good that comes out of it. I really don't understand how anybody could be that optimistic and how they could throw themselves into a project 100% without knowing that it was going to be acted upon.

The men took turns making statements in which they emphasized how strongly they felt about the need for the chief to accept their recommendations:

Officer 1:   Now when you ask [the next generation group members] to change in the streets and you just sit there and say "if you don't change you're going to get punished," it just means that they'll figure out another way to do it. That's all. But if you show them at the same time you're asking them to make these changes that Chief Gain is going to make some changes in the department that are favorable to patrolmen, to make it nice, to make it a little bit better, that he's coming around and he's going to listen to patrolmen, this is going to be very important. And I believe it's very relevant to what's going on here. You're interested in violence; I'm interested in departmental change, too. I think the two go hand in hand. If you have a department that's changing and it's because of patrolmen—like if you bring these guys up here with the idea that they're here because they are the reason for the necessary changes, it's not going to work. If you bring them up here and you tell them, "We're bringing you up here to help us make the changes" it's going to work. . . . Because they're going to see it not only as a group that's studying violence. They're going to see us as a group that's doing something within the department. And they're going to see themselves when they walk in as being in a position of being able to do something also, which is important, something constructive, something directly related to what they're doing down there.

Officer 2:   Now if we can show that we're successful in having some recommendations accepted by the chief, that we as a group are successful, then it will lead these other people to believe that they can be successful. If we fail, they're going to believe that they're going to fail. Therefore, they're not going to work on these projects, and why should they work on them? Now if they're not working on these projects, what are they going to do up here? They're not going to work on projects unless we show them that we're successful. If we tell them about five projects that we worked on here and we had a lot of fun and we documented a lot of stuff here. . . .

The group was concerned about the impact of the presentations it had scheduled. The men had labored hard, invested much, and were hopeful of a positive reception, but understandably afraid. They needed acceptance but could not risk assuming that they had earned it. Reluctant to express hope, they instead voiced their trepidations.

A Full Measure of Success

The subgroups met with the chief all afternoon, and the chief met with the total group briefly. The chief's reaction throughout was unambiguously positive, and the officers were stunned.

One surprise stemmed from the fact that wherever written material had been available, the chief had studied it. As one of the officers put it,

> Jack and I met with the chief on the field-training-officer study. He had a copy of the study beforehand and as he indicated later, he read it in some detail. I don't know about Jack, but I was totally surprised at his first reaction. He indicated to us that he thought we had a heck of a good thing here and that we'd researched it and we'd come up with some real good ideas, which right off the bat gave us the impression that he'd bought the program in totality—and in effect, at this point he has.

The men also discovered that the chief was determined to give them a role in implementing their proposals:

> He threw the ball right back to us: "You guys have got it started, now . . . you can follow it through by doing the staff study routine." I think what he's saying to us in effect, you know, "You've come up with a good thing here, and you're familiar with what you want, and if we just hand this paper to somebody else and have them working on it, that a lot of your ideas are going to be lost. Since you are familiar with it, it's more or less your responsibility to go into the staff studies and learn that these things are feasible or not feasible and keep as many of the points in your original proposal as possible, in the end product." . . . we've impressed him with this thing to the point that he's willing to give us the responsibility of carrying this thing on through.

The chief had thought of possible extensions of the project, and had proposed these as additional group activities:

> Another ball he kind of threw to us just in passing, which I don't really think I got the impact of until later, although I think I turned to Jack and thought "Oh my God, now what are we getting into," was the fact that he was talking about what the course content should be for this field training officer training class. There were some little words passed there to give me the impression that we may be involved in writing the program, what's going to be taught the field training officers.

The chief's reaction to the survey data the officers showed him was similar to his thoughts about the proposals:

> He thought of all these things that this could be used for, which I thought was very good. And he said he's very interested to see further analysis of this thing by putting out more of these. I did mention we were going to do it. In critiquing, for instance, feedback-wise in the recruit academy. He said he would be very interested to know just what point they were at in the academy when they fill out the questionnaire and the study material that had been covered when this questionnaire was given to them, because there was an obvious ignorance of the particular laws that were involved in some of these incidents.

The chief stressed that some of the material presented to him was new information:

> I feel that the chief was very surprised at the results of the questionnaire. It was pointed out to him—I got in kind of late on this thing, but it was pointed out in the analysis that we had done and Bill presented to him that there was a very great difference in a lot of his thinking and policies and what was going on in the department. His indication was more or less amazement, I guess, that so many people had made arrests in some areas that he could see no legal basis for. We both pointed out to him that this was happening all the time and it was more or less accepted in some areas.

The chief also appeared pleased with the competence demonstrated by the officers. A staff member who had observed the chief's reaction commented,

> I think all of the studies, all of the presentations, did convince the chief—something he may have thought of or not—but convinced the chief of the ability of patrolmen given time and inclination to do staff studies and make recommendations within this department. And this came up very strongly and it sort of bubbled to the top in regard to his comments, in regard to "well, maybe I ought to detach all you people and put you to work on specific projects."

The group, following their meeting, expressed themselves relieved, stunned, and elated. The session had the air of a victory celebration. The experience had drawn the group closer and had made it conscious of the importance of its mission and its responsibilities for the future. Bill commented,

> I don't know whether it's been a real pleasure or not. I think we said before, it's a hell of a lot easier to go out on the street for 16 hours and kind of do our thing on calls in a relaxed, nice atmosphere. Because this has been a lot of work. It's been a good experience for me, because I'm lacking in formal education and I probably got something here that I would never have gotten otherwise. And I am appreciative of everybody here, especially of the staff members. It's been a good association. There's been a lot of name-calling and a lot of kidding, and I think most of it has really been in jest on my part. My sardonic, morose attitude isn't bad all of the time. Generally I feel very close to you assholes, and I'm looking forward to seeing you again next summer.

A Profile of Morale

We had attempted no formal measurement of group process and morale. To trace progress through the summer, we resorted to a rough content analysis of session summaries. Figure 6.1 depicts the profile resulting from this review. (See the appendix for the form used for systematic monitoring of subsequent sessions.)

Figure 6.1 shows a fever curve alternating between "high" and "low." There is a possible "Thursday Slump" syndrome: Three of four "low" days fall on Thursdays. On the other hand, "very high" Thursdays outnumber "very high" Wednesdays.

More significant may be the nature of the task (or absence of task or anticipated task) facing the group. High profile points seem to involve (a) substantial group efforts yielding immediate new information and (b) products of long-term group activity. Group morale appears to hinge on documented group achievement.

Conversely, low morale appears related to (a) difficulties in seeing a purpose in group activities, (b) worry about the value of group products in a larger context, (c) unsuccessful effort, and (d) work in which the product was not as yet clearly available. Low morale seems tied to the unsatisfied need for documented achievement.

The cycle of group development appears to comprise (a) elation over learning from a new activity, (b) doubts over the significance of new learning, (c) evolution of redefined new tasks, (d) involvement and contentment, (e) restlessness over the lack of tangible product, (f) elation over a product, and (g) worry about the significance of the product.

Several personal roles had evolved in the group. There was a group barometer (Bill) whose moods anticipated and stimulated feelings; there was a group superego (Waterman) whose responses to nondirectionality catalyzed activity; there was an agent of reassurance (Sam) who promoted faith through optimism. The group also contained a group skeptic (Mills) and a group amuser (Young), although such functions were exercised by all group members. A final stabilizing element was the group editor (Jack), whose tolerance for paper work overrode the restlessness of his peers.

The officers had acted as a problem-oriented group and their problem-oriented activities had progressed in logical sequence. They had engaged in problem definition, had formulated questions, obtained data, analyzed data, drawn inferences, and initiated implementation of proposals.

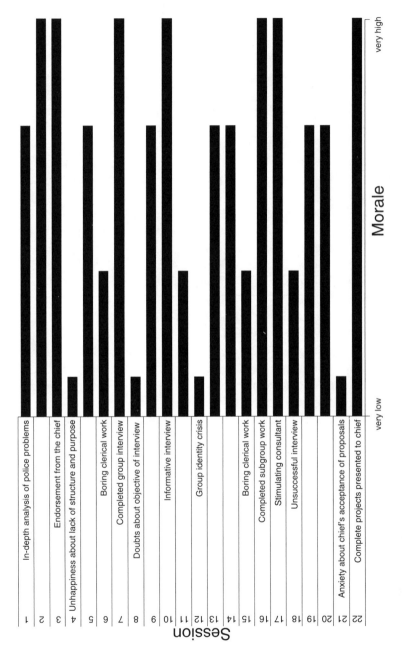

Figure 6.1. Profile of group morale derived from content analysis of session summaries.

In the next two chapters we sample phase 2 of the project, in which the phase-1 officers had become group leaders and catalysts. The phase-2 groups were composed of violence-experienced officers who were asked to evolve strategies for reducing Oakland's violence problems. They did so in several ways, but we shall concentrate on one of their projects, the invention of the peer review panel. Chapter 7 describes the officers' thinking leading to the inception of their proposal. Chapter 8 follows up the officers' intervention after it was implemented, to ascertain how well it had worked.

Note

1. The focus on arrests for resisting arrest (PC 148) confirms that the officers regarded such arrests as a plausible measure of police–citizen confrontations. In other words, the officers assumed that the charge (resisting arrest) would be lodged if a physical conflict had occurred.

7

Addressing the Problem:
Inventing the Peer Review Panel

F ew ideas are as much of a challenge to Taylorism (chap. 4. this volume) and to management derived from Taylorism as the notion of worker peer review.[1] The Oakland project eventually led to a peer-review prescription for police use of force. The group that invented and fleshed out this prescription was a second-generation group of the project (hence, a group composed of officers with a history of violent involvements), chaired and cochaired by members of the first-generation group. This seminal group began life as a free-floating late-evening seminar. There was bemused talk of the possibility that unhappy experiences at home could affect a man's equanimity on the street. There was talk of the dangers of being seduced into "mob psychology" in a crowd situation. There was talk of "thresholds" of explosiveness or emotionality. The bulk of the talk, however, focused on the likelihood that young officers could enter the arena of police work with undesirable psychological dispositions, insufficiently corrected by training and experience.

After an early morning lunch, the group listened to a tape that had been made the previous week by one of its members while out on a call. The production of the taped incident was a gesture of goodwill and an expression of willingness to play ball. What was accomplished, however, was that the fate of the group was ordained. The group was being serendipitously treated, during its first meeting, to an exercise in systematic analysis of a behavior sequence. It is this analysis that culminated, several sessions later, in the peer interview project.

The Interview Experience

The incident taped by the officer was a violent encounter that started with an effort to examine a suspect's eyes with a flashlight. Our officer was the first person to have contacted the individual in question, but his subsequent role was that of supporting cast to the officer who arrived later.

The tape of the incident suffered from relatively poor fidelity. Our officer—who we are calling Jones—was able to fill in from recent memory. He played the tape, supplemented it with narration, and answered questions that were posed by the group. The group leader (who happened to have internalized the staff's typological approach to the analysis of violent encounters and had a penchant for systematic interviewing) began a more detailed reconstruction of the incident; a staff member joined in early on to further the analytical reconstruction, and this in turn led to an animated discussion by the group.

As it happens, Jones had proposed that the discussion of his incident be taped. We thus still have the discussion on record and we can draw excerpts. These excerpts show how our group happened to witness, during its first session, the results of a diagnostic process on which the group's thinking could subsequently capitalize.

The reconstruction of the incident started with Officer Jones arriving on the scene, where he encountered the suspect (in the vicinity of a reported burglary) working under the hood of his car. The analysis starts with this encounter:

> Jones: I arrived first, and I talked to him and got his driver's license. And he was trying to tell me about the car, but he wasn't making any sense at all.
>
> Officer: Was he cooperative with you?
>
> Jones: Yeah.

Staff: So he didn't seem to be alarmed at your presence at all at that point, huh? In fact, he was sort of viewing you as a source of help and advice with his mechanical difficulties?

Jones: No, I don't think he was doing that. He appeared that he had this problem and he was going to do it himself.

Staff: But he was telling you about it. He wasn't viewing you as a menace?

Jones: I don't think so.

Staff: And you asked him for information and he at least gave you that.

Jones: Yeah.

Staff: And then what did he seem to be expecting?

Jones: He went right back to his car. He said he wasn't going to drive it, though. I got his license and he said the car had rolled down the hill and on the sidewalk. And he said "I don't care if I ever drive it again." And then he went back under the hood and started playing with these wires. He had a real concoction of thin electric wires rigged up under there for some reason.

Officer: Maybe he was practicing putting a bomb in it.

Jones: He mentioned that. He said "There's a secret bomb under here."

Staff: So he was sort of joshing you.

Jones: Well, maybe joshing at that point, but with everything else he seemed to be serious.

Staff: Did he seem to be scared of you at all? Did he seem to think that you'd do anything next?

Jones: No.

Staff: So as far as he was concerned the interview was over and he was going to go back to work on the car.

Jones: Yeah.

The degeneration of the incident was explained by Jones as resulting from the suspect's presumptive drug intoxication. Jones indicated that he had become apprehensive about the suspect almost as soon as he met him. The group was intrigued by this fact and probed further:

> Officer: And then what? Did he show any type of belligerence to you before your cover got there?

> Jones: No.

> Officer: Well, then, why were you apprehensive? That's what I can't understand.

> Officer: Because of his physical condition? Was there any difference in your sizes?

> Jones: Yeah, he was bigger than me. Everybody's bigger than me.

> Staff: But when you say "high" now, that means he was nervous, incoherent, sort of happy. It does not necessarily mean that he's aggressive or nasty, does it?

> Jones: No.

Jones explained his apprehensiveness on the basis of his experience. He said that his fear grew as the suspect dropped a piece of tinfoil on the sidewalk (subsequently the foil proved empty) and the apprehension reached its high point as Jones's partner, Dave, arrived on the scene. Jones tried to communicate some of his impressions to Dave, without apparent success.

Dave meanwhile had independently decided to verify the suspect's condition by shining a flashlight in his eyes. The man had no warning of this contingency. Jones, for his part, said he expected trouble:

> Officer: Did you or Dave, one of you guys, tell him what you were going to do with the flashlight, or did you just come out and put it in his face?

> Jones: We just stuck it in his face. Dave said, "Let me see your eyeballs."

> Officer: Nobody explained, "I want to see your eyeballs. I think you're under the influence and I want to give you a sobriety test," or something like that?

Jones: No.

Leader: You said that you anticipated him making a move, you expected that he might move. When did you first get the feeling that he was going to make a move against you? Did you have the feeling before the other guy got there?

Jones: I had the feeling from prior experience that if I tried to take him to my car, he would probably resist.

Leader: This is before the other guy got there.

Jones: Yeah.

Jones confirmed that the suspect—up to this point—had given no indication of apprehensiveness or concern about the presence of two officers. As he was suddenly faced with the flashlight in his eyes, however, the man struck out at Dave's arm; Jones at once grabbed the suspect around the neck in a choke hold, and Dave used his mace on the man's face:

Coleader: What was his first resistance? You said something about shining the light in his eyes and he shoved it away or something?

Jones: Yeah, Dave said something like, "Let's see your eyeballs." And he stuck the light up in his face. And he pushed the light away from Dave, and then I grabbed him around the neck and started choking him out. He wiggled out of that, and that's when Dave said, "If you keep it up you're going to get hurt." And he poked the light in the guy's stomach a little—he didn't jab him, he just kind of pushed it. And he started coming back at Dave again, so I grabbed him again and Dave pulled his mace out and maced him and me.

Leader: Were you close enough to see when Dave wanted to look at his eyes—apparently you were, because you grabbed him, right?

Jones: Yeah, I was right next to him.

Leader: How did he do it?

Jones: You mean how did he push the light away?

Leader: Yeah. Stand up. You're the suspect. Jim is Dave. How did Dave shine the flashlight on the guy? Did Dave have ahold of him?

Jones: No. He was standing right next to the car, his back was to the car, and we were standing in front of him.

Leader: Show us how to get it. Now how did the suspect do it—he went like that? That easy?

Jones: No, he hit it hard. He didn't have a chance to do anything, because I grabbed him around the neck then.

Leader: Why did you grab him?

Jones: To control him.

Leader: What were you thinking about then?

Jones: We were in such close proximity, he could have just taken a step and started in on Dave. Because we were just inches apart. So I grabbed him so that he wouldn't.

Leader: What did you think the guy was doing when he made his move?

Jones: Well, the first thing, getting the light out of his eyes?

Leader: Is that what he thought?

Jones: Yeah, because I had the feeling that he was high and he didn't want this light in his eyes, and I knew he was going to go to jail eventually.

Staff: But if all he wanted to accomplish was to get the light out of his eyes, and he had gotten the light out of his eyes, what made you start assuming that he would then go and do other things?

Jones: Well, the way he did it, he hit, you know, hard at the flashlight. It wasn't just like a swatting away. It was a good hard jab at that light.

The group analyzed the sequence in several different ways. Their first concern was with breaking the incident down into steps and exploring the assumptions of the officers at each juncture:

Leader: I think what we're interested in is the sequence of events, and Joe was trying to sort of draw a diagram of what was happening between you and this guy when you were alone with him; of him ignoring you, a feeling that you would have that would control your next move which is, one, you're apprehensive about him because you've arrested people that have used drugs before, and they have always resisted. Or you've always had a problem with them. So, this guy is going to give you a problem. Two, you were expecting him to make a move toward you although we brought out that there were really no signs or cues that gave you that reason, merely because this has happened before. So these two cues that you have, rather unconsciously on your part, are going to govern what you do next. Officer Two drives up. You try and tell him the guy is high, but he doesn't catch it. He doesn't talk to you, so there's no consultation. You haven't gotten rid of your uptight feeling about this thing, you know, [by] talking to the other guy about it. You kind of feel like you might have to handle this whole thing yourself, because the other guy isn't aware of how dangerous this man is. This is probably what you were thinking.

Jones: Yeah.

Leader: When he shines the light to check his eyes and the guy says, "Keep the light out of my eyes," maybe he moved the flashlight away and all your expectations have at last been fulfilled. This guy moved and showed that he's done what you expected him to do. That would cover your maybe hasty move in grabbing him around the neck. . . .

Jones: Yeah.

The group then proceeded, in a positive and sympathetic fashion, to guess at Jones's motives and premises and to illustrate their plausibility by citing experiences with encounters in which comparable feelings had been evoked:

Leader: Like this guy really wasn't playing your game until you shined the light in his eyes, because you kind of anticipated all kinds of things to happen, and none of them were happening. The fucking guy's cooperating, talking kind of slow, fumbling around like he's high, sort of clumsy and nonchalant about the whole thing, and that's not really what you want to play right then. You've got a real dangerous dope fiend on your hands, and you know he's going to make a move at you, but the cocksucker won't do it.

Officer: How many of you have gone to the door of a live party? I hate that call more than anything else. I hear that report on the radio and I'm ready to fucking quit, you know. I worked six Saturday and Sunday nights and there was always parties I'd have to take. You'd go to the door, and there'd be 100 people inside this little apartment and they're gassed and having a fucking ball. The stereo's blaring out, and they're all dancing and drinking and having a great time, and you go up and you bang on the fucking door, and usually a couple of them saw you come in, and they go and say "he's coming." A lot of times you're by yourself, and somebody will swing the door open and say, "Well, come on in" and they'll just leave you. They swing the door open and tell you to come in and then just go back to dancing and drinking and having a great time and just leave you standing there with your thumb up your ass. Nobody comes forward or nothing. Maybe you can latch on to someone and talk to him and then they'll shuffle off and ignore you and you're really frustrated as hell. And then once in a while you'll manage to get a hold of the host, and then somebody in the background will say "Let's barbecue that motherfucker," or "Let's throw his ass out the window. . . . " I know when that feeling gets to me the most, where I'd love to get a bunch of goddamn guys and wipe the place out, just because I'd been treated so rude when I was there.

Leader: I haven't had that happen to me, but I find that when you try to stop a car for a traffic violation, a lot of times they just stop where they wanted to go in the first place. And they get out of the car and you get out, and they just sort of walk away, and there you are with your headlight going. Like if you ignore the guy, he'll go away. He's not real. I say, "Where the fuck are you going? You know, I haven't got that light on for my health!" And they'll say, "Oh, yeah, I didn't see you." But could that be what was happening? You've got the other guy's strategy all figured out in this game, and he wasn't doing that? . . . I guess if I was standing behind the guy and he made a swift, very forceful jab I'd lose control somewhat.

The sympathetic concern and the "but-by-the-grace-of-god-it-could-have-been-me" approach to the postulating of motives made it possible for Jones to seriously consider some unpalatable possibilities, and to admit to them:

Officer: Is that the way you felt?

Jones: Well, I think the gun was maybe in the process of going off, but this might have been the situation. Or I thought it was going off and maybe it really wasn't.

The group not only attempted to reconstruct Jones's perceptions and concerns but also those of the suspect. This type of analysis enabled the posing of questions about the interaction of motives and about the transactional genesis of the violence:

Leader: Maybe you wouldn't have to say he was scared so much as he's surprised. He's making what he thinks is an innocuous move—hitting the flashlight out of his eyes—when he's attacked from the rear. And he finds himself being choked. Trying to look at it from his point of view—he sees a light in his face and all he wants is to get it out. So he makes a move and then he's being choked. That's what he sees happening. I'll bet you ten to one if you talked to him, that's what he'd say. "Shit, I wasn't doing anything, and the next thing you know a light was in my eyes. It hurt my eyes and I wanted to get it out." He would probably add, "I said please, and I didn't slap it—I just reached up to move it, when all of a sudden this fucking maniac is grabbing me around the neck and trying to choke me to death!" That's what he would say. And maybe that's how he really saw it. Because there were some things that he drummed up in his head about you maybe, because of a contact with another policeman.

Jones himself also became involved in the analysis of the suspect's motives and began to see the other side to the interaction:

Staff: Now this guy is panicky because he has been grabbed about the neck, right?

Jones: I would say he was, yeah.

Staff: And the rest from there on in is more and more panic.

Jones: Yeah.

Staff: So he's really getting scareder and scareder and scareder until he's sitting in back of the car screaming.

Jones: Well, he's screaming because he hurts.

Having reconstructed the possible contributions of participants to the evolving incident, it became possible to explore alternate courses of action, and to discuss these with Jones:

Coleader: You don't think there was any way you could have talked to him, just talking, talking until he was in the car? I'm not talking about a "you're under arrest, you're going to get into the car one way or the other" approach. Don't you think you could have talked him over to your car? Like you could say, "Well, we got a call about a burglar. I'm going to check into this. You want to come over . . . " and you're walking while you're talking, and you open the door for him just like you might open the door for your wife, and the first thing you know you're sitting in the car talking.

Jones: It didn't even enter my mind. . . .

Officer: Do you think macing this guy was necessary?

Jones: I wouldn't have maced him, myself . . . I was surprised when Dave came out with it. . . .

Staff: At that point he was really pretty effectively restrained?

Jones: I thought he was. I thought I was doing a pretty good job. He was starting to gag a little bit. He was just starting to feel the lost air, I think. In fact, after he was maced, I kept the hold.

Staff: What do you think gave your partner the impression that he required mace?

Jones: That's a good question. I didn't expect it.

Leader: Why do you think he thought he needed macing?

Jones: Well, like he said later, the guy didn't have his shirt on, so he didn't have any clothing to control him with. Or he thought that was the best way to control him at that point, to mace him and let him worry about himself.

At this juncture, Jones had to admit to some lapses in communication that might have contributed to the outcome of the incident.

Officer: If he was being cooperative when your cover arrived, how come you didn't . . . take time to relate the situation to Dave?

Jones: Because he's the senior man, and I usually let the senior man do what he's going to do.

Staff: Could [Dave] have assumed that you had already gone into all the explanations necessary, because he didn't know what conversation you had with the guy? So he might have thought the man had been briefed.

Leader: Could he have also assumed that you had already talked to a complainant and this in fact was the guy that she felt was a burglary suspect?

Jones: He could have, yeah.

The incident had been systematically dissected by the group, and key decisions had been highlighted. Still missing at this point was the working out (in the group context) of alternative solutions. This last stage, however, was soon to be supplied.

Foundation Building

The second eight-hour session of the group can be described as a period of exploration, leading to the building of trust and group purpose. The conversation ranged widely, as is illustrated by the following summary excerpt:

We discussed police states, crowds that gather at scenes of arrest, and how sometimes it would be beneficial if you could get across to the people that gather why you have taken the action—why the guy's all bruised and sitting in the back of the police car and bleeding. Why it takes an ambulance so long to get to a scene. Why they can't talk to a prisoner in the back of a police car, or maybe that they can talk to him, maybe they can give him cigarettes, things like this. A____ brought out an example of a call that he'd been on that was very touchy where he assisted a person that had been shot by a policeman and gained the sympathy of the crowd. And then we discussed the using of a person in the crowd to assist us in our work so that the people that gather can get some kind of identification with us, that we're there to help. That we have one of their group sold on whatever it is that we're doing, and therefore they should be sold on it. We discussed the locker-room talk, the locker-room atmosphere, and how it could possibly influence new policemen in their actions out on the street. How locker-room talk can be used by different officers in a kind of status-seeking thing. Then we got off on a discussion of marijuana, alcohol, and the justifications for making it legal or illegal.

The officers uniformly described the session as "rambling"; several characterized the topics as "tangents" and called for the initiation of project-related work. On the other hand, the group noted with pride and pleasure that ideas were presented openly and freely. Several members stressed that the session was "honest." As the following statements illustrate, they became pleasantly aware of a developing propensity to speak without constraints.

B____ mentioned to me at a break that he felt that it was very good that we were getting down to talking to each other and being fairly honest about it, and that the ice is sort of being broken, and this is going to be very good for the unit. I think that the first four hours that we spent here, although it did seem rather rambling and blah blah blah, was very valuable for group development. People today opened up and said things, even though they may not be directly, right then, relevant to violence, they might not directly be relevant to a project that we could study, they are honest opinions that maybe we're a little surprised to hear. Things were justified, feelings were rationalized, other people opened up and admitted a few things that they probably wouldn't have said if this hadn't happened. So although we didn't get any work done, I think we reached a level of a high degree of honesty and openness with each other which will be beneficial in future discussions.

On the whole the one thing that's come out of this that strikes me, that stands out very much in my mind, was that we found out tonight that although we're all policemen, we don't all think alike in any particular instances out on the street. And I think we'll see as time goes on in here that we'll all have a little bit different ideas of what our roles are out there on the street as police officers.

I believe this is a beginning to break down our own feelings to each other and strip to the bare truth what our own feelings about issues are in the process of becoming honest with each other.

The lack to this point of project-related effort led to the request by one group member for guidance from staff. This request provided an opportunity to reiterate the rule that project ideas had to originate in the group. A staff member indicated that

Part of the problem with this sort of a project, and one of the problems that came up very often last year was the questioning of "what do you want us to do?" And while you didn't say it quite that way, you were talking about what are the directions of the unit, and the aims and the objectives. And we can't answer that. We can say what we want to do generally. The title of the unit implies that. But in terms of telling you what to do, or what projects, that would destroy the intent of the project. It simply would, because if we tell you what to do, then it isn't a group of officers deciding what should be done. And while there are ground rules—we can't teach molotov cocktail making or anything like that I suppose—the ground rules are very limited in that regard. And that's my reply generally. Now, it's not a cop-out. It's really and actually true.

The group leader confirmed the point, and recalled that in the previous summer, "We went through that crap for hours and hours and weeks and weeks," but that the group had become convinced that it would not receive substantive guidance from staff. He concluded that

we're going to have to come up with it. And it's a son of a bitch when somebody says, "We're all sitting down now. Think of something good." There's no harder task in the world than to think of an original idea. It's an utterly unbelievable, frustrating, bastard experience.

Another source of anxiety that emerged in the session related to the question of expected impact. Here, also, the group received reassurance, but the result was inconclusive:

> Officer: It's a little hard to believe after four years of having people tell you, "Well, when you want to make a change, wait till you become a captain," it's hard to believe that anyone around here will say to 25 patrolmen, "You come up with some ideas and we'll make the changes." It's still a hard thing to accept that whatever ideas we come up with, even if they're really good, it's still right now hard for me to believe that they would be implemented even if they meant saving the lives of five policemen next year. It's still hard for me to believe that these organizational changes would be implemented.

> Staff: The only reply I would have to that is test it.

> Officer: Well, I'm willing to give it a chance. It's just that right now I'm still skeptical.

Germination

The next session was the fifth project meeting of the summer and the third group session. It was during this meeting that our principal project—the Action Review Panel—was born.

The session started with Smith (later categorized as the "group filibusterer") bringing up a television show that had impressed him. The discussion quickly branched out, became increasingly germane, and grew quite spirited:

> Smith somehow brought up the fact that he saw two New York policemen on television, and they had long hair and long sideburns and is this a good thing? Do policemen have certain rights that are taken away from them that might help them on the street to identify with certain groups of people? We got into talking about conformity to sets of rules and do the police have to conform to a certain degree. And this of course led into the ideas of rules and regulations, general orders. Are we given too many general orders and rules and regulations to the point where maybe the men on the line

level don't even know what the rules and regulations that we have are? That we just sort of know that they're a vague set of laws in a Great Big Book. And that even if we know the rules, that a lot of times we will violate them to do the job out on the street. Knowing that possibly nothing's going to happen unless we get caught and unless the administration has a big thing about the rule that we do violate. This then led into the idea of the militarism of the police department, or is there militarism in the police department and are we a quasimilitary organization, and is it in fact necessary to be this in order to accomplish the "police mission?" And then C_____ [asked whether] in the realm of rules and regulations, can line patrolmen come up with guidelines that would be followed by other members of the department?

At this point Officer Jones, who had been thinking about his experience in the first session, initiated the topic that led to the project idea:

> About this time Jones came up with the point that the attitude of a particular officer, if he's an old-timer or if he's been on just a little while, greatly affects a new patrolman out on the street. And that maybe when he's been working with the old-timer and he gets out and he works with a little more aggressive police officer, that he's suddenly finding himself in the midst of a large conflict in how to accomplish his police mission, because of the diversity between the two approaches.

It was this posing of the problem that set off Officer Kent—the author of the panel idea—in search of remedies. Officer Kent (not his real name) has remarkable facilities: He is not only equipped with a strong theoretical bent but has the capacity for working ideas out on paper, in detail, in the midst of noise, distraction, and sometimes chaos. He himself summarized the birth of his idea and described it as follows:

> And about here I started scribbling. . . . And I started making little notes about maybe coming up with trying to work up some sort of system where we can have line patrolmen or

the peer group meet in some sort of order review or some sort of review unit where you can analyze the problems that the specific officer might be having on the street when it becomes apparent: Recommendations from superior officers, numerous trips up to Internal Affairs, just numerous violent incidents on the street. This would not be a disciplinary unit or anything like this and it wouldn't really come up with any particular finding pro or con about the officer's actions.

This idea was immediately praised by a staff member, by the leader, and by Officer Jones:

Jones mentioned that he certainly could have used (such a) unit and would have come up here willingly had a unit offering this type of service been available, because he did have a judgment problem. But that the problem wasn't prevalent enough, although he was aware of it and felt it, he didn't feel that it made sense to go to anybody else in the department. I would imagine for a number of reasons—that they would have thought him this incompetent guy, or he doesn't have self-confidence, or what the hell's the matter with him? Which is a problem all of us have—if we have something that doesn't go right on the street, it's very hard to go to somebody and say, "Hey, Joe, I need a little help." Most of us just don't do that.

The group leader not only noted the importance of Kent's idea but spelled out the need for the development of skills necessary to implement it. He pointed out that the acquisition of such skills involved continued experiences with systematic interviewing and pattern analysis:

The idea Kent came up with about perhaps offering the VPU [the Violence Prevention Unit] as a service to guys in the department kind of showed me that after 400 hours seven of us couldn't come up with everything, and it encourages the hell out of me, because this is only the fifth session and bango, we've got something that we can work on and look into. And as an offshoot of that suggestion we're going to have to be able to somehow learn to skillfully extract information from a particular officer who is in need of aid from the unit. We're going to have to get that information out before we can really get down to the crux of anybody's problem.

The group immediately implemented this advice by proceeding to interview Officer Graham, one of its members. The interview was mainly conducted by the leader and proved incisive but inconclusive. Graham (a former skeptic) participated in the summary by expressing surprise and satisfaction with his experience as a subject:

> The first time we brought out someone's reports I was very disappointed in it, in comparison to listening to the tapes, in comparison to some of the more interesting topics that we got into. But now after going over my reports, I think that I now feel that it can be good. But the person who gets the most good out of it is that one individual, not everyone in the group. . . . I may have forgotten a lot of the incident, but I still remember well enough that I remember getting the call and most of the general appearance of everything, from the house to people who were there, emotional flare-ups, little things that I remember about these things but don't go into length to describe and that aren't reflected in the report. . . . I didn't think too much of going over reports before. But for the individual who is having his report on the chopping block, it is beneficial and little things can be conceived as a possibility that may be applicable to that case. And in the future I think maybe you'll be looking for maybe a couple of those little conclusions . . . whereas I didn't think much of this before, I do see a lot of benefit now, for the individual who's getting his report reviewed.

The leader disagreed with Graham's point that the beneficiary of the interview was the interviewee, and pointed to the possibility that patterns might be generalizable:

> I saw myself a few years ago in every one of your incidents, as a matter of fact. In fact, I had a couple of little analogies here that matched mine so much that I'm not going to go into it now because every one of you will hate my guts.

Graham, however, was validated in one respect: Although the group rated the session enjoyable and moderately productive, their participation ratings proved low. The group was beginning to see the point of Kent's scheme but had not yet moved to fully share in its implementation.

A Side Trip

In the first half of the next session the group continued to explore the pattern analytic theme; in the second half, a different concern took temporary precedence.

The officers concentrated for a time on the premise that had inspired the panel idea—the fact that an officer who had developed destructive patterns could perpetuate these through contagion.

The group also conducted a short, relatively impromptu interview of one of its members. This interview developed in fairly circuitous fashion through exploration of tangential topics:

> And then we discussed how members of the community would react to this incident, and how the police react. And then we discussed whether or not police should be more sensitive to cultures. Whether or not they should be aware of the individual culture of the people that live in the area in which they work. We stressed more positive ways to stop people on the street, and we got into Al Cole's approach to stopping people. And Al was more or less criticized by the other participants because he at least said that he was rather impatient and he didn't go to any length to tell the people exactly why he had stopped them and what the reason was, what the crime was in the area that may have precipitated that stop.

During the discussion following the interview, the group's coleader stressed the fact that one could learn from the problems of others and that one could infer behavior rules from the analysis of incidents:

In reference to Al's walking stops and things that we discussed, it ought to be remembered that when we're bringing things out and discussing them that although you might be on the hot spot at one particular moment, everybody in the room is kind of listening to the discussion going back and forth . . . on your methods of stopping people on the street, we're taking all of this in. A lot of us do things at times that aren't correct also, and when you're discussing your case with someone else, all of us are learning something at the same time. Whether or not it's actually true that you do this, it's important this discussion did go on. A lot of us picked up tips on walking stops at the same time you two were discussing it.

The remainder of the day was spent in session with the sergeant of the internal affairs unit, exploring questions related to discipline. The group felt that this interview was "informative" but not focused. More positively, the willingness of an outsider to meet with the group was encouraging for the men, even though hasty planning and unclear objectives deprived the experience of more concrete benefit.

Defining the Mission

The fifth group session was probably the most constructive and fateful in the life of the group. Paradoxically, the meeting started with a free-floating, rambling exploration of tangents. The summarizer noted,

When this meeting started off, I actually thought nothing was going to get done tonight at all. It was the most rambling start—from Internal Affairs back to [a] shooting—the most idle conversation that we've had so far. It went just on and on without even talking about anything at all.

Other officers made similar observations. One member of the group noted (on the back of his reaction form) that "the meeting started slow and rambling—not staying on the same topic, but going back and forth." As the session gravitated to an early (2:00 a.m.) lunch, prospects for constructive work appeared slim.

Directly after lunch, however, Officer Kent pulled out a thick stack of notes and began to expound the details of his panel idea. He proposed "some sort of review unit made up of patrolmen. When another patrolman gets into a behavioral pattern (such that) he is having violent incidents on the street—and it becomes apparent that he is . . . help him out, help find where he's going wrong, before he has to go up to Internal Affairs, before he gets hurt on the street."

Kent stressed the necessary informality of the procedure, the desirability of an "off the record" approach, the need for a positive, constructive emphasis. The sessions of the panel, he indicated,

> Would be conducted more as an interview rather than an interrogation. And what you're going to try to do then is review the behavioral patterns of the person and analyze what he's doing and somehow make him, in this process, come up with some self-critique, like we do here. You know, after he reads the report somebody asks questions. "There's some questions in some of your reports that you'd probably want to go over"—"why did I do this this way?" And you'd have to stop and think, "Do I do that very often?" I think this type of review is going to be helpful. In other words, just sort of as an assist unit for the individual patrolman.

The group quickly took up the discussion. One point that was repeatedly emphasized was the desirability of having relevant insights originate with the officer being interviewed, rather than with the review panel:

> Officer 1:   Wouldn't it be good if we could sort of switch it around that he bring out his own problem?
>
> Officer 2:   I think that's the only way.
>
> Officer 3:   You bring out his problem and you're another Internal Affairs.
>
> Officer 2:   That's why I said we've got to have a system or technique in order to bring it out. It would be a self-awareness

on his part. In the interviewing and talking to him all of a sudden the bell would go off.

In connection with the need to have the interviewee arrive at his or her own inferences, two other points were made: first, that prejudgments of their problems would remind officers of traditional supervisory technique, and second, that this diagnostic approach could produce retreat into inactivity. Officers who did not spell out their own difficulties in their own terms were apt to equate a delineation of their deficiencies with a mandate to lie low:

> Officer: You're never going to get to the crux of the problem by pointing to the problem. Because this is the M.O. [*modus operandi*] that this department has always used. When there was a big purge in patrol division, all these guys were called in and told if they have any more 148s [resisting arrest arrests] they're going to be fired. The M.O. has always been, "Look, Louie, you've got a problem. And you'd better stop whatever you're doing, although you don't know what it is, or you're going to be fired." And the guy walks out of the room saying "son of a bitch." I did when I was called in by a captain several years ago. I really thought that I was doing a good job. I'm a hell of a cop. I get involved, I get out there and I fight crime, and I'm running into nothing but assholes—bad luck. You know, right, we all do good police work and it's the citizen's fault. Resistances. And I thought, "Fuck them. I'm not going to do nothing."

Probably in an effort to convince itself of its integrity, the group became concerned with the need to "sell" its panel to the interviewee, while remaining completely honest with him or her. Both the ethical implications and the pragmatic aspects of approaches to the interviewee were ventilated:

> Officer 1:   You could destroy a good tool by being completely honest. Why don't you tell your wife about all your extramarital love affairs and say, "But, baby, I love you!" I did that, and it's going to cost me $4,000 a year for the rest of my life. I was completely honest with her.

> Officer 2:   I think you were a dumb shit.

Officer 1:   Right. That's exactly the point. Now, would we be dumb shits?

Officer 3:   Are you going to tell that guy that's 6 feet 9 inches, 250 pounds as you walk up to him and you know he's a burglar and you walk up to him and your cover ain't there, "You're going to jail." I wouldn't do that. I'd walk up to him and say, "What's your name," as I look over my shoulder, "Where the fuck is that cover?"

Officer 4:   Jack, what you say does make a lot of sense. I guess this is it—these could be some guidelines to think about. If the guy says, "Why am I up here?" we tell him, "Your supervisor recommended that you come up." If he doesn't say, "Why am I up here" I guess you don't have to say it.

Kent: In your initial interview, state the purposes of the VPU [Violence Prevention Unit] as a whole. Very, very basically state it as a whole. "Lower the violent confrontations, fewer cops get hurt, and in order to do this, this program has to come up with new changes. In other words, this is a program of change." Get that across there somewhere. Then tell them, "You've been recommended by your supervisor. Now the reason you've been recommended is because apparently you've been getting involved in the street. So since you're getting involved in the street and you seem to be concerned with what's going on, two things can happen from it. One, you can help us and then we can help you."

There was general agreement that the panel had to be introduced to the interviewee by stressing its benefits to the police in general and to endangered officers in particular:

Officer 1:   Maybe we could say we don't want to emphasize [the issue of violence], because he's going to be aware of it, and I guess that would sort of be adding insult to injury, you know, to emphasize it. "You know why you're up here, Charley, you vicious bastard you!"

Kent: You've got to get across to them that the purpose is twofold. One, to prevent the violent confrontation, and because you're doing this you're going to help policemen (1) not get fired, (2) not get hurt. Whichever order of preference you want to make it.

Officer 2:   We could say we want you to help us to prevent people from getting fired, screwed up. Not you necessarily, but everybody.

Officer 3:   What you are able to offer us may help some other guy coming up next.

A number of procedural alternatives were explored by the group, and their advantages and disadvantages were considered. One such alternative was that of "embedding" the interviewee in a discussion group or involving him or her with other officers who also had demonstrated difficulties:

Officer 2:   There's just a slight hazard to doing it that way. . . . Let's put it this way. If we had three people up here at one time who were recommended or were having problems and needed a little consultation, it wouldn't be too smart to give them even odds. You know what I mean? It's kind of hard to talk to a guy and bring out an incident when you have two other guys sitting there saying, "Bullshit, he did the right thing. I think we ought to kick the shit out of all of them sons a bitches, you know, mow them down."

Staff: Of course there is another complication to this which one ought to consider, and that is that unless you pick three guys awfully carefully—your problems are different enough from mine so that we can get awfully confused if we start trying to discuss them all at the same time and the same place.

Officer 3:   A lot of confidence is supposed to be here. If a man comes to a psychologist, he wants to tell him his problems. Say he's a businessman and he's got a lot of hang-ups. Well, he doesn't want two other businessmen sitting there listening.

A related possibility that was mentioned was that of involving the interviewee indirectly, by dissecting the patterns of other subjects with the interviewee's participation:

Officer 1:   Or we could do it this way. We're going to have to do the homework on the guy before he comes up here, right? . . . We all know who we are. If we see his reports and hit on some where we have that same type of pattern that got us into shit, start talking about that pattern as related to ourselves first—criticizing ourselves, and then as the discussion goes around the table to him, maybe by that time he's reading his own report, he can more or less see that same pattern, but never referring directly to his reports. Do you see what I mean? In other words, if you're always having trouble with women, like the one guy did as an example, pick out our reports where we had trouble with [women], and then maybe in the discussion, while we're talking about, "Well, this is what I did," you say something like, "Son of a bitch, I have a lot of trouble with women." And maybe this guy will look at his report and say, "So do I."

Officer 2:   He's probably going to say, "Do you assholes really think I don't know what you're trying to do?"

The group moved from discussing procedural variations to the planning of sessions in which techniques and strategies of interviewing could be tried out. The proposed sequence was to start with members of the unit and subsequently to branch out to volunteers secured elsewhere:

Kent: I think initially (we ought) to continue what we're doing now. From within our own group here. Within the three groups that we have. To see if we could work out some kind of interview system here, since we are as close-knit groups as we are now, the guy being interviewed would say, "Now look, you're beginning to piss me off" or "I'm beginning to feel in a corner. I don't like the way you're doing this. Let's forget that line of approach in questioning me regarding these particular incidents." Things like this. Because really, as you look through the three groups, it's a pretty good cross-section of patrol.

This discussion led to an unexpected testimonial from Officer Graham, who revealed that in a postinterview session in the cafeteria he had arrived at unexpected insights into his difficulties and now saw a pattern in his involvements:

Kent: As an example, and this struck me very much, what you and Graham went through the other day would have been a tremendous thing. . . .

Graham: Can I say it, because I went over it? . . . I had a problem and didn't even know it—wasn't aware of it. Me and Bill (the leader) were really having a lot of laughs on my reports, and I walked out the door and still didn't have any awareness or conclusions. It was a lot of talk. But then we started bullshitting out there and he related a couple of incidents and then I remembered the Angels and I pointed out the one about the Angels and then Bill pointed out something. And I found that I was, without even being aware of it, anytime there were insurmountable odds against me I was tearing-ass into it. Three Angels in the [tavern] and no cover. "Outside, all three of you, let's go. Take you on." No cover. I could have waited. Two men inside already slammed the door in my face made a statement they're going to kill the mother-fucking pig. I didn't care—I went right on through anyway. "Here comes supercop." Without even realizing it.

Staff: With a slingshot.

Graham: Yeah, that's what he said—David and Goliath. And I never realized I was doing that. I'm surprised I haven't got my back busted or my neck broken. I don't really know whether I was trying to prove anything, because I wasn't expecting anyone else really necessarily there.

Graham himself indicated his satisfaction with the interview as a procedure and so did other group members. The session was universally characterized as "constructive"; it was rated extremely high in productivity and morale. The group leader summed up his own impression of the occasion by exclaiming that

I never cease to be amazed at how you people are getting through these eight hours as compared to how we did. It's unbelievable. Everything I've got on this session rating form tonight is very high. I can't think of anything bad about it. I think we've come a hell of a long ways in coming up with this idea. And it's going to take more work, but it's going to be worth it. And I just want to say that I feel real good about it.

The session ended with a collective determination to expend whatever time and energy it took to get the review panel idea firmed up, so that it could be proposed to the chief as a strategy worthy of adoption.

Constructive Conflict

The sixth session represented a forced departure from group project development. The leader of the group had been scheduled to instruct the recruit academy in "violence prevention" and requested help in the preparation of his class outline. Collective drafting exercises generally proved painful to our groups, and this one was no exception. The period was enlivened, however, by spirited divergences of views relating to training concepts and techniques.

One of these conflicts related to the word *game*, which had become a staple in the working vocabulary of our first-generation officers. For us, the term was synonymous with interpersonal interaction and denoted moves and countermoves with latent purposes and assumptions. The new group had bypassed the conceptual exercises leading to the development of vocabulary and thus was unfamiliar with "in-group" language. One of the officers objected to references to violence-prone "games"— arguing that the word was unnecessarily flippant. A lively discussion—initiated by the group's coleader—followed the objection. The new members joined the "old-timers" in defending the word, and the dissenter declared himself eventually satisfied.

The second argument was not similarly resolved. Again, it stemmed from a prevalent first-generation assumption, relating to the value of role-playing as a training tool. One of the new officers (Graham) objected to the technique, classifying it as artificial and unconvincing. (The point was a carryover from a retreat session, where the same subject had come up.) The group spent considerable time on the pros and cons of various forms of role-playing and even staged an impromptu demonstration. The debate terminated in a proposed subcommittee on role-playing, which was never constituted.

Probably of more interest than the subjects of these conflicts was the form that they took. A staff member noted in the summary that

> Part of what we ought to be looking at is what happens here other than the content of what we are talking about, just in terms of, for instance, how we get along. It would seem that

from that point of view it was rather interesting that what we had after what Jim calls lunch was a complicated kind of thing. We had a lot of fun. We were all chuckling pretty well, but along the line we also did quite a little solid fighting which we wouldn't have done if we didn't trust each other enough to say all kinds of pretty forthright things; in the process I think we discovered how we really feel about a subject in terms of where we all stand with respect to it, and now we can all start working on it constructively.

As noted in this statement, the relaxed group atmosphere could be viewed as indicative of the development of trust. Another such test arose when two group members reported that they had been adversely received in the coffee room by three officers to whom they broached the subject of the unit. They discussed the incident as follows:

Officer 1:   There were two patrol officers and one from traffic and (we) were sitting there talking to them, and they were entirely negative to the VPU idea, period. If their thinking is contagious. . . .

Officer 2:   Were they negative because of their lack of knowledge of it, or because of what they had heard by rumor, or what?

Officer 1:   We tried to talk to them a little about it, and it was like talking to the wall, wouldn't you say?

Officer 3:   Well, I said, "I like you and everything, but I can't help it if you're not progressive and have a very narrow mind."

Officer 4:   That was a very forceful, diplomatic way of putting it.

Officer 1:   Well, if you had seen how negative he was!

Officer 4:   Did you feel like getting violent with him?

Officer 1:   Yeah, like reaching over and knocking his head in.

One of the officers who complained about this encounter suggested that the reaction might be more general and pervasive. He recalled that he had been previously subject to negative feedback:

A lot of them . . . really think that we are a peace and flowers organization, "turn the other cheek, run up and kiss them." You know what I mean?

"Blazers with flowers on them"—what else did he mention? "Take your gun off." Those two points they both mentioned.

And I think that a lot of them feel that way. Because I went all the way up around Clairmont or somewhere to cover somebody on a [complaint involving] two hippies who went up behind a building and ran up in a middle of a block of apartments behind some stairs. One officer comes in this way and is blocked by a fence and yells, "There he is," and another officer literally flew over a fence and came down on the guys, put them right down to the ground, a wrestling match out to the car. And one of them in his frustration, who is a good friend of mine, looks at me and says, "How would you prevent that?" And I never even thought anything! You know, this was a guy who just splits and all they did was take him. And he looks up and he said, "How would you prevent that?" And I said, "I thought you did pretty good police work." But part of this was that we are supposed to be sitting here saying, "Oh, you pushed him down. Did you scratch his elbow?"

The group leader was reassuring. He characterized adverse views as unrepresentative expressions of uninformed envy:

I guess it's kind of like the guy who has a Cadillac. If you can't afford one or you can't get one, the normal thing to say is, "I don't want one anyway, and I wouldn't have it." My conclusion is that that's about it. You know, there's kind of a fear of it—something new. You're a little envious in a lot of respects. For instance, I wouldn't take very seriously what either one of those two individuals said. I think we both know them.

He also, somewhat indirectly, counseled patience and forbearance:

Last summer we tried to ride with the punches and not create any more animosity than was necessary. But I also got to the point where I was bugged so bad one night, for instance at the Public House, by a guy who I went along with for about an hour, and I finally got him in a corner and said, "Look, Joe Blow, you've had an awful lot of fun at my expense. And I would suggest very strongly that you change your line of conversation, or I'm going to knock the shit out of you." But I rolled with him for a long time. I'm not suggesting that you'll have fistfights. I've never done that in my life, and I hope I never do. But I think we can play the game with them, talk to them about it, maybe sell it. But it ain't going to be easy.

On a more serious note, the leader suggested that sobering experiences were the price one had to pay for commitment to change:

Getting back to what Bob said about he was kind of discouraged, I'm glad. Because if you weren't discouraged a little bit I wouldn't feel too good, because I went through an awful lot of that and I guess maybe it's just because we've got a few hundred hours under our belt and a lot of digging remarks that you sort of get used to it after a while. It's sort of like being called dirty names on the street. If you weren't discouraged, I would be discouraged. You know, I mean, if you really didn't give a shit, I'd feel bad about it.

The issue under discussion by the officers relates to the vulnerability of new (and presumptively deviant) groups in any subcultural context. The officers proclaimed that they could handle the problem. Despite this ostensibly reassuring conclusion, they felt that the session had been difficult. There were many ratings of "average," and words like *exasperating* and *inconclusive* cropped up among the (largely favorable) characterization of the meeting.

Tooling Up

Much of the next session was taken up by the first effort of the group to prepare itself systematically for a panel interview through analysis of background information.

The prospective interviewee (slated for the following evening) was a member of the project consensually regarded as violence-prone and impervious to influence. This characterization was not only shared by the group but was part of the officer's general reputation in the locker room.

The group agreed on the point that, "If we can make impact on this guy, we can change anyone." However, they were not hopeful. As one of the men put it,

> I'm a bit pessimistic insofar as he's concerned, because I don't really think he's the type of individual we're going to make much headway with. He obviously knows what the attitudes of his fellows are here and he's obviously uninfluenced by this attitude; and I think he'll be similarly uninfluenced by our attitude toward him or by anything we say to him.

But others noted that the interviewee's anticipated obduracy made him an ideal test case for the interview procedure:

> While we're all probably pretty pessimistic about this particular individual, especially those of us who have had an occasion to work with him even if it's only one time, that if this particular individual who had such strong convictions can be made aware of the fact that he does in fact have a problem—because I don't know that he's really aware of it—there shouldn't really be anybody else that we would have as much of a problem with as I think we're going to have with this one.

The first approach to the background analysis was a qualitative one. Members of the group read reports aloud, and hypotheses were formulated about general themes. The group also solidified its impression of the magnitude of the interviewee's problems:

> It was a bit thought-provoking to think that such an individual actually goes out there among the citizens. I'm a little staggered by it. I'd heard all the stories, but it's another thing to see the man put it in his own words and tell it the way he sees it!

In digging deeper, a system was devised for tabulating salient features of the report. This innovation again originated with Kent, who recalled the following:

> While we were all sitting here talking, everybody had a report or a series of reports in front of him, and we were all just generally making comments. And it began to hit me that there were certain areas or patterns that were developing just from the casual conversation that we were having before we were even really going to analyze these reports. So I just took a little piece of paper and drew a bunch of white squares on it in order to pick out some of these things.

The group thoroughly enjoyed the classification exercise that followed. Almost all session ratings were high, and the adjectives most frequently used in descriptions were *constructive, relevant,* and *purposeful.*

The Opening Night

The group arrived the following night full of anticipation and curiosity. The interviewee (whom we will call John Spark) appeared on time and reacted positively to the introduction. He spoke freely, although at times he showed apprehension or nervousness.

The group leader conducted the first portion of the interview and did so incisively and with surprising success. Spark was taken through various reports step by step and a pattern emerged, not only for the group but for Spark. The pattern showed a propensity for personal vendettas against citizens who had challenged Spark's supremacy on his beat. These vendettas invariably culminated in a relatively petty arrest in which Spark used the municipal code to retaliate against his perceived opponents. The following are excerpts in which the summarizer (Jones) details the manifestations of the pattern:

> When we discussed his first report, I noticed that he kept track of a witness and he stated, "I didn't particularly like

her." So he's been running a warrant check on her about every month and he finally came up with a $39 warrant which he is bent on serving. This brings up the personal involvement that he gets in these things, and I think this leads him to having difficulty. He also stated in that report that he can't stop doing the job because a suspect has a gun . . . and he has the attitude that he's going to get the guy no matter what.

In the second report . . . he was challenged on how much officers will take in the eyes of the public. . . . And then he reacts with arresting somebody for something. . . . They weren't using profanity so he couldn't use that for a crutch. So he used littering when somebody picked up some papers and threw them on the ground again. He also wrote the driver eight violations on this second stop, after he'd already cited him for speeding. Going on to the next report, it was a high-speed chase. The driver gave him a funny look; he explained that he thought that the driver was hoping that he wouldn't notice and wouldn't turn around and chase him. He almost begged for a high-speed chase—he turned the red light on two blocks behind him. And he stated that he hadn't been in a chase for a while and he was kind of hoping that the guy would run. This sort of indicates to me that he appears to go looking for trouble.

Jones characterized the pattern as he saw it. In doing so he included concepts adopted by our first-generation officers (e.g., "playing in the opponent's ballpark"), which had spread to our new trainees:

At this point it was appearing to me that he was being drawn into the other guy's ballpark, and he was trying to win in his ballpark when actually he wasn't, and he was looking very bad. He stated that the cop is the ultimate authority, and this is the way he works. That's his Territory and he's the guy who's going to run the show, although going over these reports, he's running the show rather badly. And he's not playing in his own ballpark, although he thinks he is. Again, when he loses control in a situation, he reverts to an arrest. This seems to be the only out that he can use. . . . These were personal challenges: [In] the first one this gal that he's running the warrant on called him a "motherfucking pig," I believe it was. And he was challenged there. The funny look on the driver's face in the high-speed chase challenged him. He takes all these things personally. He's using these personal challenges, and the way he wins them is by arresting these people on anything he can think of.

The process of elucidating Spark's motivation through interview, after study of his reports, proved to be especially instructive. Hypotheses based on the written material were helpful in directing the questioning but had to be reformulated as new data emerged. One officer summarized the positive contribution of this experience by saying,

> We had a lot of material to work with, we had a good background study last night, and I personally felt good with myself because I began to pick out these traits of people that are being interviewed. And [with] some of the other people in the group [that] had been interviewed I had had a little bit of trouble finding the things that they did leading to the problem that they had. And of course Spark had some pretty glaring problems that weren't too hard to follow, and I think this has helped me find these traits and be able to follow them to a problem.

The discrepancy between the written and interview versions of the incidents led to speculations about the function of the written report. Here the "official" version of the incident was seen as a rationalization of the private encounter—not only for the benefit of superiors but also for the officer's own use as a tool of self-deception:

> Officer: There's a lot of things you wouldn't put in a report, like the kids—he declared war on them. He told them that they were fair game several days, months, or weeks before, "I'll have you—I'll get you—I'll take care of you at a later date."

> Staff: I think part of the pattern is the real stuff never goes on his report. Because he uses the letter of the law to accomplish some other purpose, and that other purpose is only in

his mind and it cannot go on the report. He cannot say, "I got this guy for turning around this corner because I wanted to curb prostitution." He can't say that. He has to say, "failure to signal." He has to say, "litter." He couldn't say, "I was in a war against these kids and that's the first excuse they gave me." The report is the excuse he uses. What we got today was the reason why he's in this business, which is to get people. And it's to get people who have shamed him in public or who he disapproves of because they are making a mess of his turf there. Which he's in charge of. And there is no way you can put that in a report.

Another learning experience was related to the issue of insight and change. The first part of Spark's interview was insight-centered, with Spark responding like a textbook case. At the conclusion of this interaction, when Spark warmly thanked the group for helping him to understand his past conduct, the leader moved to terminate the interview. The group, however, continued it, focusing on Spark's current practices and his future plans. The leader, who retreated somewhat into the background, later complained,

> I thought, "Goddamn. We won this battle—we really did. And now we're blowing it. Because we're giving him too much room for justification." Now that was my opinion. However, it was explained to me, and we talked about it quite a bit over lunch, that there had to be some way that we could go into future contacts that Spark would be having with people on the street and somehow relate them to past contacts which have resulted in a whole pile of 148s. I didn't see that—I didn't see that.

Group members noted that while Spark was freely conceptualizing his past conduct, he showed little indication of willingness to extrapolate from these hypotheses. As a staff member put it, Spark

> was filling in a picture which was neatly detailed, made absolute sense, was completely coherent, and every additional piece of information he gave us tied into it. And it's quite understandable that when one has it all together, one

should say, "Well, thank you and goodbye." What happened, however, is that we kept on saying yesterday, as you'll remember, "If we can break this guy, we can break anybody." And we lost sight of a couple of little cues. Namely, he kept on saying, for instance, "Yeah, that's the way I used to be." And the clear implication was "that ain't the way I am now." Obviously if that's not the way I am now, then all of this is history and it doesn't have any relevance. Except you're giving me some pretty good insights into the way I was when I was young and inexperienced and green.

Indeed, as the interview progressed, Spark showed an exasperating propensity for justifying his escapades and for refusing to acknowledge the contribution of attitudinal factors to his current problems. As the interview concluded, the group felt that they understood Spark but that they had made no impact on his conduct. They nonetheless felt elated at their success in securing data for analysis and at their role as interviewers. The coleader (generally predisposed to skepticism) asserted the following:

The main thing that I could see tonight was that we did achieve the purpose that we set out to do. That is, that we had an interview with someone with regard to the 148's that he's been involved in. And after Bill's initial introduction, probing and discussion, everybody here did enter into it in some degree. And this is what the hell it's all about. It was real good. Then after it was over it was even better in that everybody had an awful lot to say about what went on— what they saw developing or happening. We had a real good discussion.

He stated the feeling of the group in noting that the information secured from Spark testified—among other things—to its developing interviewing skills:

And I think that if we had an interview with anybody now, that any three or four members in the group, regardless of who they were, could conduct an interview and keep it moving. . . . He threw out some real big stuff that wasn't in those reports. And that was after we started chipping away.

And I think maybe we tonight were working on our own particular M.O., our own interviewing M.O., in that you get a guy talking and there's a hell of a lot not written in that report that he will tell you. Like I say, there were large gaps in most of these reports, yet when we went back through them chipping away on some of the little stuff, picking through and going back through the hours and the location and were there other people around, what was the crowd situation. . . .

As for failure to produce impact on the interviewee, questions were raised about how much of this could be expected. A staff member observed:

The element which may have been a little hidden by what happened today is that somehow, despite all the guff yesterday about this is the last man we expect to change, everybody came in here today deep down inside expecting a tremendous conversion to take place in this room. Now actually we got a long ways toward something happening. That is, we got some insight here. And we got the guy on the defensive here and there. And we just have a large question mark here as to what's going on in his mind. . . .

We needn't castigate ourselves for not getting him to walk out of here a convert and a changed man. I think we have given him some room for thought. I think he did say some things in this room that he has never said before. I think we have made a good start.

The staff member recalled that Sparks was due to be assigned to the group (by mutual agreement) as a temporary member, and noted the following:

We'll have an opportunity, since [Spark is] going to be with us in the next month or so, to do a little more observing and see the results, if any, of our session with him. I suspect there are bound to be some. I think we shook him up. We'll also have an opportunity, if we like, to bring him in for a follow-up interview anytime that he feels he's ready.

In addition to discussing the possibility for reinterviewing Spark, the group considered outside candidates for additional "practice" interviews. One such candidate, a notoriously trouble-some officer, had been recruited as a volunteer in a neighborhood tavern the previous evening. The group decided to invite him next. Other prospective candidates were also named and dis-cussed. The profusion of subjects—and the feeling that the group knew what it was about—produced much self-congratulation. Officer Graham, who announced his departure for two weeks of military training, said in parting that

> I can remember about a week ago Paul and I came in here with a stunned look on our face, like it's hopeless. Two officers just talked to us and condemned the hell out of us—it's hopeless, we'll never get anybody up here. But my last thought as I'm preparing to go out the door is, there are more people right now during this test time than we have time to prepare for. Volunteers. We've got more people right now that may want to hold a mock interview to learn how we're going to do this in effect than you have time to prepare for them. We're already talking about, "No, you can't have him Monday. We don't have time to prepare for it." And you've got another one lined up who I'm totally surprised is coming up here no matter what game he thinks he's going to play . . . if you have him in here that's a hell of a start right there. So I'm totally encouraged once again with the idea of the VPU board.

The group's ratings of the session divided between high and very high; the leading adjectives were *promising* and *valuable*. The group had developed a sense of purpose and a feeling of confidence.

The Man Who Came to Dinner

The next session put the group's self-confidence to a solid test. They faced their first outside interviewee, and—as if this were insufficient—the individual was an officer whose record of activ-ity (and to some extent, of physical involvements) had made him a legend in the department.

Officer Beam had volunteered for the interview, with some persuasion from Bill, the group leader. As one member put it, the preceding evening,

> at the Public House over his Ballantine scotch that Bill bought him after losing a game of dice to an unnamed officer, he very skillfully directed this officer into coming up here. I was a little surprised that he thinks that he volunteered to come up here.

The origin of the idea aside, Officer Beam expressed interest in serving as a subject and did so for his own ends. His ends included clearing his reputation by demonstrating the clear-cut justifiability of his physical encounters; pointing to changes in his conduct (but maintaining that these had not sprung from changed attitudes), rectifying false impressions about the nature of police work, and helping others who might have problems.

Whichever the dominant motive, Beam's appearance was self-defined as that of an expert witness, an officer without problems who had wisdom and information to impart. In the face of this fact, the group set out to analyze Beam's pattern of conduct with a view to arriving at some understanding of it. The result was a standoff that left both parties satisfied. Whereas Beam departed with the conviction that he had enlightened the group, the officers (in their postinterview analysis) felt that they had arrived at a meaningful diagnosis.

Descriptively, Beam's pattern involved a propensity for arresting narcotics users and a tendency to physical interactions with some of them at the point of arrest. In the words of the officer summarizer:

> People that he has arrested, and has had problems with, have been people that he has known or knows to be using narcotics. And this appears to be a very important thing with him. All through his interview he repeatedly referred to people who used narcotics and the way that they will act, and the way that he handles narcotics when he is going to arrest them. He stated that he makes the first move on a hype [a person under the influence of drugs] "If I think I'm going

to have to fight them, because they're nervous, paranoid, and overall dangerous." He also stated anyone who doesn't cuff a hype either is a fool or the bravest person on earth. "They're all fighters"—and he emphasized this over and over—all hypes are fighters. They're the most dangerous people. He says, "I'm always prepared to fight, I'm careful, and I've never been nailed"—meaning that he's never been hit by one.

In an extended lecture, Beam defended the proposition that narcotics users were unpredictably violent people, dangerous to deal with, and that it became necessary, at times, to act to prevent injury. He admitted to being "specialized" in his interest in narcotics users. Bill, the group leader, classified this interest as a "crusade" or "war," and this characterization resulted in a brisk exchange, with Beam defending his activity as rational and objective. According to the summarizer:

> He said, "Everybody's happy including me, because I put this person in jail and I've solved some burglaries and maybe some robberies and maybe some violence, plus I've also got this narcotic that no one else could catch but me."

The group inquired into the origin of Beam's interest in narcotics users, and he referred to two precipitating events:

> We got into why he developed this interest in narcotics. And he related an incident about when he first was on the street that he arrested a person that was high on narcotics and this person told him that if he would have arrested him 15 minutes earlier that the guy would have probably killed him. This made him think about people that are on narcotics, and he became concerned about the violence of these people, and also the narcotics problem. . . . Again, in his background, he evidently went home to Boston and he was talking to this sister and some friends about drugs, and he found that his sister had been using drugs a little bit, and some of his friends were now in prison for serious crimes because of their narcotics use. And he has a feeling that he must protect them from their own actions.

During the analysis session, the group speculated about the role that fear—and its suppression—might play in producing Beam's pattern of conduct. As one officer (the group coleader) put it:

> Maybe I'm all wet in this little analysis that I have here, but I think that he's operating out of fear. I think that he's so goddamn afraid that he probably came into police work to prove that he could overcome this, which he does—and I think that's one of the reasons I have so much respect for him. I think he's got the shit scared out of him, and that's the main reason he's chosen narcotics work and specialized in it. But he's not a dummy; he's armed himself with all the laws on narcotics and a hell of a lot of information, a lot more than normal patrol procedure calls for out on the street. He's always talking about snatching people first and never losing control of the situation, and then going through with some physical thing to restrain a guy—getting the handcuffs on him, getting him out of circulation real quick. And I think the reason he does this is also based on fear.

Another officer (Bill) pointed out that Beam tended to target

> incomparable demons in narcotics. I really believe he believes that, although I don't buy his story about being scared to death by a hype in a men's room, and this is why he's on this personal vendetta. I think that's some sort of mental justification.

This point was elaborated, later in the session, by one of the staff members, who argued.

> If you were trying to build a case of, "How do I handle this feeling in myself, that I can't rise to challenges, that I've got to make up a challenge where I can really overprove to myself that I really can make it, that I really can do it," it would seem to me that he's done a rather beautiful job. And we all agree he's bright, and he's made up a bright rationale here of the evil of these guys who use drugs. And then for a safeguard he puts in this, "I hit first."

You've certainly got a beautiful pattern here for actually getting a physical confrontation over and over again. We don't understand enough of it, but from what he's been telling us, giving himself reassurance that he can take on challenges and can meet them. And I would think of the drug addict as actually a relatively safe challenge. I don't know that I'd buy that he's really taking on anything that's rough.

Another staff member, in a fairly lengthy statement, produced a different version of Beam's hypothesized vulnerability. He reminded the group of the following:

When people hunted witches they prided themselves in being able to locate witches by marks that were left under their crotch or under the armpit or by various little indications that they gave. Beam considers himself an expert at locating these bad guys with a physical indication. He's able to separate them from the rest of the world, and goes about this business very assiduously. And it's extremely important to him to separate them from the rest of the world, which means that he has the world sort of divided and the people who are drug users—the ones that he can locate as bad guys—represent something very intimate to him that upsets him terribly. And he has to control them, which means, I think, that he has to control whatever it is in himself that he somehow senses in them. Now, I guess it's Bob who said before Beam came up here, "It must have something to do with his neighborhood, and the people he grew up with." And then that proved to be an extremely well-confirmed hypothesis because it's one of the few things that Beam was quite willing to answer . . . he started talking about what it is that really was the occasion for this need to control hypes, as he calls them, and it had to do with two friends he had whom he was apparently close to who ended up in serious difficulties after they started using, or he thought they started using, and his sister. I don't know what to make of his sister, and we might think about that a little bit, but one can venture two possible guesses as to what it was about his friends. The first one was that he felt acutely disappointed by them. Now, that doesn't seem very plausible. The second one was that he said to himself, "There but for the grace of God go I."

That is, "These are people that grew up with me and this is how they ended up, and whatever it is in them, I got to fight it in myself." And he fights it in himself by fighting it out there in the world.

He recalled that Beam had presented as a reason for his campaign the fact that narcotics users do harm to themselves. He then went on to suggest the following:

Part of what that means is that "they are extremely vulnerable," which means, "I'm extremely vulnerable." Then the other part of the answer I think is related to that, in that they become very "irrational." Their mind gets tampered with. They lose control. They become aggressive. They become evil. They become stupid. They become irresponsible. Which means that I guess in part what he's saying is that "In order for me to keep control over my mind," and the fear element may enter in this, "I've got to fight like hell this tendency for people to have their minds tampered with, and to become irrational monsters, which I can become myself given half the chance."

The discussion later returned to this point, stimulated by an afterthought:

Staff: He says that he's in the business of controlling them. . . . I think he means "subdue." I think he means "suppress."

Kent: He said their personality changes when they use it, they resent authority, and you can't tell them what to do.

Leader: He did in fact talk about suppression.

Staff: Which may kind of lend some support to the feeling that this is sort of a metaphor. That is, that he is really trying to control what he thinks of as the drug problem, which is the change in a person's mind from rational to irrational. And this is a very intimate, personal type thing.

Officer: That's where someone like Beam has an advantage. He has the answers.

Leader: Yeah, but you see he doesn't have the alternatives to his answers. And furthermore he doesn't believe they exist—that's the problem. I think he might think about it.

The group concluded that Beam might be relatively difficult to change—and that the interview probably made relatively little impact on him:

> What he essentially wants to do is go out there and fight his private crusade, or as Bill put it, his private war. And he would like as much approval as he can for this. He would like to convince as many people as possible of the rightness of his cause. But if he can't, he'll do it irrespective. There's no amount of pressure today that has had much effect, simply because the sources of the pressure are irrelevant, because people, he feels justifiably, don't have any feeling for this crusade that he's on. And he's right. They don't.

The group also agreed, however, that if any officer was worth preservation, it was Beam. As one officer put the case,

> I have a hell of a lot of respect for him, because in each line of work somewhere along the line there's something outstanding in whatever he does. Most people just go along and they do a job. There are people who play violins and then there's people who are damn good violin players. And then there are guys who are policemen. There are some 700 policemen, and then there's Beam.

One staff member, who had never encountered Officer Beam before, observed,

> Of all people, you hate to see him go down the tube when you get to know him. This is a very powerful guy. . . . It seems to me besides talking, there ought to be some strategy developed to get him to be a real participant.

The group concluded that additional interviews and other follow-up activities involving Beam were worth the effort, even if Beam—like Spark—was admittedly a "tough nut to crack."

Ratings of the Beam interview testified to the feeling that the time had been constructively invested. The assessment of productivity reached a peak unequaled except for the first session. Group morale was rated higher than ever. And members felt they had participated fully. They also felt they had learned much and classified the experience as *instructive* and *informative*, as well as *constructive* and *valuable*.

A Command Appearance

During the group's next meeting, the members found themselves faced—at the initiative of another group—with the opportunity of a summit meeting with the chief. They arrived at this encounter without advance warning, completely unprepared, and were unable to present their ideas. As a result, the chief occupied himself with other matters. He responded to questions from members of a second group and (during a lapse in the questions) reported on his recent experiences with a police department in another city. As Bill summarized the situation later:

> With the chief, you can't give him 30 seconds of silence, because the man is extremely intelligent, he manipulates group conversation. He dominates it because he's extremely brilliant and he's a very eloquent man. He is; there's no doubt about it. And that's what happened. He shot the whole thing. He carried the ball the whole time. He's never in a corner. Joe drew a beautiful picture of a Southern Pacific Railroad Roundhouse, and let me tell you something. He was in the middle and we were all revolving around him like the earth and the sun.

As a constructive by-product of the debacle, there was strong incentive to structure the review panel idea in proposal form. In response to Kent's vague description, the chief replied that he'd like to know more. As Joe (the coleader) pointed out,

> He stated several times, "That's a great idea—you guys work up the finished package and show it to me." And I think

that's what we're going to have to do. I think before you get anything across it can't be a generality or any vague idea. It's got to be the specific facts, a finished product all ready for him to sign and send on or it's not going to get anyplace.

Kent, who felt personally responsible for the failure to inform the chief, immediately set to work drafting his proposal. Amid much pleasantry and aimless conversation, he sat grimly formulating the document. As a staff member observed in the summary,

> Kent has made a great deal of headway there—he is well on his way to writing this proposal. We can give it to the chief as soon as it's done. So we may have in fact moved faster in this area than if Bill had been eloquent, although it's quite obvious that the chief would have listened, and from what several of us know about the way he thinks, he would have been extremely sympathetic and supportive and excited.

The group, however was still largely discouraged. Their session ratings reached an all-time low and hovered around average. The two main rating terms were *fun* and *exasperating*. Similar ambivalence was reflected in words such as *rambling, irritating, monotonous*, and *enjoyable*. The meeting had offered entertainment, but the group members did not feel materially furthered in their mission, nor were they proud of any accomplishments.

A Study in Complexity

During its next session the group was back on course, with another volunteer interview. The volunteer, Officer Kennedy, advertised himself as a changed-but-unreformed practitioner of violence. Kennedy had had contact with our original group in the context of research into the Hell's Angels incident. At that time Officer Kennedy had impressed the group with his willingness and ability to conceptualize events. Thus, when he declared his interest in assisting in subsequent inquiries, the offer was welcomed.

Officer Kennedy is in fact a brilliant young man, with a distinguished academic record (including a graduate degree). Despite his excellent mind, however, Kennedy had placed a premium on muscular prowess, with emphasis on boxing. He had also accumulated a reputation for explosiveness. He said he was successfully working to overcome this propensity, but that he was otherwise far from a pacifist. According to the interview summary,

> He stated that violence is attractive to him. He liked the idea of street justice. He liked to draw people in to make them move so that he would have an excuse to hit them when he decided that they would have to go. He said that he must restrain himself in violent situations; he has an impulse to strike out when he is mad.

Kennedy's recipe for producing violence was to "come on soft" to give the impression that he is a pushover. This encouraged prospective opponents to assert themselves and provided occasion for a confrontation. In encounters such as these, Kennedy asserted, he has never been beaten:

> He said, "I will always fight to the end. I will never be beat. If I am beat that time I will remember the person and I will get him later. I can't lose." [He recalled] some of his high school days when he was in a tough crowd and it was kind of a big thing and you got into a beef and won the fight. Also, when he was in the Marine Corps he evidently didn't lose too many fights.

In his early associations, Kennedy recalled, his physical confrontations had brought status with his peers:

> He said that he fought for status and he mentioned the codes. The code that he had in the Marine Corps and the code he had here dictated that he must fight for his status, that he had to demonstrate his fighting ability, to acquire his status here or in high school or in the service. And this status was

what his peers expected, or this is what he feels is expected. He feels that in order to be worthy of their expectations, he'd have to be a competent fighter.

He contended that the same circumstances obtain in the police as in other settings:

> He thinks there is a code among police officers, probably gathered from the locker room, that you are cool because you got into a beef and you beat the crap out of somebody. This makes you feel good and you talk about it and everybody looks up to you.

Simultaneously, he felt that the police organization—particularly at the command level—kept the level of violence in line and suppressed it:

> And were it not for this pressure, the pressure of command and the pressure of Internal Affairs, he would conduct himself as he sees the police, and that is as commandos. I guess that's kind of the bit where you swing from the ropes and kick down the doors and go in there with machine guns blazing, and you leave the bodies there for the Graves and Registrations Crew to come through and pick them up.

The same characterization of externally suppressed violence ran through Kennedy's discussion of individual motivation and, particularly, of his own motivation. He indicated that when a status issue arises—when he is challenged—this liberates "anger" or impulses and permits him to fight:

> His violent encounters start when someone is running away to avoid arrest or when someone is degrading the uniform and he becomes upset. He says that "I hit people when it is necessary and I lose my cool." When "I've lost my cool or when I'm angry, I'm letting that person know who is the boss."

The image Kennedy sketched of himself was that of a dormant volcano, with a propensity for occasional eruptions. The result of eruptions, in addition to the discharge of violent impulses, would be the consolidation of status or dominance; the image being compounded when Kennedy also claimed that he reacted against the angry eruptions of others. However, as one of our group members noted, this paradox is resolved if one considers the suppression of others as indirect self-control:

> He constantly mentions when you act in a violent way, this is giving way to some animalistic tendency. Real animals doing vicious things are violent themselves. All men are animals down inside. And he says when he sees somebody acting in this animalistic nature, it gets on his nerves, and he tries to stop it. And maybe it's because he has the fear of the same thing in himself. And by doing so, he comes to fight the fire with fire, fight the animal on his own terms of being an animal.

Officer Kennedy made a point of telling the group that the department had checked his violent propensities and that he could expect to engage in no further physical involvements on the street. "I go out of my way to avoid fights," he maintained. With respect to this stance, one of our officers (Kent) speculated,

> I think he came up here to tell us that he had changed. And to give us some sort of reasoning for his sort of joining the Establishment. I think he was looking for approval from us. I think maybe one reason for this is that because he . . . had already decided that he had to change in order to advance, that maybe he wasn't finding the peer group approval from the locker room. So he had to find it somewhere. And even more so, I don't know—like I said, the guy is no dummy— maybe in the back of his mind he felt that this information would get passed on somewhere else, the fact that he's changed his approach. I think the reason that we saw so many of the contradictory statements was that he's still got to maintain a partial identity of the tough guy with the peer group that he finds down in the locker room. And this is where we find our contradictions.

The group saw additional complexities and inconsistencies in Kennedy's self-portrait. Bill, the group leader, categorized some of the themes in Kennedy's interview, which he labeled "the idealistic tough guy," "the introspective marshmallow," and "the justifier." There was some speculation that at least some of these roles were being played for the benefit of our group:

> Here's a guy saying, "I enjoy violence," and some of us get upset. And we say to him, "Don't you see all these alternatives? And how can you enjoy violence, and isn't this terribly shocking?" And I think at that juncture what was happening to us is we had a game of honesty played on us, where the fellow says, "I'm going to be completely honest with you" and then proceeds to say all kinds of really deep dark things about himself and at times you almost want to stop him and say, "Look, I've got to protect you because you're really exposing all kinds of terrible things." And he says, "Well, you know, I'm making sort of a monster out of myself," with a little snicker. And sure enough, you take a look and the guy is making a monster out of himself—there he is, "I'm enjoying violence, I've got all these deep dark urges. When I repress them I sit there clenching my teeth and have my hands in my pockets and I've got to go to a sex orgy to let all this energy out, because that's the kind of guy I am." You start having the feeling that you're being tested, that you're being goaded just like these people out in the street. You're being goaded this way because you're the Violence Prevention Unit and this is the way that you can be goaded, by my saying, "I am the Violent Man—I'm what you're fighting." But then you also have this business where he is trying to suck us in. He says, "I enjoy violence, we all enjoy violence." Meaning, "You guys enjoy violence." And, "What nerve do you have having me up here for being a guy who joins the police force to get a little action when it's quite obvious we all do. Let's all cop out to how we are all really violent and the only thing that's keeping us from being violent is Internal Affairs."

Role-playing aside, the picture presented to the group was clearly paradoxical and considerably more complex than the patterns emerging from previous interviews. The group considered various ways of reconciling disparate elements. One of these was summarized by a staff member:

> Now this commando or Green Beret model of policing that he has is a little odd, because he gets something here that says each of us is sort of an uncontrollable force and it's the job of the police department to squelch us. And it sounds like if that happens you can be proud both of being potentially violent and also of being squelched, so that you can't really lose. Because essentially Kennedy can say, "Look, I am still capable of winning fights, and the only reason why I don't win them is because the police department is not permitting me to fight. And I don't mind in one sense the police department not permitting me to fight because I am also in this police game. That is, I don't like people out there stirring up trouble. But at the same time I myself am still capable of doing the things that I have been doing. And it's only the system that keeps me from doing them." Which I think is sort of in miniature the feeling he has about himself. . . . There's all that adrenaline there that is flowing. But still, there is the mind over matter bit, and he emphasized this very early in the game. He says, "I don't lose my cool—I choose to lose my cool. And now I don't choose to lose my cool as much as I chose to lose my cool before." So he has to feel that he's in control, but he also has to feel that he can get out of control and can have these highs and can have this fun and can be this monster, whenever he can get away with it. That is, he does not like the self-image of being a guy who had the controlling forces in command. It's got to be sort of a precarious balance at all times. A constant battle, where the only time you can be nonviolent is when you can give yourself some pretty solid reasons for being nonviolent. Then you can stand there saying, "There but for the grace of God goes another corpse. And it's only the system, or these things that I choose to give way to, that keeps this guy from being a corpse." And that way, save face. I must say he has me convinced when he comes in and says, "I am a violent man, I am a monster." I think he is. I think, however, that's just one part of the picture. I also think he's a guy who's very capable of coping with this, but in a situation in which he doesn't get any excuses for coping with it, he isn't going to. I think that's part of what he was trying to tell us.

The group decided that some of Kennedy's self-description was more revealing than he suspected. Thus one of the officers observed nonverbal indicators of discomfort or apprehension:

> Whenever Kennedy gets into any kind of a confrontation like he was here tonight, you'll notice that right around his collar line it starts a brilliant red color, and it creeps right up. I was watching it as he started taking us on here tonight. It finally covered his whole face. Evidently there's some physiological change that goes here and maybe this is this apprehension that we're talking about.

Except for group participation ratings, the session brought the quantitative indices back into the high category, with the group members feeling that they were developing the group's procedure and learning much. The most frequently checked adjective was *valuable,* followed by *thought-provoking* and *constructive;* other recurrent rating terms were *challenging, promising,* and *informative.*

Back to the Drawing Board

The next meeting was a two-part working session. During the first half, the group met with a captain who had requested that one of his officers be interviewed. The purpose of this session was to brief the group on the interviewee's problem, as assessed by the captain.

The group was pleased by this session on two counts. First, there was pride in having been perceived as a resource, particularly by a member of management:

> I think we can be flattered somewhat that a command officer sat down and told us that he has exhausted just about every means that he has available to him in an attempt to help this officer, and now finds himself [working with] patrolmen who have come up with a proposal that might do the job better than he himself can do it. And, I think that is something to be damn proud of. I really think that it is something that we can kind of wallow in for a while.

The second source of satisfaction was the fact that a commanding officer might become sufficiently concerned with helping a patrol officer to take the trouble to explore available resources. Simultaneously, the group felt that supervisors might not be equipped with information or skills relevant to the diagnosis of problems. The group discussed the possibility that the supervisor's role might make it difficult to exercise constructive influence:

> Like he was aware of several danger signs, he went through the standard procedure of calling a man in and talking to him, not really having any plan or pattern or any idea what was bugging the guy, what the man's individual problems were. And it's an indication to me that something's lacking around here in all ranks. That possibly a training program could remedy.

In the second half of the session the group broke up into subgroups to work on the details of projects. One of these subgroups, chaired by Kent, worked on the review panel idea. The other group dealt with a questionnaire exploring possibilities for using lineup (change-of-shift) time for short-term remedial training. The lineup survey group reported progress, but added that "everybody subverted each other all night long." The action review group characterized their session as "an agonizing exercise" from which they "emerged a bit torn up mentally."

Session ratings ranged widely, with some men classifying the evening as productive and pleasant and others declaring themselves exhausted. The most frequently used adjectives were *thought-provoking, challenging,* and *inconclusive.*

Running Out of Steam

At the next meeting the group was faced with the prospect of more planning. No activity was scheduled, nor was there a consuming pending task. One assignment was the record review session relating to an interview the following night. The remainder of the time was occupied with drafting and discussion. This portion of the meeting was somewhat slow. Its most negative assessment came from one group member, who said,

> After lunch I felt that we all fell apart. As I looked around the room, I found everyone . . . doing something other than the work that was going on or should have been. We spent an unproductive second period of joking, doodling, and making obscene gestures at one another.

The group leader viewed the session somewhat more favorably. He observed,

> There comes a time when you kind of think you run out of things to do and rather than think about something and rather than really push yourself on it, you have a tendency to want to not do anything. And I think we were damn near at that point tonight, because that's how I felt. I seem to relate everything to how I feel. And I wrote down that the group seemed to move tonight simply because it wanted to. I really didn't think I'd be able to get on board tonight, but I found it really easy when things started moving. And it was merely because you guys started participating and producing something.

A staff member's assessment fell somewhere in between:

> I think Bill put it very accurately—it was a tough session, we had a lot of thinking to do today; we didn't have anything entertaining to do, like interviewing somebody. And we sat around for eight hours, and we did some solid talking and thinking and looking at information and reading, and we got through it and we survived it and we got some ideas to take with us that we didn't have when we arrived.

The interview planning session did capture the interest of the group. It produced some observations, but no conclusion:

> We sensed that there was a person here who has a tendency to put himself in a situation where some people have given him some warnings that they're going to be unfriendly if he

orders them to do things that they're not going to do. And
then he jumps on them when they predictably respond, or
fail to respond. There is still a certain amount of mystery
about this which is healthy, because it kind of shows the point
to which one can proceed with these preliminary reviews and
the gaps that are left, which is a lesson that we have to learn.
And we will learn it filling in tomorrow.

The group also formally decided to adopt its new member,
Officer Spark. Spark had belonged to a group in which he had
become the focus of tensions. Adopting Spark was a calculated
risk, and the officers took it freely and unambivalently. Several
members of the group observed that as things stood they need
not fear potentially destructive influences. The group also felt
that it could regard itself as a regenerating environment.

Except for morale ratings (which were high), the officers were
disinclined to boast about their accomplishments. Nor did they
despair. Almost all rated the meeting as *constructive*, and some
thought it was *creative* and *valuable*. However, there were complaints about occasional *rambling*.

Accomplishment

In a sense, the interview of the man referred by the captain
represented movement from the sandbox into the battlefield.
Whereas previous interviewees had presented themselves as volunteers and as participants in the design of the project, Fels was
neither. Here was an officer who had been ordered up for an
interview, with reason to be wary and resentful. The order had
emanated from a superior who had previously voiced strong
reservations about Fels's conduct—and who had remonstrated
with him, ordered, cajoled, sermonized, and threatened him.
Officer Fels suspected that his conduct was the issue, and assumed that the proceeding was adversary. He knew nothing
about the group, nor had he more than superficial past contact
with any of its members.

Fels entered into the situation coldly, sullenly, and determined
to remain silent. He started by refusing to read his reports, and

responded "I don't recall" to every one of Bill's questions. According to an outline chronology by Kent, the first hour and a quarter of the interview transpired as follows:

> My first entry on this little conglomeration of notes that I keep says, "He's extremely defensive, stern." At 8:05, this is 5 minutes after he sat down, I wrote, "His responses will be like testimony." At 8:12 I made a notation, "Things are going bad." At 8:20 I made a notation, "Bill sounds like a cross-examination." Also, I put down the first report in this case that we thought was a good report was bad actually, I think. Because it put him way on the defensive. We picked up a few things. At 8:45 I made a notation that we were belaboring that first report. Then we go to the second report; then we jumped right to the third one. This is 9:15.

Fels's initial reluctance to respond had an adverse impact on the questioning. The issue began to revolve around a concerted effort to wring a concession or acknowledgment from Fels. In one report, for instance, the group worried about Fels's reluctance to permit an intoxicated woman to be taken to her nearby home. As one officer (Graham) summarized this incident:

> In an attempt to get him to open up, everyone kind of got on a bad bag. Whether they couldn't find another one or not, or what it was, but you wanted to try to make him open up and think about alternatives. So you're trying to come up with an alternative in this drunk case. And you couldn't get him to come up with one, so you suggested one, and then everybody took it on and you wanted him to admit something which he didn't believe. And everyone kept bringing up the aspect of possibly letting the suspect go, which may have been an alternative. But nothing else was mentioned, and then it went on with "haven't you ever done this before?" "Let her go, let her go, let her go." I kept hearing this cry from the group. And he kept sitting over there saying, "Well, I don't see why I'd have to let her go—isn't there any other alternative? Is that all you've come up with?" And I felt that possibly at that time, that he might, since he's new and hasn't heard all this, be thinking along the lines of, "Is that their

alternative, period?" No "s" on the end. "Do you have to
make these arrests just because she's a little drunk?"

Eventually, after an indigestible Mexican lunch that produced
innumerable complaints from the group, the atmosphere began
gradually to relax and Fels talked. He started "remembering"
details, including those not entered in the report. He began to
speculate about motives and to discuss his premises. He became,
ultimately, voluble. It became clear, as Bill later noted, that Fels
"was ready to talk to somebody . . . really wanted to talk to
somebody."

Fels speculated that at some juncture he had developed a
pattern of reacting personally to suspects and bystanders. He
indicated that he had permitted people to "get under his skin";
"respect" had been an emotion-laden issue. He confessed to
feeling "challenged" by lack of respect. "He was out there thinking of himself as having to uphold the whole legal structure
when anybody defied it by saying something to him or by not
responding to him."

The group was not surprised by this analysis because it corres-
ponded to hypotheses formulated the previous evening in the
review of Fels's reports:

> We did a very good job confirming all the hunches that we
> built up during the agonizing four to eight hours that we
> looked over this stuff. That is, almost everything that he told
> us about himself we had thought through, and in a sense
> this was a kind of confirming session. . . . Which meant we
> did some solid thinking.

Like Kennedy, Fels presented a picture of having been suppressed. He produced two versions of this sequence. His first
model was that of a "pendulum" movement, which he thought
was fairly general with police officers:

> He definitely thought when he was coming on and he first
> came on he was very susceptible and quite liberal and open-
> minded. And then some training officers in the peer group
> and some of the observations got to him, and also his person-

ality, as he puts it, got molded to the point where he was taking these things personally. . . . And then he was able to get out of this into another period in which now he can view things more dispassionately.

In this model, Fels attributed his transition to education:

He said he had been taking college courses and reading Black literature. His view had broadened. He can see why Blacks act the way they do and how they view the police. And this affects the way he acts.

He described the result as a set of insights, and indicated that he had found them to be valid, confirmed through experience:

Fels has realized recently that he approaches people different. He talks and listens, he smiles more, he can get their view as to their actions and get their side of the story. And he can relate to them better. His first words made a difference. He tries to give the person an out . . . "It used to be my attitude if I am saying it, you better do it. Now I feel I ought to explain." He said, "How can somebody call you an MF if you walk up smiling?"

Fels's second version of change represented a strict compliance model, in which the new pattern resulted completely from administrative pressure:

He's changed not really because of any changing in his mind, but he's changed because of administrative pressure here, which he thinks is unfair. He realizes that this is the environment that he's living in. If he wants to stay here he's going to have to do certain things.

In elaborating this version of the sequence, Fels characterized himself as apathetic and asserted that he was working less hard and deriving less satisfaction from his work:

He says, "I enjoy the job less. I don't go after crime like I used to. I don't know how to be aggressive and keep out of

148s." . . . He said he hadn't thought about any alternatives to being aggressive and being effective and staying out of 148s. He says now he doesn't have any initiative. . . . "The department is telling me I'm bad because I have a lot of 148s. Yet I don't think the department has the facts."

According to Fels, the reason for his low productivity had to do with the indiscriminate nature of the censure to which he was subjected. By subjecting his street conduct to criticism, the department had failed to distinguish between his constructive activity and his corollary problem behavior:

> He's in a straitjacket when he's going out there. . . . The point he made several times [is] that just telling him that he has a lot of 148s without any explanation made him very angry, especially because when somebody tells you that you have a great many 148s they also say you're a bad police officer. They don't distinguish that 148s and quality police work are definitely tied together.

In the course of the interview, the group pointed out to Fels that his supervisor was concerned with his problem, as witnessed by his high opinion of Fels and his desire to "save" him. Fels acknowledged that these arguments were reasonable and indicated that the discussion had been helpful. In general, he reacted to the evening positively and appreciatively. As he left the session, he said that he was prepared to support the review panel project, which he viewed as necessary and obviously constructive.

The group, in turn, was uniformly elated. Bill, the leader, introduced his summary by indicating that he had been "trying to think of how I can talk into the tape . . . without sounding like a kid who just woke up on Christmas morning." Jones, on his reaction form, waxed lyrical ("It's been shown that a rough road can end at a beautiful meadow"). Officer Spark, the new group member, characterized the review unit as "great," and expressed the hope that he could be used on future panels.

Productivity ratings averaged very high, as in the first session of the summer. Almost everyone rated the session as both "tense" and "constructive." Other adjectives (in order) were *enjoyable, purposeful, valuable, relevant, promising, instructive, inspiring,* and *beautiful.*

An Interlude of Alienation

Joe, the coleader, introduced his contribution to the next session's summary by saying,

> We really didn't have anything going that anybody wanted to bring out right off the bat. There are a lot of things that are on policemen's minds today and we brought some of them out. . . .

As another officer put it (on his reaction form): "The before-lunch session *screamed* many frustrating things felt by police-men today."

The "frustrating things" had to do with recent snipings at police officers in various major cities. Once this subject came up, it branched into increasingly remote areas. At first, there was concern about the sufficiency of protection—was there enough "backing"? Then there were issues of priorities, strictures, the arbitrariness of rules, and lack of appreciation. At one acrimoni-ous juncture, Joe advanced the following proposition:

> It's going to be a hell of a thing to sell a violence-reduction program in police work when you're getting policemen snuffed out left and right all over the country.

Bill, who had tried (unsuccessfully) to curb the discussion, "dropped out" of it and did not participate much. Eventually, the group returned to business half-heartedly and turned to reviewing the records of its next prospective interviewee.

In the summary, the evening was penitently reviewed, with the only positive note injected by a staff member, who indicated that the evening's discussion might have some bearing on the concerns of several interviewees:

The idea is, "Well, they . . . are trying to make me stop doing work." Which then gets to the issues of is this police department or is the chief really serious about doing police work? Or is he in the community relations business? And although the discussion itself may not have been terribly relevant, the more I think about it, the more it's obvious that there are some indications in this kind of discussion that are relevant. They have to do with the issue of good people like Fels for one, and maybe even possibly at some juncture Spark, saying "I feel like I'm being forced into a position of not being able to do my job. And I'm going to be unhappy and I'm going to be inactive and I'm going to view this department as in a sense not designed to get the job done." And on another level it relates to the feeling of maybe they aren't serious about protecting me from snipers. Or maybe the Chief isn't really on our side, maybe he's just a politician as opposed to a guy who's out there trying to facilitate our work. So in a sense the theme is related.

The group remained resolutely depressed. The session was rated relatively low, and the adjectives reflected considerable ambivalence of feeling. The top four rating terms were *enjoyable, constructive, inconclusive,* and *rambling;* these were followed by *valuable, frustrating,* and *subversive.* The group had permitted itself a cathartic experience and was now determined to return to business.

The Interviewer as Theorist

The next session, on September 1, was the last group session of the summer and the penultimate meeting of the project. The evening started off somewhat disappointingly, with the scheduled interviewee, for whom preparations had been made, not appearing. Fortunately, Officer Chico Bond, a member of one of our other two groups, had stayed in the building and volunteered for an interview. The men spent an hour getting ready for Bond and then subjected him to a review session. In the final portion of the meeting the conclusions reached about Bond were compared with those obtained with other interviewees, and some general assumptions of a theoretical nature were advanced and discussed.

Bond was an amiable, relatively young, slight officer, whose physical encounters had taken place almost exclusively with Mexican American suspects, most of them youths. He admitted that he sometimes felt personally challenged in these encounters and that he felt compelled to respond:

> He said . . . "The suspects failed to comply." "The suspect appeared hostile—looked like he was mad at being stopped." . . . "I put myself in a position to lose face if this suspect didn't leave." And also the suspect would lose face if he did leave, so they had kind of a standoff here.

At the simplest level, the hypothesis about Bond was that there was some resonance or similarity between himself and his young Mexican American suspects, which led to a collision of patterns:

> He isn't in some respects an imposing, muscular physical specimen. And it's entirely possible to speculate that he's also out there occasionally trying to make a case for his being an imposing figure. And he runs into other people who have the same case to make. You get a collision there, on account of there's only one imposing physical figure at any given altercation of this kind. And there is not room for both unless there is some kind of compromise possible. And you don't get the feeling that there was much compromise.

A more sophisticated (and more general) formulation was advanced by Officer Kent, who summarized it as follows:

> What I've noticed here, and I don't know if it's going to come out with the rest of the people we're dealing with, but the word I've got here again . . . is fear. Here you have fear of Mexican Americans just like earlier we saw fear of hypes, fear of [Blacks], fear of the crowd inciter, and now we have fear of a Latin American. It seems to follow a pattern. And I'm wondering if when he has this particular fear when he approaches a person on the street, a person tends to get tense, and when he's tense because he has this fear that he's trying

to control, if this causes a breakdown in his ability to verbally communicate with somebody. And when you have the breakdown of this verbal communication—this willingness to get out and talk to the person on a police officer–citizen contact— it almost seems like it's going to be a corollary that you will have physical contact, because you have this mutual misunderstanding. Because the citizen's going to be afraid of the policeman, too, at a particular point. And consequently, if you have just orders coming out and he doesn't want to comply, you have both people that are nervous, tense, tight, and sooner or later somebody's going to take some sort of action. Because obviously the verbal communication is broken down.

The application of this view of a fear-induced communication impasse was elaborated by one of the staff members:

I do think there may be something to this. . . . That when Chico gets afraid he becomes a different person. That he isn't the mild, sweet gentle Chico we all love. And you kind of have the feeling that maybe the one game that is going on with these Mexican Americans is that he is in effect challenging them. That is, he isn't so much being challenged as he is challenging them, and there is communication going on here, and they are getting the message. I'm impressed, by the way, by the fact that we are putting some life on this bone of people refusing to comply with orders, which is in fact how 8 out of 10 148s start out according to the statistical analysis. The statistics just give you that fact. One thing you get from Chico is that very often the order that is given or the instruction that isn't being complied with is really impossible for the person to comply with, not physically but in terms of the way he has already pointed out in some way or other to the officer he's going to be able to act. And it seems to me that one thing that you get with Chico is he does present difficulties to the civilians that they can't resolve. And it isn't so much that he gets mad with people who don't follow his orders, like another guy we had up here, but he has a tendency to give people orders that are boxing them in and then he gets into trouble. It's interesting that in many of the instances, that is, at least those instances that we've looked at, you've got a 148 where there's no real grounds for arrest in the first place.

This formulation led to a long and spirited discussion among the group. Joe, the coleader, demanded a dictionary definition of *fear*; Graham worried about the implication of manifest fear among police.

There followed a more intimate discussion in which officers who had been interviewed speculated about the role of fear in their incidents. Jones maintained that he could detect fear in his own encounters; Graham (in response to comments by other officers) began to see a possible involvement of fear in some of his own incidents:

> Jones: This reminds me of this incident that we've got on tape that I went over. Remember when I snatched the guy when he swung? This is probably the same type of thing that we're talking about here. I reacted so fast because of apprehension, fear of what might happen.
>
> Graham: Do I really need to prove myself when I go through the door, or is it because—well, I find that hard to believe about me. . . .
>
> Officer: In your ideas about fear, you've rationalized in your own mind that you've corralled fear. . . .
>
> Graham: The group mentioned [fear] as an observation about Beam. And then I just took it like an explanation. And now Kent is actually making a kind of theory out of it. And I don't know how you're bringing in fear, but I'm having a hard time imagining policemen out in the street afraid.
>
> Bill: You've never been afraid?
>
> Graham: Not as a running emotion, as constant a factor as this theory suggests.
>
> Officer: Every time I get in the car I've got it.
>
> Graham: Well, on a particular incident, yes, but I find the theory being presented as a constant.
>
> Bill: Could the fact that an officer could or could not act out of fear be because he's in a position where he can't make

an exit? I would say that if a person was in fear or afraid other than a policeman it's obviously possible for him to get the hell away. A cop can't do that; he's got to stay there, although he feels that fear. Which makes him act out of that fear. You can't leave the scene like a truck driver or a banker or an insurance salesman or anybody else. You've got to stay there; that's your job. It makes it pretty goddamn awesome at times.

Graham: At times, but no one answered this question about the fear as a constant.

In response to Graham's request for a more comprehensive formulation, a staff member elaborated on the possibility of behavioral patterns based on habitually suppressed fear:

All right, lets say it's a constant in some respect but not in others. For instance, forgetting for the moment about the fear but thinking about what would happen if it were there at some level. . . . One thing is you can run in there without cover just to show you're not afraid. Another is you can go out there and be a man of steel and exaggerate the danger of all these people, and the more danger the better. That's another thing you can do. Another thing you can do is pick the first little guy you come across and beat him up, which is as a matter of fact the most terrible way of all. That's the way bullies do it. That is, you make other people afraid, and the more afraid they are, the more you feel you're an inspirer of fear rather than a feeler of fear. Another thing you can do is brave it out, and this is where you get the Chico Bond type of thing. That is, you come on more harshly than you would if you weren't afraid. The point being that all of these maneuvers and some others are designed for two purposes. One is to fool yourself, in the sense of making it hard to view yourself as a guy who's capable of fear, and the other one is fooling the other people involved, or the spectators or the opposition. . . . It's possible that one of the main problems in the police business is how to make yourself accept fear as a perfectly decent, respectable emotion to have if it doesn't run away with you, obviously. Not panic—fear. Admitting it. You know, the locker room doesn't compensate you if you go in there and say, "You know, I was scared out of my pants today."

The staff member argued that the suppression of fear could be a reaction to a self-image that labels fear as a symptom of vulnerability or weakness:

> If you can admit that you're afraid, you admit that you're *weak*. And you may have a big problem about feeling weak. So you can get the Man of Steel type thing, which says, two steps removed . . . "I'm really not much of a guy, I'm really pretty vulnerable," and then you end up making yourself invulnerable. But in between is this feeling that you've got to fight off because it would make you admit what you don't want to admit. . . . On top of everything else, this is a dangerous job. We've got fear running through this whole business and then we've got some guys who seem to have more of a thing here than others.

The group at this juncture returned to the fact that several interviewees (including Officer Bond) had reported that their conduct had changed. This led to a discussion of the review panel as a context in which constructive movement (whether real or fictitious) could be discussed freely and rehearsed:

> They wouldn't go around the locker room saying, "I have changed." They say it here. And I think the exercise of saying "I have changed" and documenting it is healthy. That is, one of the purposes of this interview might in fact be to give an opportunity to a guy of emphasizing those things about him that are positive, which otherwise might be submerged again by talking about inactivity, which is quite popular. It's quite respectable. Even Joe would regard it as respectable for a guy to say, "Well, this department has gotten me down and so I'm not doing any work." No one in the locker room would look down on you for this. But if they are talking more, "And I used not to tell people much and now I talk to them," that doesn't strike me as something that would get you many pats on the back in the locker room.

The session had thus provided an opportunity to begin generalizing about the dynamics of problem officers and to discuss concepts meaningful to the analysis of patterns. Despite the fact that some of the discussion had involved disagreements, and despite the abstract nature of the ideas, the group felt good about the session. The ratings were high. The only negative adjective used in the evaluations was *puzzling*. Other terms used to describe the session were *academic* (as a positive attribute), *enjoyable, sensible, constructive, relevant, promising,* and *thought-provoking*.

An Activity Profile

Figure 7.1 presents a profile of quantitative ratings for activities of the group. The high points of the productivity graph are identified and they all tend to relate to the review panel. Interviews and interview analyses produced favorable ratings, and interviews with "outsiders" ranked higher than the less worrisome "in-group" exercises.

The group morale rankings proved relatively stable, except for three low-productivity sessions, in which morale dropped, and the first group session, in which morale was uniquely high. Participation was often closely tied to productivity but occasionally proved independent.

A General Comment

The first impression that might strike an observer is of this group's high degree of task orientation. It may be noted that almost every session had some relation to the peer review project. On the first day the stage was set and a preliminary rehearsal actually took place; the discussion of the second meeting proved germane; the idea was formalized in the third meeting, and in almost every subsequent session a task was performed or concepts explored that fed directly into the review panel project.

Several other activities were stillborn during this period. Their life consisted of explorations of rationale, discussion of practical problems, and, in one instance, the design of an instrument. In no case did a side project occupy more than a fragment of meeting time and the attention of a few members.

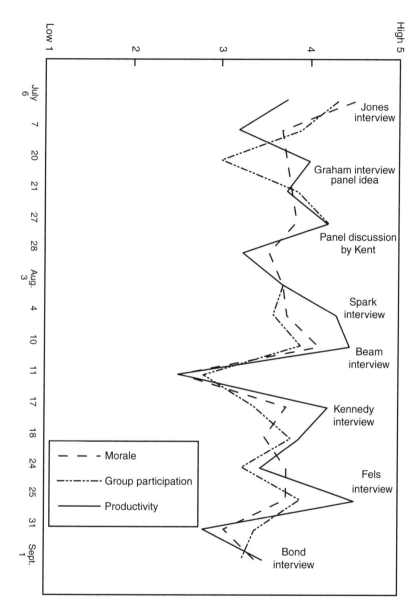

Figure 7.1.   Profile of self-assessed group reactions to problem-related activities (peer review panel).

The success of the group (if we use summaries and rating forms as criteria) can be attributed to three factors. (a) Time was taken up with consuming tasks that were related to an objective with which the group identified. These tasks (the interviews) were intellectually stimulating, controversial and challenging, and produced information that could be generalized. As the officers developed as interviewers, they gained insight into the conduct of their peers and into their own behavior, and they became more thoughtful about their jobs. They increasingly saw the value of interviews; even the interviewees saw the experience as extremely relevant for themselves and for others. (b) The group enjoyed sophisticated leadership. Not only were the sessions conducted with sensitivity to group and individual dynamics, but group leaders showed that they had acquired useful information the previous summer, which was deployed at critical junctures. Both leaders (especially the main leader) had perfected pattern-analytical and interview techniques before the project was born; both had become familiar with concepts that provided a framework for discussion; both had undergone an extended group experience that helped them deal with victories and defeats to which they were exposed. (c) The group contained key members who were stimulating and self-stimulating and who were able to originate ideas for the group and work them out in detail. It is obvious that Kent would be a figure of power in any group setting. Somewhat less obviously, other group members (particularly Jones) and even some of the guests made key theoretical contributions.

The role of staff members in the group was admittedly not that of completely nondirective observers. Typically, staff made two types of contributions: (a) They added to the analysis following interviews by building on concepts advanced by group members and (b) they produced observations about group process, especially in the session summaries. Staff members also participated in interviews, especially at first. In this connection, one important element was the obviously unqualified trust between the staff and first-generation officers. This trust spread rapidly to the group, so that staff were accepted as credentialed fellow members.

Concluding Note

We started this chapter by observing that the group had implicitly challenged the prevailing assumption that police must be tightly managed to control potential misbehavior. The peer review concept, which the group originated, implied that officers can help monitor and control each other's behavior.

This assumption of peer review in general defies a widely verbalized objection to the exercise of responsible discretion by rank-and-file officers, which is that officers tend to be either unqualified or untrustworthy.

In our project, police misbehavior was the problem the officers were asked to address. In the course of addressing this problem, the officers discovered that police conduct can be broken down into patterns that can be analyzed, studied, understood, and remedied through interventions. This discovery is indistinguishable from the process that must be invoked by officers in problem-oriented policing to deal with issues of crime and public disorder, which are far less sensitive, delicate, obdurate, and controversial than those effectively addressed by the group.

Note

1. *Peer review* means that workers control the quality of their own (or each other's) work. More broadly defined, the concept implies that workers can take over supervisory functions—such as monitoring and evaluating performance—by having peer groups review the work of their members. The process of peer reviews is a key ingredient of team management (French & Bell, 1999).

8

Documenting the Solution

I n chapter 7 we traced the evolution of the peer review panel idea. We summarized rehearsals of the procedure that helped the panel take shape. We discovered that even suspicious interviewees could become cooperative. We discovered also that the panel could be seen by supervisors as an adjunct to effective management; that novice panelists could become skilled interviewers; that the paper record could yield hypotheses that could channel questioning, without impeding discovery; that after half a dozen interviews, common denominators emerged that could expedite interview analysis; and that patrol officers could act as social scientists in evaluating data and as clinicians in reviewing clues to personality dynamics.

However, we also discovered that single interviews could be more productive of insight than of changed conduct. Some of our early interviewees did in fact end up showing improvement after their experience with the panel. But in these cases, the panel was one of several concurrent experiences; we can, at best, hope that it played a contributing role. With other interviewees, the prognosis following their one interview was guarded, particularly when the interviewee continued to defend his modus operandi conceding that he might have erred in the past. Such experiences led to the suggestion that the original procedure would have to undergo modifications to strengthen its impact.

In its original form, the review panel consisted of the following stages:

1. The necessity for the panel is documented. Typically, the process would be initiated when an officer reaches a threshold number of incidents on an up-to-date inventory of violent involvements. The number used would not be the number of raw incidents but a refined index in which the active role of the individual in question had been established. It would exclude situations in which unwilling participation had been secured. It would include instances in which another officer had filed an arrest report despite the individual's active role in bringing violence about.

   Other ways of mobilizing the review panel would include requests by supervisors or by the individuals themselves. In such cases, however, the record would have to bear out the man's eligibility by showing a substantial number of recent involvements.

2. A preparatory investigation for the interview is conducted. Data relating to the interviewee's performance on the street are obtained from available secondary sources. This includes interviews with supervisors, reports by peers, and all information on record. The investigation culminates in a "study group" where panelists formulate hypotheses and draft questions that streamline the panel session.

3. Then comes the interview itself, which can be subdivided into three stages:

   a. Key incidents are chronologically explored, including not only actions taken by all individuals involved in the incident but also their perceptions, assumptions, feelings, and motives.

   b. The summation of these data in the form of common denominators and patterns is undertaken primarily by the interviewee, with participation by the panelists. An effort is made to test the plausibility and relevance of the hypothesized patterns by extrapolating them into other involvements.

c. The discussion of the pattern occurs last and includes tracing its contribution to violence. This stage features the exploration of alternative approaches that might be conducive to more constructive solutions.

As experience with panels accumulated with additional rehearsals, so did reputed success stories. Some of these sounded convincing, but they obviously fell short of proving that the panel could modify behavior. What was needed was information about individual officer performance pre- and postpanel participation, and comparable data for non-panel-participants. Fortunately, an evaluation could be conducted easily because we left in our wake an entity that was in a position not only to operate and coordinate review panels but to collect performance data and to analyze them with our assistance.[1]

An addendum to the department's organizational chart had been introduced in 1970. An *Information Bulletin* described the new addition to the departmental roster (later renamed the Conflict Management Unit) as follows:

The Violence Prevention Unit

Mission
The Violence Prevention Unit has as its major goal the reduction of violence during police–citizen contacts. Specifically, the unit will identify violence-producing situations and aid personnel found in these situations, undertake detailed analyses of circumstances and individuals, design and implement preventive and remedial approaches for violence reduction, and evaluate the success or failure of such approaches.

Organization
The Violence Prevention Unit is directly responsible to the chief of police. The unit is organizationally assigned to the office of the chief of police.

The unit consists of three sections. These are the action review section, the training research section, and the experimental projects section.

The action review section will analyze in a nonpunitive manner the activities of individuals who seem to be having difficulties during interpersonal contacts. Its activities will include the identification of such individuals, the review of their handling of interpersonal contacts, the convening of action review panels, the discussion of cases, and the recommendation of remedial actions.

The training research section will engage in a variety of developmental activities. It will plan, execute, and evaluate training programs dealing with violence reduction for clientele both inside and outside the department. Of particular importance will be the section's involvement in exploring new training approaches and applying them in the program of violence reduction.

The experimental projects section will design, execute, and evaluate new organizational approaches to the problem of violence. Operational activities in areas where there is a high potential for violence will receive considerable attention.

The analysis we present below is an effort at evaluation of the peer review panel prepared by the new unit, in which we provided technical support for the officers in the unit, who had collected the data they needed to perform the evaluation.

The Incidence of Conflicts

California has three charges referring to citizen–officer conflict: resisting arrest, a misdemeanor offense; battery or assault on a peace officer, a felony offense; and assault with a deadly weapon on a peace officer, also a felony offense. In the discussion that follows, these are referred to as *charged incidents.*

Formal charges do not, of course, cover all instances of physical confrontations between citizens and officers. Many of these, in fact the majority, do not lead to a formal charge against the citizen; they become "invisible." In a special study undertaken by the unit, all arrest reports were reviewed and coded for the presence or absence of physical confrontations.[2] In the discussion that follows, these are referred to as *not-charged incidents.*

Figure 8.1 shows the incidence of each of the three charges for the years 1970 through 1973 and of the not-charged incidents for 1971 through 1973. The total charged incidents show a decline from year to year over the four-year period; this holds for the not-charged incidents (over a three-year period) as well. It will be seen that the drop in charged incidents is a result of the decrease in misdemeanor charges (resisting arrest) rather than in the two more serious felony assault charges. The latter, it might be argued, result from situations that offer less room for officer discretion in whether or not to make a formal charge. However, because the not-charged incidents decreased as well, it cannot be argued that the drop in resisting-arrest charges represents a shift from the charged to the not-charged category. Nor can it be argued that the recording of actual incidents became more lax. The chief, concerned with reducing the number of citizen complaints, had made it clear that any behavior of which a citizen might reasonably complain must be documented, whether with a formal charge or not, in the arrest report. The climate he set makes it reasonable to suppose that most, if not all, confrontations appeared in the department's records.

Injuries to Officers and Citizens

Many physical confrontations between citizens and officers may be more show than substance, but they sometimes result in real injuries—to officers, to suspects, or to both. Table 8.1 reports data on injuries to each group over each of the four kinds of incidents displayed in Figure 8.1.

As would be expected, injuries resulted from the misdemeanor offenses far less often than from the two felony offenses, and injuries resulted from the not-charged incidents less often than from the charged offenses. Unlike the year-to-year decrease in number of incidents, the proportion of these in which injuries occurred to one or both participants showed no such clear-cut trend. The number of injuries to officers rose somewhat from 1970 to 1972; the number of injuries to suspects, at least in the misdemeanor and not-charged incidents, showed a slight

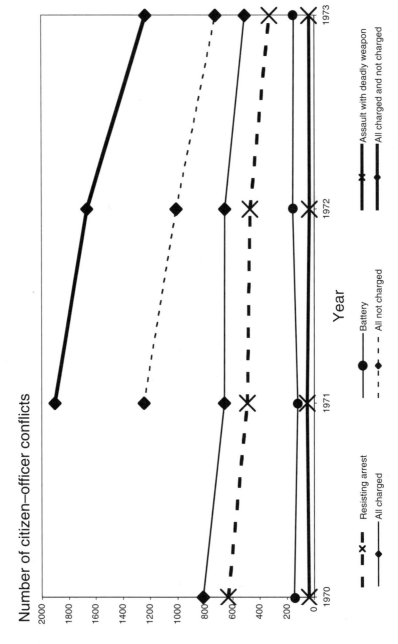

Figure 8.1. Incidence of three charges for 1970–1973 and the not-charged incidents for 1971–1973.

TABLE 8.1

Injuries to Citizens and Officers in Citizen–Officer Conflicts

Type of incident	1970		1971		1972		1973[a]	
	Citizen	Officer	Citizen	Officer	Citizen	Officer	Citizen	Officer
Resisting arrest								
Total	23	48	24	32	26	33	8	12
Percentage	3.7	7.6	4.9	6.5	5.5	7.0	3.2	4.7
Battery								
Total	38	37	44	28	50	39	13	11
Percentage	26.2	25.5	37.3	23.7	32.5	25.3	11.2	9.5
Assault with deadly weapon								
Total	9	8	10	11	9	6	1	4
Percentage	23.7	21.1	19.6	21.6	27.3	18.2	3.7	14.8
All charged								
Total	70	93	78	71	85	78	22	27
Percentage	8.6	11.4	11.9	10.8	13.0	11.9	5.5	6.8
All not charged								
Total	NA	NA	12[b]	54[b]	21	44	0	9
Percentage	NA	NA	1.0	4.3	2.1	4.4	0.0	2.0
All charged and not charged								
Total	NA	NA	90	125	106	122	22	36
Percentage	NA	NA	4.7	6.6	6.4	7.3	2.6	4.2

[a] Injury data were not collected after the first three quarters of 1973. The number and percentage of injuries are for the first nine months.
[b] The 1971 figures are extrapolations based on the data available for the last four months of that year.

decrease. Both dropped sharply in 1973; we have no explanation for this sudden change.

In reviewing resisting-arrest injuries, we find that, although it is the citizen who is being charged and arrested, the alleged aggressors' injuries exceeded (consistently) those of the officer-complainants. The same point holds—although not as surprisingly—for uncharged violence.

Complaints Against the Police

Under Chief Gain's administration, the department encouraged the filing of complaints by citizens. Complaints were accepted in any form, including those made anonymously, by a central complaint office. Case records were kept on all complaints; feedback was given routinely to the officers who were the subject of complaints and, on request, to the citizens who made them.

Table 8.2 shows the complaint data for each year from 1970 to 1973. The total number of complaints made by citizens can be taken as a gross measure of citizen dissatisfaction with police. The number of complaints sustained (i.e., the number in which the department formally found a valid basis for the complaint) can be taken as a measure of inappropriate officer behavior. The percentage sustained may be considered a minimum measure of the legitimacy of the complaints made.

TABLE 8.2

Formal Citizen Complaints Against Officers

Complaints	1970	1971	1972	1973
Number sustained	96	77	44	23
Percentage sustained	14.9	21.6	17.5	11.2
Total number of complaints	645	357	251	206

Note. χ^2 test (number sustained versus number not sustained over four years); $p < 0.01$.

It will be seen that total complaints dropped dramatically from 1970 to 1971 and continued a downward trend after that time; the total in 1973 is one third that of 1970. Despite encouragement to make complaints, this expression of citizen dissatisfaction sharply decreased. The number of complaints that were found to have validity also decreased from year to year (differences are significant at the .01 level); the total sustained in 1973 is one quarter that of 1970. The percentage sustained rose from 1970 to 1971, a result of the fact that total complaints made dropped far more sharply than did the number sustained. The first may indicate the chief's success in working with the community; the second, his success in working with his officers. The latter came more slowly. After 1971, however, the percentage of complaints sustained decreased.

The Initiation of Interaction

A police officer may become involved with a citizen when dispatched on a call through the radio room or the officer may initiate the interaction ("on view"). In the former situation the officer's interaction is not a matter of choice. On-view incidents, on the other hand, are always "precipitated" by the officer in the sense of making a physical overture or contact. Table 8.3 shows the number of officer involvements in incidents in each type of citizen–officer conflict by the way in which the conflict was initiated.

The picture presented by Table 8.3 is striking and dramatic. In all categories, we see a strong, consistent decrease in the proportion of violence resulting from on-view incidents. In fact, we conclude that the time trends we have noted are disproportionately a function of on-view trends.

We also see that resisting-arrest incidents occurred more often with officer-initiated (on-view) activity than did felony-assault incidents; and of the latter two, assault on the officer occurred more often in officer-initiated actions than did assault on an officer with a deadly weapon. But for each of the three types of charge the ratio of officer-initiated to dispatched activities decreased from year to year over the four-year period. The same

TABLE 8.3

Initiation of Citizen–Officer Conflicts

Type of incident	1970 No.	1970 %	1971 No.	1971 %	1972 No.	1972 %	1973[a] No.	1973[a] %
Resisting arrest								
On-view[b]	474	50.1	383	42.6	352	41.5	147	27.2
Dispatched	415	43.9	458	50.9	449	52.9	392	72.6
Other[c]	57	6.0	58	6.5	47	5.5	1	0.2
Total[d]	946		899		848		540	
Battery								
On-view	116	46.2	90	38.3	144	38.4	53	20.5
Dispatched	113	45.0	121	51.5	205	54.7	206	79.5
Other	22	8.8	24	10.2	26	6.9	0	0.0
Total	251		235		375		259	
Assault with a deadly weapon								
On-view	21	35.6	33	34.7	26	28.6	17	22.1
Dispatched	31	52.5	53	55.8	59	64.8	58	75.3
Other	7	11.9	9	9.5	6	6.6	2	2.6
Total	59		95		91		77	
All charged								
On-view	611	48.6	506	41.2	522	39.7	217	24.8
Dispatched	559	44.5	632	51.4	713	54.3	656	74.9
Other	86	6.8	91	7.4	79	6.0	3	0.3
Total	1,256		1,229		1,314		876	
All not charged								
On-view	NA		846[e]	46.4[e]	784	38.8	425	35.2
Dispatched			906	49.7	1,174	58.0	781	64.6
Other			72	3.9	65	3.2	3	0.2
Total			1,824		2,023		1,209	

continued

TABLE 8.3   *(Continued)*
Initiation of Citizen–Officer Conflicts

	1970		1971		1972		1973[a]	
Type of incident	No.	%	No.	%	No.	%	No.	%
All charged and not charged								
On-view	NA		1,352	44.3	1,306	39.1	642	30.8
Dispatched			1,538	50.4	1,887	56.5	1,437	68.9
Other			163	5.3	144	4.3	6	0.3
Total			3,053		3,337		2,085	

Note. χ^2 test (on-view versus dispatch over four years):
Resisting arrest $p < 0.005$.
Battery: $p < 0.005$.
Assault with deadly weapon: NS.
All charged: $p < 0.005$.
All not charged: $p < 0.005$.
All charged and not charged: $p < 0.005$.
[a]Data on initiation of conflict were not collected after the first three quarters of 1973. Thus the number and percentage of incidents are for the first nine months.
[b]"On-view" refers to an officer-initiated interaction.
[c]"Other" refers to occasional situations in which the interaction is neither initiated by the officer in question nor results from a specific dispatch from the radio room: For example, two officers may be dispatched on a call from the radio room and a third makes a decision to join them on the call.
[d]Comparison with Table 8.1 will show larger "total" figures. Figures presented are for total number of officer involvements in incidents. Figures for Table 8.1 are for total number of incidents (which may have involved more than one officer).
[e]The 1971 figures are extrapolations based on the data available for the last four months of that year.

is true for the not-charged incidents.[3] Thus, it seems plausible to argue that the decrease in citizen–officer incidents reflected a decrease in field contacts or an improvement in field-interrogation conduct. In the resisting-arrest category the number as well as the percentage resulting from officer-initiated activity decreased; the number resulting from dispatched actions actually showed a slight increase.[4]

The Type of Arrest

To what extent is the amount of citizen–officer conflict simply an expression of how active officers are? In the extreme case, if officers snooze or drive aimlessly about, they will clearly have no difficulties with citizens. The more work they do, the more risk they take of physical involvement with citizens. Thus, the decrease in conflicts over this four-year period could simply reflect a decrease in the number of arrests made.

Table 8.4 both confirms and disconfirms this argument. This table presents the percentage change in the number of arrests made for each year from 1970 to 1973. Offenses are divided for this purpose into the reporting categories used for the FBI Uniform Crime Reports. Part I offenses include the major felonies (criminal homicide, rape, robbery, aggravated assault, burglary, larceny, and auto theft). Part II offenses include victimless crimes (e.g., drunkenness, vagrancy, disorderly conduct, and drug, gambling, and prostitution offenses), some white-collar crimes (forgery, fraud, and embezzlement), and a variety of others (e.g., arson, simple assault, family or child neglect or abuse, vandalism, carrying illegal weapons, receiving stolen property, curfew violations, and runaways).

The table shows that total arrests were down considerably— 25%—over the four-year period from 1970 to 1973, but this decrease was almost solely a result of a decrease in the part II offenses. Productivity in the sense of major crime fighting showed relatively little change over the four years. There was a marked decrease in arrests for the less severe criminal offenses, with drunkenness constituting 30 to 40% of these over this time period. The concomitant decrease in citizen–officer conflict seems

TABLE 8.4

Arrests by Type of Offense: Percentage of Change From Preceding Year

Type of offense	1970	1971	1972	1973	1970–1973
Part I					
Number	8,718	9,401	8,974	8,469	
Percentage change	+12.8	+7.8	−4.5	−5.6	−2.9
Part II					
Number	31,500	25,233	21,588	21,699	
Percentage change	+0.2	−19.9	−14.4	+0.5	−31.1
Total Part I and II					
Number	40,218	34,634	30,562	30,168	
Percentage change	+2.7	−13.9	−11.8	−1.3	−25.0

thus to be related to a change in police behavior toward troublesome but not seriously criminal citizen activity. Such change is, of course, precisely the thrust of antilegalistic police reform.

The arrest figures we have cited must be evaluated in two contexts. The first is change within the department: the advent of new activities—an increase in nonarrest productivity (including such service innovations as family crisis intervention and landlord–tenant intervention); the desire for nonenforcement reactions to street situations formerly resulting in arrests (e.g., drunken behavior, disturbance calls); and, to a lesser extent, the deployment of personnel into activities such as violence reduction, training, and other work concerned with reorienting the department.

The second context is the crime picture. As we note in Table 8.5, Oakland experienced a slight but consistent decrease in reported crime from 1970 on, resulting for the most part from a drop in larceny-theft and auto-theft offenses. An exception is aggravated assault, which spiraled steadily upward, doubling in number from 1970 to 1974. Thus, the decrease we find in police–citizen confrontations occurs against a backdrop of increased citizen–

TABLE 8.5

Crimes Known to Police in Oakland, California

Year	Total crime index (using 1973 FBI formula)	Type of crime								
		Nonnegligent manslaughter	Negligent manslaughter	Forcible rape	Robbery	Aggravated assault	Burglary, breaking and entering	Larceny theft	Auto theft
1970	42,872	69	37	212	2,497	1,088	13,787	20,166	4,993
1971	42,699	89	26	220	2,932	1,224	14,311	18,528	5,395
1972	41,836	78	25	261	2,907	1,646	13,080	18,445	5,419
1973	41,595	100	11	220	2,879	1,853	14,734	17,063	4,746
1974	40,507	78	3	246	2,883	2,175	14,144	16,702	4,279

Note. Federal Bureau of Investigation, Uniform Crime Reports, 1971–1975 (1976). In the public domain.

citizen conflict. This suggests an improvement in police response to assaultive citizens rather than a change in citizen assaults.

Individual Productivity and Violence

What of the individual officers? Is the amount of their arrest activity related to the frequency with which they have trouble with citizens? Does their involvement in incidents increase with their productivity or with certain kinds of productivity?

Some law-enforcement personnel contend that citizen–officer conflict is most likely to occur in situations of serious criminal activity—that is, in association with felony arrests. Observational studies have reported, however, that many uses of force (and some uses of excessive force) take place during misdemeanor arrests, in field contacts, and in police activity that evokes resentment from suspects and bystanders (Geller & Toch, 1996).

To shed light on this issue in Oakland, a special study was undertaken to allow accumulation of arrest and conflict data for individual officers. The year selected was 1971. A count was made of the number of felony and misdemeanor arrests for each of 489 officers and of the number of citizen–officer conflicts associated with each type. Officers were then classified as high or low in productivity for each type of arrest and for total arrests.

Table 8.6 presents the average number of citizen–officer conflicts during the year for officers classified as high and low in terms of various measures of productivity: number of felony arrests, number of misdemeanor arrests, number of total arrests, and ratio of number of felony arrests to number of misdemeanor arrests.[5]

It is clear from Table 8.6 that officers with more citizen (arrest) contacts do have more conflict with citizens. This holds for felony, for misdemeanor, and for total arrests. The differences between the average number of conflicts for officers with high- and low-arrest productivity are significant beyond the .001 level for each type of arrest and for the two types combined. Thus, although the data in Table 8.5, which show a large drop in the number of arrests for less serious offenses over the period when citizen–officer conflicts were decreasing, tend to support the argument

TABLE 8.6

Citizen–Officer Conflicts by Officers With High and Low
Productivity: 1971

		Different productivity indexes		
Level of productivity (median split)	Felony arrests	Misdemeanor arrests	Total arrests: felony and misdemeanor	Felony– misdemeanor ratio
High				
Number of officers	275	244	270	235
Average number of conflicts	3.2	3.3	3.1	2.8
Low				
Number of officers	21	245	219	254
Average number of conflicts	1.3	1.4	1.4	1.8
Total number of officers	489	489	489	489

Note. T-test (high versus low production). Felony arrests: $p < 0.001$. Misdemeanor arrests: $p < 0.001$. Total arrests: $p < 0.001$. Felony–misdemeanor: $p < 0.001$.

that conflict is more likely to occur in connection with misdemeanor than with felony arrests, the data in Table 8.6 support the reverse position. One explanation for the discrepancy may be exposure: Those officers assigned to areas with a high amount of criminal activity and thus more arrestable behavior had more opportunity for conflict with citizens.

The felony–misdemeanor argument raises the question of the quality of arrest as distinct from arrest productivity. If the law-enforcement function of the police is seen as one of attending to greater as opposed to lesser crimes, then an officer whose arrests are primarily for felony as opposed to misdemeanor offenses might be considered more effective than one whose arrests are primarily for the latter.[6] Conflict may be more common among the less effective officers when effectiveness is defined in terms of the quality of arrests that they make.

As a crude measure of the quality of arrest, we calculated the ratio of felony to misdemeanor arrests for each of the 489 officers during 1971. The officers were then divided into those with a felony–misdemeanor ratio equal to or less than 1.0 (i.e., those who had no more felony than misdemeanor arrests during the year) and those with a ratio larger than 1.0 (i.e., those who had more felony than misdemeanor arrests). According to our argument, the latter would be said to show more effective arrest quality and we would expect them to have fewer citizen–officer conflicts. They did not. The last column of Table 8.6 shows that the high felony–misdemeanor ratio group had an average of 2.8 citizen–officer confrontations during the year compared to 1.8 for the less effective (low felony–misdemeanor ratio) group. This difference is significant beyond the .001 level. Thus, citizen–officer conflicts were not associated with poorer rather than better quality of arrests (defined crudely by the felony–misdemeanor ratio). The data support the opposite position.

Let us look at the data again, however, across columns. Officers who made relatively few felony arrests tended to have relatively few conflicts with citizens. But officers whose number of felony arrests was low in relation to the number of misdemeanor arrests they made had substantially more conflicts. Officers who were high in felony–arrest productivity had a high number of citizen–officer conflicts; those whose number of felony arrests was high in relation to the number of misdemeanor arrests had somewhat fewer conflicts. This suggests that not all the variance in frequency of conflict is accounted for by a simple measure of arrest frequency and that quality of arrest behavior contributes something to the variance in number of conflict incidents.

The Peer Review Panel

Data we have cited earlier tend to support the position that administrative policy change can make a difference in officer behavior. We turn now to consider the impact of the peer review panel.

TABLE 8.7

Total Citizen–Officer Conflicts: Before and After Panel Participation
(Participants Versus Nonparticipants)

Review panel	Before (Jan.–May 1970)	After (June 1970–July 1972)		Difference (expected vs. observed)
		Expected[a]	Observed	
Participants (n = 72)				
Average incidents/ officer	2.39	12.48	7.90	4.58
Average/month/ officer	0.48	0.48	0.30	0.18
Nonparticipants (n = 434)				
Average incidents/ officer	0.64	3.38	2.44	0.94
Average/month/ officer	0.13	0.13	0.09	0.04

[a]Expected figures were obtained by multiplying the average number of incidents per month by the number of months, June 1970 to July 1972.

The panel, after it had been institutionalized, reviewed departmental arrest reports and maintained full records on every officer on street assignment. When any officer's level of "incidents" became statistically unacceptable, the officer was scheduled for a review session. The review session involved a rotating group of officers, with most being former panel interviewees. Sessions were repeated if high incident levels persisted.

We find that there is evidence that panel experience had a positive effect on an officer's street behavior. Table 8.7 compares panel participants with nonparticipants in the frequency of citizen–officer conflicts for the five months before instituting the review panel and the 26 months following. Only officers who were on street duty for the entire 31 months were used in the comparison June 1970 to July 1972 period.

Using the five months before the panel as a base, the average number of incidents expected for the next 26 months was determined. The actual number that occurred was less than the number expected for both the participants and the nonparticipants. The decrease was much greater, however, for the participating officers, their expected–observed discrepancy being 4.5 times that of the nonparticipating officers. A covariance analysis shows that a difference of this magnitude has less than a .001 probability of occurring by chance. The conflict-prone officers who had designed the panel had developed an intervention that significantly reduced the incidence of police–citizen conflict.

Although the review panel began in June 1970, participation in the panel was spread over the months following. The figures reported for the participants for the "after" period in Table 8.7 include varying numbers of months before participation. More precise measures were obtained by taking each participant's average number of incidents for the actual months before and following participation in the panel. This analysis is reported in Table 8.8. The average monthly incidents for the participants dropped from .37 to .16 following participation. Monthly averages for the nonparticipants (using randomly assigned comparable time periods) dropped from .10 to .08. A covariance analysis shows that the differences among these averages have less than a .01 probability of occurring by chance. Time is controlled for the nonparticipants by proportional random assignments, to correspond to the monthly proportions of participants.

What Could We Conclude?

In chapters 6 and 7 we described how we worked with groups of officers as costudents of a problem that had meaning both for them and for us and how we assisted their planning of interventions to cope with this problem. One concern for the police department had been the high number of physical confrontations between officers and citizens, leading to tensions with the community, and the concentration of those incidents among relatively few officers.

TABLE 8.8

Average Monthly Citizen–Officer Conflicts Before and After Panel Participation: Participants Versus Nonparticipants

Review panel	Before	After
Participants (n = 88)		
Average	0.37	0.16
Variance	0.13	0.02
Nonparticipants (n = 434)		
Average	0.10	0.08
Variance	0.03	0.02

Note. In contrast to the figures in Table 8.7, time before and after participation varied for each participant. Actual months on the street before and after participation were used to determine monthly averages. This allowed the inclusion of 16 additional officer–participants who could not be included in the analysis reported in Table 8.7 because they were not on the street for the full before and after periods.

One of our assignments was to help the officers assess the result of any interventions they originated. In assessing the panel intervention, we followed one kind of officer behavior, participation in physical conflict with citizens, over a period when the department was undergoing rapid policy and administrative change.[7] We have shown that police–citizen conflict can decrease sharply with a deemphasis of legalism and that citizen resentment (as expressed in complaints to the police) can also decrease. We have found that this decrease is associated with changes in kind of arresting behavior, with less emphasis placed on the less serious offenses and on-view stops. We found these changes occurring against a background of an increase in total assaultive crimes by citizens.

We found a link between productivity and police–citizen conflict. This link is neither surprising nor disheartening. It confirms that productivity, even if refined, entails paying a price in violence. It tells us that a police force of any orientation must precariously balance its values. It must decide how much to prize arrests and how much to "trade" for them. Not all trade-offs are inevitable, and moderation in arresting—as elsewhere—pays decent dividends.

We found some evidence that frequency of conflict may be associated with arrest quality. This last is an issue that needs to be explored more fully. We need arrest-productivity indexes (such as conviction rates) and ratings of nonarrest productivity. We need to know more about different types of officers and about different patterns of productivity. We need to know how these patterns change when change is imposed from without and when it comes from within.

Finally, we did find that officer behavior can be changed by an intervention designed and implemented by other officers. Although incidents were decreasing in the department as a whole, officers who participated in the peer review panel showed a larger decrease in incidents than officers who did not. The panel might not have been implemented without the background of change in the department, but its relative success is a testament to the importance of involving the officers themselves in change efforts.

But Was It Replicable?

The 1960s and 1970s saw surprising experimentation in police departments with organizational reforms (chap. 2, this volume). The Oakland project differed only in degree rather than kind from activities in progressive departments elsewhere. In Kansas City, for example, the Northeast Patrol Division organized a number of task forces to study problems faced by the department and to make recommendations. One of the task forces was called Conflict Management: Analysis/Resolution, and it studied the relationship among violent incidents such as disturbances, domestic conflicts, aggravated assaults, and homicides (Northeast Patrol Division, 1974). The task force (three patrol officers and a middle manager) issued a scholarly report, prefaced with the self-effacing caveat that "the paper was written from the viewpoint of police officers within the framework of a police organization.

The project members have not tried to . . . deceive themselves into thinking they are social scientists" (p. ii).

A second Northeast Patrol task force went into the peer review business. It

> was created in late 1971 with a mandate to study current innovations in the police patrol function. During the course of their review of existing programs, the task force members became interested in the Action Review Panel Program of the Oakland, California, Police Department. The task force decided that the program was applicable to problems in Kansas City. In April, a second [of two] visit[s] was made to Oakland to gather extensive data regarding the operation of the panels. A formal proposal for a Peer Review Panel Program was subsequently submitted to and approved by the [Kansas City] command staff. The Peer Review Panel Program drew heavily on the design of the Oakland program, with the exception that the Kansas City program focused on citizen complaints as well as resisting arrest charges, as indicators of negative police–citizen encounters. The first Peer Review Panel was held on August 4, 1972. (McCullough, Bowers, & Ferrara, 1976, p. 6)

Despite input by members of the Oakland Unit, the Kansas City panel differed in emphasis from its West Coast counterpart. Most significantly, the process had become directive, hortatory, and confrontational. The program was not a success. Although officers claimed that panel members had been inducing "insights," evidence of behavior change was not forthcoming. Moreover, the members of the panel accumulated increasingly high rates of complaints and resistance arrests, raising questions about their credentials as change agents and role models (Pate et al., 1976, p. 57). Most fundamentally, the evaluators noted that "the application of ['participation' models] requires that the targets of change become actively involved in the change process. The [Kansas City] Peer Review Program . . . was an incomplete model because it did not involve the subject officers as change agents" (p. 57). Finally, it had become clear that if the intervention were to be again replicated, evaluators would need to know about what could have transpired during panel sessions.

And Was It Problem-Oriented Policing?

Peer review panels do not sound like a problem-oriented intervention that deals with what Goldstein (1979) defined as police problems. For Goldstein, police problems are troublesome events in the community to be addressed *in* the community. The panels by contrast were an intervention operating inside the police department. Panels did not intersect with citizens, nor did they involve citizens as panelists. But what defined a "problem" for the panels were arrests that occurred in incidents taking place in the community. Such arrests do not make a different pattern from one of criminal or disruptive acts that become police business.

Of course, the panels were not the beginning of our story. We started with a concern about incidents involving conflicts between police and suspects. These incidents created tensions in the community and adverse publicity and complaints. Some of the incidents inspired lawsuits and others cost officers their jobs. This was indisputably a problem for the community. It was also a problem for the police.

The police–citizen violence problem could have—and sometimes has—been defined as an offender-related problem, as one of patterns in the behavior of violence-prone civilians (Toch, 1969). There are suspects who in fact replay the same attacks against officers time after time. And one can think of interventions that anticipate the level of risk posed by such suspects or that attempt to reform recidivistic assaulters. One can try to stage peer review panels—or something like them—for offenders.

Our officers had a mandate to study violent incidents and to ascertain their patterns and causes. The officers might have loved to blame most of the violence in these incidents on resistant citizens. But in the end they did not do so. Honesty prevented the officers from taking this route, because the data pointed elsewhere. In this respect the officers proceeded as we had hoped they would proceed. Our studies, and those of the police department, had highlighted individual officer contributions to the incident variance. The groups rediscovered this contribution in their deliberations.

We had especially selected violence-involved officers for our project, hoping that they would combine their experience with science to evolve expertise. Such expertise, we felt, could then be transmitted to others, as through training. Problem-solving skills could similarly be applied to future problems. It was our view that an intervention like review panels could make a strong case for problem-oriented reforms. If police officers can accept the import of self-critical data, their capacity to intervene after dispassionately studying problems is established. There are few institutions in our society that can match the commitment shown by the police department and by our officers to the problem-oriented process. The officer's uninhibited exploration of intervention options in the project yielded departures from familiar responses. In problem-oriented thinking, this is not a liability but a prized virtue.

Notes

1. Most of the data we review in this chapter were collected under NIMH grant MH 20757 ("Research on Violence Prevention by Police") from the Center for Studies of Crime and Delinquency. We are indebted for this support.
2. Elements of resistance, battery, or assault with a deadly weapon were present in the arrest report but not charged by the arresting officer.
3. Differences between the proportion of on-view and dispatched incidents over time are significant at the .005 level for all but "assault with a deadly weapon."
4. As noted in Table 8.4, 1973 figures are based on nine months only. Extrapolating to the full year would give 96 on-view and 523 dispatched incidents in the resisting-arrest category.
5. The data were compiled originally for a study of officers who participated, or were eligible to participate, in the peer review panel during its first year of operation. These constituted 171 of the total. The remaining 318 formed the criterion group for determining high and low productivity—high in each case being all numbers above the median for this group, low being all numbers at or below the median.
6. It is recognized that this does not take into account the nature of an officer's assignment—its location and time of day—which may have an influence on the primary type of arrest the officer makes.
7. Police departments do not commonly keep the kinds of records that allow systematic study of change efforts nor the tracking of individual officer behavior. The Conflict Management Unit (the rebaptized Violence Prevention Unit) had to set up an information system that allowed study of the citizen–officer conflict problem over time. The data presented in this chapter derive from this system.

9

A Decentralized
Problem-Oriented Activity

Three decades after the experiences described in the preceding chapters, a group of us at the University of Albany became involved in a problem-oriented venture that covered a number of geographic locations in New York state.[1] Our partner in this project was the first state police department willing to experiment with problem-oriented policing. The experience provided us with a unique opportunity for comparing different approaches to permutations of the same problem. The subject of inquiry was that of traffic accidents. As it happens, many people believe that traffic control is the only concern of a state police agency. Although this impression is erroneous, a prized goal of the organization with which we worked was "to reduce traffic accidents and minimize fatalities and injuries by . . . compiling data on accident causation for internal analysis" (New York State Police, 1989, p. 2).

Data analysis may inform statewide approaches to a problem such as traffic accidents, but variations in strategies are needed where traffic patterns vary, and different types of drivers become involved in different types of accidents. In some counties in New York, for example, commuter traffic represented a challenge; in others, problems had to be dealt with that resulted from seasonal variations in traffic associated with tourism or the influx of weekenders or summer residents. Factors that are overrepresented in serious accidents—young age, substance abuse, substandard road conditions, and so forth—can substantially vary in prevalence from county to county in a large state. Such factors can also play larger or smaller roles in accidents, depending on how they intersect with each other and with other factors.

Local strategies can accommodate local variations in the prevalence and type of accidents, to the extent that relevant patterns can be uncovered and causal hypotheses can be generated to explain them. This task is tailor-made for problem-oriented policing because it can profit from the focusing of professional experience on the interpretation of patterns of incidents revealed by statistical analyses. One table can tell police officers that personal injury accidents have peaked on Friday evenings; cross-tabulations can identify types of drivers (disproportionately young male, for example) and driving habits (a tendency to speed, as noted in police reports of accidents). But officers who have responded to some of the accidents at issue are also ideally situated to generate sensible and plausible hypotheses related to patterned dynamics (such as that the drivers involved in a set of incidents are probably mostly young recreants who come from late-night places of amusement). Such hypotheses invite verification, which again can be entrusted to the responding officers. And if pattern-related hypotheses are ultimately verified (through close reading of report narratives or a minisurvey conducted for the purpose), the same officers would be in a position to propose responses to the problem they have diagnosed and verified.

To arrive at a strategy of local problem solving in a statewide agency one moves from larger patterns to smaller ones and from regional variations to local differences. The process is reminiscent of Russian dolls that encase increasingly smaller dolls, with minidolls at their center. But as with the wooden dolls, the process must start at the macro level—police headquarters.

The New York State Police is run as a traditional, paramilitary organization, but it is a notoriously progressive organization. This means that although customarily decisions are made and actions taken moving from the top to the bottom of the hierarchy, there are numerous exceptions to this rule. This subject was mentioned at a middle-management meeting related to our project, convoked to select one of several groups of participants. According to the minutes of the meeting:

> during the course of this discussion it was agreed that there were several issues involving State Police supervision which might impact on the [problem-oriented] initiative. . . . The normal progression of events in the State Police (as in other police agencies) would include the "mission" being identified by supervisors and then regular law enforcement methods being executed by the Troopers to solve a problem. It was apparent that an integral part of this program would be to give the assigned Troopers a free hand to develop the program from the bottom up as opposed to the usual "top down" protocol. To that end it was decided that once the initial organizational meetings had been held, the commissioned officer interaction with the group would be limited in an effort to allow the Troopers to exercise autonomy in their analysis and decision making processes. It was anticipated that as interventions were developed by the group, that some requests would of necessity be made to other state agencies, like the Department of Transportation (DOT). Captain S. decided that any contacts with outside agencies would be done by sergeants assigned to this detail, and they were instructed accordingly.

It is interesting to note that the planning group pointed out in the same minutes that the delineated bottom-up approach did not violate established principles:

> It should be noted that, while this specific project did represent a departure from the regular course of business for the State Police, its predicate concepts were not completely foreign to our Members. This is attributable to the fact that, unlike most city and town agencies, we expect our Members to take appropriate action without the presence or guidance of a supervisor. The State Police has traditionally prided itself on this point, and as a result it was believed that our Members could take the initiative in this project with a minimum of supervisory prompting.

The statement emphasizes the distinction between a hierarchical organization that operates with a presumption of compliance with authority, to the point of squelching initiative and innovation, and an organization that self-consciously values both conformity to rules and the judicious exercise of individual initiative. As a testimonial to the latter emphasis in the State Police, the group highlighted its selection criterion as, "Simply put, we looked for 'self-starters' who had demonstrated the ability to work through the analysis, design and intervention phases of this project." The roster of the members who were chosen described each of them as having deserved commendations or advancement for recorded demonstrations of self-engendered achievement.

Dispensing With Preliminaries

The project opened with a ceremonial convocation in which the first prospective participants were introduced to the philosophy of problem-oriented policing. This inauguration took place in an auditorium attached to the police headquarters complex. After the session, a group of returning participants reported the following:

> Speakers included Professor HERMAN GOLDSTEIN of the University of Wisconsin, who is widely credited with establishing the idea of Problem Oriented Policing, and Lieutenant MO MOWRY of the Newport News, Virginia Police Department who has successfully implemented Problem Oriented Policing strategies in his city. In essence, the basic precepts of this approach included an emphasis on the outcomes of police intervention in a given problem area. Moreover, it was further explained that it was acceptable for involved Police Officers to employ non-traditional strategies in both the conceptualization and implementation of intervention strategies to solve problems.

On the same day as the plenary session, we organized two groups of officers into seminars to review accident statistics for their counties. Members of one of the groups described their session as follows in a memorandum they filed after the meeting:

> Items discussed included types of accidents, number of vehicles involved in accidents, initial contact, manner of collisions, location, roadway characteristics, weather related factors, time period, and age of driver involved in accidents. The statistics for [our county], for a three-year period, indicated that the majority of accidents involved personal injury, involved only one vehicle and involved a collision with a fixed object. The majority of accidents occurred at non-intersections, on dry surfaces with a split between straight and curved roadways. The time period of accidents, age of operators, and gender of accident victims was also discussed.

The group hypothesized, based on their preliminary review, that many of the single-vehicle accidents in their county might be the result of hazardous topography. They also suggested that "a significant number of one car accidents on non-interstate highways involved contact with an animal." This was an observation that we were able to corroborate for two critical high-accident highways. The group subsequently followed up by delegating one of its members to contact representatives of two state agencies with expertise in deer–car accidents to obtain their advice. This inquiry produced the following information:

> Lt. L. [of the Department of Environmental Conservation] indicated that there was no way to target specific areas or roads concerning these accidents. Deer change their patterns frequently and there is no way to predetermine which trails or paths they will follow. He indicated that his department had also determined that the car whistles affixed to bumpers of vehicles have no effect on the deer entering the roadway. . . . He indicated that the only method to reduce car/deer accidents is to reduce their [presumably, deer] population. . . . Mr. M. [of DOT] advised that his department has done two studies with special reflector devices on the side of roadways to prevent deer from entering the path of vehicles. Both studies showed no improvement in lessening car/deer accidents. . . . He feels that there is no positive way

to stop car/deer accidents besides reducing the deer population. The patterns they exhibit while crossing various roads
changes continuously.

Because deer genocide did not qualify as a problem-oriented-
policing project, this line of inquiry was eventually abandoned.
Other contacts with state agencies, however, were effected in a
different connection.

On a regular basis, the officers met with our research group
to review information "on possible sites to target for the problem-
oriented policing project." We, in turn, obtained data from Department of Motor Vehicles computers, increasingly centering
on two stretches of road the members of the group selected,
based on their conclusion that "these two areas both contain a
significant number of accidents and high traffic volume." Thereafter, the group's minutes tell us that "the data collected on these
two areas were further broken down into specific targeted areas
including target days, target times, and specific roadway segments." The officers then initiated their own preliminary surveys
of driver misbehavior, recording that "collection sheets were
distributed to members to be completed on speed related
violations."

In relation to one of the locations, the group members
pinpointed a pattern that they felt they could themselves address and a set of physical conditions they felt would benefit
from remedial interventions under the auspices of other agencies.
With respect to this multiproblem location, they reported the
following:

> Investigation into this area indicated that speed was the most
> contributing factor to motor vehicle accidents. Specific days
> and times were targeted from the material obtained from
> Hans Toch's research group. Radar details were held and
> documented. Information obtained from local Troopers and
> POP [the group] members indicate that the geometry of the
> existing roadway did not appear to be adequate and the slope
> of the roadway angled in the opposite direction from what
> would be appropriate for the turn. This situation would defi-
> nitely be a contributing factor in weather-related accidents.

The officers called the alignment problem to the attention of the Department of Motor Vehicles, which delegated a group of its engineers to make a study of its own. Based on this assessment, a roadway reconstruction plan was drafted and submitted for financial approval. The estimated cost of the project was $5.124 million.

Lukewarm Collaboration

The group's second interagency overture was not commensurately successful. The roadway segment of concern to the members of the group was a stretch featuring shopping centers and other business establishments and associated levels of traffic, resulting in a high rate of accidents. The group felt that given these conditions, a reduced 45 miles per hour speed limit would be an appropriate response. A proposal to this effect was submitted to the state DOT, buttressed with records of radar studies that had been conducted by the group. A subsequent confirmatory radar study by the DOT's engineers led to a counterproposal for a compromise resolution (a possible 50 miles per hour speed limit), which was, however, temporarily placed on hold. The DOT in its unenthusiastic reply gratuitously observed that "a 45 mph limit would place 82% [of drivers at the time of measurement] in violation, an undesirable situation." Even more gratuitously, the DOT wrote the following:

> Apparently, this section of highway surfaced as a high accident location under the "Problem Oriented Policing" program. We are not sure exactly what criteria is [sic] used in the NYSPD accident evaluation program, but it appears that a "high accident" location may only be a section of a particular road where the number of accidents is greater than on another portion of the same road. Every road will have sections where more accidents occur due to varying factors such as intersections, roadside development, traffic volumes, etc. This does not necessarily indicate that the rate is high compared to similar sections of other roads.

The DOT staff indicated that it had an "ongoing study" covering a portion of the target area. "Please advise," the DOT spokesperson inquired, "if a delay to obtain more data is not objectionable." The delay at issue could by implication be appreciable, because studies by the New York DOT routinely require three-year observation periods.

Liaison activities by the POP group, however, were not confined to contacts with agencies such as the DOT. Each group member had been assigned individual responsibility for obtaining information and advice from key informants in specific local communities. Their instructions read as follows:

> In addition to the computer data, the above mentioned troopers will make contact with all Troopers in their stations, Town Highway Superintendents and their crews, Police Departments (including Village Police and Board of Water Supply Police), wrecker services and whoever else can provide input as to:
>
> (1) where the majority of motor vehicle accidents are occurring within their respective towns;
> (2) who was operating the vehicle at the time of the accident;
> (3) why these accidents occurred; and
> (4) how they perceive we can proactively reduce the number and severity of these accidents in their respective jurisdictions. . . .
>
> Obtain their suggestion as to what we can do to solve a particular problem in their area. Their input is important and required for this project.

A Penchant for Quantitative Analysis

The second of the groups was inaugurated concurrently with the first. Starting with their first meeting, the members of this group demonstrated a warm and sustained interest in quantitative methods and statistics. With preliminaries out of the way, they began the session examining our graphs and tables, which detailed accident data in the county for the years 1980 through 1993. According to minutes of the meeting:

During the ensuing discussion, the group raised a number of issues relative to the veracity of the data along with several requests for site-specific data. In addition, the group requested that some of the site-specific data be "sorted" by demographic indicators, like age breakdowns on accident victims as well as a breakdown on accidents which occurred during peak commuting hours. Among the issues raised by the group about the available data were . . . problems with unknown, unavailable or missing data [and] reliability and uniformity of data among the reporting agencies.

In preparation for the next meeting, stacks of tables of accident-related data were generated for seven intersections and other locations specified by the group, and these tables were carefully scrutinized by the group and inspired a great deal of discussion and animated speculation. The group members then manifested their voracious and insatiable appetite for additional information, and further circumscribed their locations of concern. As noted in the minutes for the meeting,

It was determined that additional data would be needed for some of the locations. . . . Further refinement of the suggested locations was made by the group utilizing additional data supplied by the SUNY Albany staff. It should be noted that there was much discussion among the group about weather related factors and the agencies which could impact upon these problems, principally, the State Department of Transportation.

In the two meetings that followed, the discussion increasingly turned to matters requiring liaison with the DOT. This agency among other duties is responsible for road maintenance and for providing services to state highways under all weather conditions, including the inclement conditions that proved of increasing concern to the officers. In drawing inferences about causal patterns, the officers had found that they were gravitating to scenarios in which the weather played a contributing role. Consequently, proposals for remediation appeared to the officers to call for changes in service response patterns during the winter months, including those of DOT crews. The following was a scenario in point:

> LOCATION: State Route 6 (Long Mountain Highway) from Woodbury Traffic interchange to the traffic circle at the intersection with Palisades Parkway.
>
> PROBLEM: This section of roadway becomes particularly hazardous during times of freezing weather when a cover of moisture is present. The roadway ices up quickly and accidents frequently occur, causing personal and property damage as well as tying up the flow of traffic. The area is served concurrently by salt/sand trucks from the Newburgh and Palisades DOT locations, resulting in long response time when road sand/salt is needed.
>
> SOLUTION: There is a DOT location on State Route 218 which is much closer to the involved area. Response from this location would solve the current problem, ensuring that the roadway can be cleared quicker.

In the case of a number of problem locations, rapid response became an issue, and "the group felt that all Members could notify the Department of Transportation of problems, particularly with regard to snow removal, in an effort to get them to act more proactively to reduce problems." For one stretch of road, the group recommended changes in snow removal routes.

Because group members were obsessed with the need for continuing data collection, they suggested that "each station maintain a log to track the number of calls to the State, County or Town Department of Transportation and the response," and "a log of civilian calls regarding poor road conditions." Other proposals called for the installation of warning signs and flashing lights at specific locations, with provision for follow-up study.

In communicating with agencies to be involved in these efforts, the group members did not encounter bureaucratic resistances, nor did they receive snide or sarcastic rejoinders. Two circumstances may account for this fact. One was that members of the group conducted all their liaison with local agency (DOT) representatives, who enjoyed a measure of autonomy. The other reason was that a key member of the group (its technical sergeant) had functioned for 26 years as the station's supervisor of traffic services. In that capacity (according to his biography), the sergeant "worked extensively with other government agencies, including all of the area residencies of the State Department of Transportation." Not coincidentally, the speed limit signs that had been recommended by the group were almost immediately installed in the specified locations. Concurrently, the group engaged in a two-month speed enforcement drive in one section of highway, which according to the data they had analyzed yielded the highest incidence of speed-related accidents.

The activities of both groups of problem-oriented officers illustrate the power of the confluence of professional experience and social–scientific expertise, focused on the solution of problems. The further we move from statistics at the aggregate level (the outer Russian doll) to those relating to local conditions (the sequestered mini-doll), the more critical it becomes to mobilize first-hand experience to inform inferences and hypotheses. At the macro level, personal experience can mislead as a source of inference because it is potentially unrepresentative. In interpreting local conditions, however, statistics alone can obfuscate the key variables that may be uniquely at play. No table could illuminate the conditions at the Long Mountain Highway Interchange "during times of freezing weather, when a cover of moisture is present." Once accident-rate tabulations have pinpointed an intersection as a problem location that we must attend to, the "problem" becomes a clinical, as opposed to an actuarial, one. At this juncture, it is the officer who has responded to accidents at the location who has the missing data with which to consider issues of dynamics and causation.

The attribute that particularly distinguished the officers in our project was the evenhanded enthusiasm with which they resonated to challenges posed by statistical compilations and local patterns of variables. They pounced on tables and graphs, in search of differences that might matter. They strained to make sense of trends and highlights in the data. Simultaneously, they zeroed in on the particulars of recurrent accidents to sort out the relative contributions of driver, road, and circumstance and their fateful combinations. Finally, they struggled with the question of what one might accomplish by way of solutions that required the assistance of occasionally inflexible bureaucracies. Even in this realm they persevered, and frequently prevailed.

Note

1. Professor Robert Worden participated as codirector in the project activities described in this chapter.

10

Top-Down Problem Solving: The Compstat Paradigm

Problem-oriented policing is one of several contemporary police reform movements. In chapter 11 we discuss one of these movements, community policing, which inspired a merger of sorts, producing an almost inextricable (community-oriented, problem-oriented) composite. As noted in the foreword, however, no such linkage is in the offing with a third reform—the so-called Compstat model, which also stresses problem solving. One reason for the presumption of incompatibility is that both problem-oriented policing and community policing are grassroots organizational reforms, whereas the Compstat approach is centered on middle management and places emphasis on data-based surveillance and control.

In chapter 4 we have described the classic version of this prescription as originating with the work of Frederick Taylor, who was an industrial engineer by profession. Taylor was an advocate of efficiency, and he felt that efficiency could be attained by planning work in detail and motivating workers through rewards and threats of punishment, including the loss of employment. Taylor demonstrated that one could keep track of the performance of tasks through time and motion studies, using quantitative data to define the "one best way" of performing each task. The advent of computers has given rise to a massive resurgence of data-as-control systems in industrial engineering, replacing primitive time and motion studies with information gathered through computers embedded in the work process itself.

Taylorism was a feature of the progressive police reform movement (chap. 2, this volume), inspiring surveys designed to enhance the command-and-control capabilities of police chiefs and to streamline their departments. The movement was suffused with an obsessive concern with locating less-than-assiduously producing officers. Compstat shares this productivity concern but prizes the decentralization of command and responsibility.

In a recent *New York Times* article (Dewan, 2004), Compstat was characterized as "the gospel of policing by data," and was described as follows:

> The system maps crime according to precise location and time, providing daily statistics that allow for strategic planning. At the meetings commanders are grilled by their bosses, in front of their peers, about crime trends in their precincts and what is being done about them. Behind them computer maps are projected on screens, blemished by crime locations. (p. B6)

The Compstat model was born in 1994 in the New York City Police Department and has been credited with reductions in crime rates attributable to increased efficiency by the department. The appellation *Compstat* (sometimes spelled "Comstat") derives from the name of a comparative statistics computer program. Compstat presupposes a planning process based on review of statistical patterns. The physical nerve center of Compstat is a "war room" to which middle managers (precinct commanders) are summoned and where they are interrogated about updated statistics displayed on the large computer screens. The interrogatories are generally focused on recent increases in the prevalence of specific crimes in the neighborhoods under the purview of the managers. According to an observer,

> the tense and theatrical NYPD Compstat meetings are the stuff of legend. All the top cops pack into a "war room," around a large rectangular table. Colorful computer-generated maps flash up on a screen, showing recent crime trends and statistics. A precinct commander takes the hot

seat, and questions start flying: "Why are robberies up in this neighborhood? What are you doing about it?" The verbal barrage is relentless, peppered with the occasional fist-pounding on the table. (Swope, 1999, p. 40)[1]

The tone of the questioning has been defined as a core element of the model. According to protagonists, "humiliation and the prospect of demotion make the sense of accountability more urgent. It locks commanders into alignment with the overall goal of reducing crime" (Swope, 1999, p. 42). Despite this feature, Compstat is seen as a way of empowering middle managers. The managers are presumed to become inspired by the assertive questioning to try to address problems under their jurisdictions. This process is alluded to as problem solving, but the standard Compstat format is far from collegial or inclusive. Dewan (2004) thus pointed out that "what New York calls accountability, the rest of America may be inclined to call public humiliation." She reported, however, that "several chiefs said they had toned down the confrontational aspect, shifting the emphasis to sharing information" (p. B6).

A common denominator in Compstat-type systems, moreover, is that they shift the focus of problem deliberations away from problems that may be of concern to neighborhood residents and frontline officers. As noted by Swope,

> police departments are not having an easy time making Compstat fit in with another philosophy currently in vogue: community policing. One of the ideas behind community policing is to empower the street-level cop to come up with solutions to a neighborhood's crime problems. When Compstat is focused on hard numbers, however, it shifts that authority away from the street cop and onto the precinct commanders in the Compstat war room. (1999, p. 43)

The implementation of Compstat coincided with the abandonment by New York City of its community policing involvements (which are described in chap. 11, this volume). A new commissioner and mayor "abandoned the previous administration's attempt to give more decision-making discretion to the rank-and-file officer (in the context of community policing and

"attempted to concentrate more power [among precinct com-
manders] to shape departmental practices. An example of his
individual-level intervention was his willingness to replace and
terminate middle managers unable or unwilling to make this
transition (about half of them in a year)" (Weisburd, Mastrofsky,
McNally, & Greenspan, 2001, p. 14).[2]

This descriptive statement was made in connection with a
survey of American police departments, which showed a widespread claim among the larger departments to having adopted
or internalized the Compstat model, sometimes before its official
"invention" in New York City. One incentive in this connection
may have been Compstat's model of organizational reform. According to the authors of the survey, the Compstat system

> did not demand that American police agencies fundamen-
> tally change the traditional hierarchical organizational struc-
> ture of American policing. Compstat does not demand a
> revolution in the organizational structure of American polic-
> ing but rather seeks to harness that structure in an attempt
> to have traditional American police organization [sic] work
> better and more effectively. Compstat thus offers American
> police agencies the prospect of improving how they work,
> while reinforcing the traditional hierarchical structure of the
> military model of policing—a structure that has been under
> attack by scholars for much of the last two decades. . . . This
> supervisory system is strongly hierarchical and essentially
> negative, relying primarily on sanctions for noncompliance.
> (pp. 58–59)

The fact that "the supervisory system" can be deemed not
only "strongly hierarchical" but "essentially negative" bears on
modifications of the model elsewhere. A southern police delega-
tion, for example, returning from a New York City orientation
visit, observed that "they're awfully rude to each other up there"
and concluded that "nobody will play along if they think they're
being abused" (Swope, 1999, p. 40). The administration of New
York City's public school system declined to adopt Compstat,
as the mayor had urged, and adjudged it inappropriate for professionals. According to the *New York Times,*

to City Hall's dismay, the quarterly sessions that [the Chancellor] has asked superintendents to attend starting this fall will little resemble the now-famous Compstat (short for computer statistics) meetings. Instead of an intense grilling in front of their peers, with public upbraidings for those who cannot explain negative trends in their districts, the superintendents will have more business-like conversations. . . .

"The mayor's office thinks the Police Department model is appropriate for every agency, but we don't accept that," Mr. Shorris said. "That is a paramilitary approach, not the approach of a professional services environment."

He added, "The notion is to give the superintendents a lot of performance data, ask them to come in on a regular basis to talk about issues we see, have them take detailed notes and make sure they follow up." (Goodnough, 2001, p. B1)

Data Review and Problem Solving

The power-coercive elements of Compstat can be differentiated from the types of data considered, the process whereby the data are analyzed, the manner in which action implications are derived, and the way interventions are implemented. The New York schools thus shared with the Compstat model a premium on the use of computerized maps that can permit the juxtaposed display of different variables. The report noted that

> a senior policy adviser . . . has just finished mapping different kinds of data geographically to make it easier for superintendents to glean trends. For example, they can now look at a map showing the percentage of different immigrant groups in every school in their district, and compare it to a map showing the percentage of students at those schools failing the fourth-grade reading test. (p. B4)

The data mentioned in the example may be displayed in Compstat-style fashion, but they are different in kind from inventories of felonious incidents implying negligent supervision. A given "percentage of students failing the fourth-grade reading test" may be deemed unconscionably high, but "the percentage of immigrant groups" defines the problem as a contextual one, which does not impugn the effectiveness of middle managers (school principals) or teachers. There is no corollary (as with Compstat) that managers had better intensify some equivalent of targeted enforcement.[3] The statistic about immigrant groups is mind-expanding. It draws attention to a set of parameters—cultural diversity and language deficits—that may call for new thinking and new programs.

The school principals had been invited to study data, draw inferences (should the data permit), and recommend courses for action. No one was on a "hot seat" or being held "accountable." Compstat sessions are sometimes defined as brainstorming, but the outcome of the process is scripted, and what is expected of the managers is the resolve to crack down on some group of malefactors.

In this sequence, subsequent developments reliably follow: The manager is strongly motivated to summon his or her underlings and to demand higher (targeted) productivity. His or her underlings are similarly apt to summon *their* underlings and to replicate the process. The sequence culminates with pressure on street-level officers who may become embittered and take out their frustrations on citizens.

The picture is at odds with the paradigm of a problem-solving organization. What is achieved tends not to be mindful behavior by subordinates who have internalized a set of goals and learned to work with others to achieve them. Instead, officers under Compstat are pressed to act (to intensify enforcement), subservient to a rationale they are not expected to share. For this they may be bribed with overtime pay, and their commander earns liberation from the hot seat after local offenders have relocated.

Another way in which the arrangement differs from that of a problem-solving organization, according to Mark Moore (2003), is that the Compstat system is "a strict liability system" in which goals are scripted and "the only question is whether someone is personally motivated enough to get the job done" (p. 486). No one is encouraged to ask whether what may be needed are new and not-yet-invented alternatives. Moore alludes to the writings of the psychologist Chris Argyris, who defined the true learning organization as one that engages in "double loop learning," meaning that it "learns to reconsider some of the basic assumptions about its purposes and means in what might be a profoundly altered external environment" (Moore, 2003, p. 487). Such a reconsideration in policing could include asking "whether the best way to deal with crime is through threatening and actually arresting those who commit crimes, rather than trying to find other more preventive modes of intervening in the large and small circumstances that tend to create offenders or the situations that produce offenders" (Moore, 2003, p. 487). Moore reminded us that officers involved in community policing generally operated under the assumption that "community problems were not necessarily limited to crime problems." Community policing had centered on problems that were locally relevant. Such problems generally "came in sizes that were smaller than those that could be seen in precinct statistics." Community problems of this kind are "at risk in a Compstat system that limits a focus to precinct-size crime problems, and depends on precinct-level initiatives to deal with these" (Moore, 2003, pp. 487–488).

Such arguments tend to carry little weight with most Compstat advocates, who contend that community policing had little impact on crime. Compstat by contrast is credited with a substantial reduction in violent crime rates over close to a decade. The point, of course, begs the question of whether crime reduction ought to be the only criterion of relevance. But should we grant this assumption, the evidence has been blunted by Eck and Maguire (2000), who point out that in New York City downward trends in crimes such as homicide had their inception well before the advent of Compstat at a time of active community policing involvements.

The Ineluctable Magic of Technology

Two advertised attractions of Compstat are its emphasis on the instant availability of updated data and its use of dramatic methods for displaying variegated crime-related information. Compstat is packaged as combining the virtues of science, technology, and sophisticated communication, which are widely presumed attributes of professionalism. Advances in data presentation or format become landmarks along which the development of Compstat was gauged:

> As computer capabilities improved at headquarters and at precincts, pin maps were replaced by overlay maps created by crime-mapping computer software. The new maps showing crime activity in the city were displayed on large video screens. The computer-made maps included narcotics complaints; time, day of week, and location of crime events; and information regarding police deployment and arrest activity. Later Compstat recorded and mapped the times and places of precinct shootings and their relationship to drug-dealing sites. A power software tool, MapInfo 94, became the NYPD's crime radar screen, with attention-grabbing colors and shapes. Red dots indicated drug complaints from the public, blue dots showed drug arrests, green triangles represented shooting incidents, and yellow dots indicated homicides. When projected on the war room's large overhead screen and on small individual screens, the overlays of colors superimposed on street locations were impressive. (Silverman, 1999, p. 109)

Correlations presumably can be ascertained when diversely colored dots converge—"demonstrating," for example, that minor-misdemeanor dots converging with violent-crime dots call for arrests of vagrants or assertive mendicants. More conventional Tayloristic inferences about police productivity deficits can also be drawn:

> Late in 1994, the Compstat Office analyzed the on-line booking system to determine how many officers had not effected an arrest during the year. The results were shocking: 28 percent of Queens cops, for example, had not produced an arrest in the first half of the year. This information was conveyed to Queen precinct patrol leaders at a headquarters Compstat meeting. . . . The story was leaked to the press and appeared on page one of the *Daily News*. Since then, arrest pie charts have regularly been generated as another stimulus to police activity and a gauge of crime strategy effectiveness. (Silverman, 1999, p. 105)

A Compstat summons is issued when data analysis suggests to Compstat staff a possible decrement in someone's productivity. (A decrement is customarily inferred from a spike in criminal activity.) The summons is always bad news in that it implies a documented accusation. The trial-like atmosphere is then undergirded by the presence of witnesses or fellow defendants who have been summoned to the session:

> This "subject to be called" approach keeps precincts on their toes and constantly reinforces the primary importance of crime reduction. If a precinct's shootings continue to climb, for example, its leaders can be recalled the following week. One entire borough's crime rate rose so quickly in early 1998 that the borough was present at two consecutive meetings— a first in Compstat's history. At the same time, all headquarters and field units connected with borough and precinct activities must be present at Compstat meetings, further emphasizing shared responsibilities. (Silverman, 1999, p. 118)

Observers who are invited to Compstat sessions are apt to be distracted from inquisitorial nuances in the proceedings by the scintillating technology involved in the Compstat system. They are apt to be further impressed by the precision with which crime problems are seemingly targeted, making the link between Compstat and crime reduction apparently inevitable.

There are, however, less obvious consequences arising out of the obsession with goals of crime reduction. No-holds-barred chasing after flavor-of-the-day offense targets overloads the criminal justice system with overvalued trivia. Obsessive crime fighting also results in the wholesale harassment of citizens and alienates segments of the community. Another liability of Compstat's emphasis is that problem-solving capabilities of the system may be negated by the narrowing of its purview. Possibilities for data analysis are foreclosed by the use of crime incident data to secure compliance with enforcement goals.

According to Silverman (1999), "Compstat's ability to control from the top ... has emerged as its dominant motif" (1999, p. 213). This top-down managerial model is hard to reconcile with contemporary thinking about work motivation (chap. 4, this volume), and especially at variance with presuppositions of Total Quality Management (TQM). The popularity of TQM derived partly from disillusionment with productivity-centered engineering approaches. TQM is heavily data-centered but concerned with having workers examine the process whereby productivity is achieved. It assumes that reliance on outcome measures (as in Compstat) detracts from a concern with quality. In practice, according to TQM, outcome data create fear by means of a "numbers game." To hound officers to make more arrests, for example, may not only lead to low-quality arrests but can also depress morale. With an emphasis on numerical productivity, quality of performance in an organization declines, and so does motivation.

W. Edward Deming, the progenitor of TQM, frequently argued that workers who are pressed for increased productivity are forced to cut corners and fudge numbers. Compstat administrators are aware of this danger and "aggressively audit precinct statistics on a regular basis" (Rashbaum, 2003, p. B3). The need for these audits is illustrated by the fact that "since the system was put in place in 1994, at least five police commanders have been accused of reclassifying crimes to improve their statistics" (Rashbaum, 2003, p. B3). According to the president of New York City's police union, "We've reached a point where some local NYPD commanders are forced to falsify stats in order to maintain the appearance of a continued reduction in crime" (Union Leaders, 2004, p. B3). In England, a police chief who had "made a routine of grilling commanders about their success rates and police work . . . discovered that one precinct was doing too fabulous a job—a few cops . . . were getting unwitting suspects to sign papers admitting to hundreds of crimes they had not committed" (Alvarez, 2003). New Orleans had adopted a Compstat supervisory model, and officers there recently "improperly downgraded complaints so they would not show up in quarterly crime figures" (Louisiana, 2003).

In TQM organizations, workers are invited to think about what they do quantitatively and are trained to study their own work. This grassroots use of statistics is antithetical to the Tayloristic (and Compstat) managerial approaches. To be sure, the core premise in all data-based reform approaches is that work can be improved. But the Compstat approach diminishes rank-and-file involvement in problem solving and substitutes a stultifying do-as-we-say-because-we-have-studied-the-data regime.

Notes

1. Updated information suggests that the physical configuration of the room has changed to one of tables aligned in seminar fashion and that fist-pounding is no longer a routine feature of the proceedings.
2. A sophisticated advocate (J. McCabe, personal communication, 2003) has contended that "if you are not prepared, or not addressing problems as they arise, you are in for a difficult morning. [But] being 'at the podium' as it is more accurately described) gives you an opportunity to get promoted, get recognized, and get rewarded for your efforts."
3. J. McCabe (personal communication, 2003) confirmed the contrast between the two approaches. He observed that

> never would the NYPD make excuses for high crime rates in a community because of its "immigrant" status. The NYPD believes that high crime areas need extra attention, and are not areas that deserve excuses because certain groups live there. Offering that excuse at Compstat would most likely get you labeled as a racist or bigot. . . . People are people and the drive is to reduce victimization, period.

11

Community Policing and Problem-Oriented Policing

T he brave new world as it is envisaged by leaders in the police field may be a world of problem-oriented policing or a world of community-oriented policing, but it is usually defined as a combination of the two. In the words of the National Research Council, "As a predominant means of doing police work, community police organizations typically try to shift away from traditional reactive patrol and investigative activities designed to threaten and arrest offenders toward the embrace of the kind of problem-solving methods of policing that are advocated by the concept of problem-oriented policing" (2003, p. 90). The National Research Council in its report stresses the following:

> There is significant overlap between [problem-oriented policing] and community policing, particularly when one is examining the ways in which these ideas challenge the prevailing means of policing. Both make a virtue of proactive as opposed to reactive responses to crime, disorder, and other community problems. Both community and problem-oriented policing focus on preventing as well as reacting to crime. Both call for solutions tailored to the particular problems and circumstances at hand rather than rely on more generalized techniques of patrol and investigation. Both community and problem-oriented policing view deterring and incapacitating offenders as only one of many different kinds of intervention that might be mounted by the police. Both community and

269

problem-oriented policing contemplate the police organizing interventions that depend on cooperation with agencies and other actors beyond the boundaries of the police organization. (2003, pp. 90–91)

Skogan et al. pointed out, for example, that "a problem-solving model forms the heart of Chicago's community policing initiative . . . officers are expected to move beyond responding in traditional fashion to individual calls and instead adopt a proactive, prevention-oriented stance toward a range of neighborhood problems" (Skogan, Steiner, Dubois, Guddell, & Fagan, 2002, p. 4). Community police pioneers Trojanowicz and Bucqueroux (1990a) wrote that "in essence, solving problems is an important aspect of Community Policing, and a department that encourages its officers to use Problem-Oriented techniques can make greater use of their potential as part of a Community Policing approach" (p. 10). Trojanowicz and Bucqueroux defined the goal of community policing as a strategy "to solve the problems of crime, fear of crime, physical and social disorder, and neighborhood decay" (1990a, p. 3). They specified in this connection that the community police officer (CPO) must be a person of tremendous ingenuity because "by expanding police work . . . Community Policing gives police officers an expanded agenda that allows fuller expression of their full range of talents" (p. 323). For CPOs, the "job challenges the individuals to see how much they can accomplish, because the boundaries of what can be achieved have yet to be fully defined" (p. 328).

The distinctive feature of community policing is that the CPO must involve local citizens as partners in his or her exercises of creative inquiry. The linkage "demands continuous, sustained contact with the law abiding people in the community so that together they can explore creative new solutions to local concerns involving crime, fear of crime, disorder, and decay, with private citizens serving as unpaid volunteers" (Trojanowicz & Bucqueroux, 1990a, p. xiii). Skogan et al. (2002) referred to this as the "turf orientation." They pointed out that maintaining turf orientation brought new challenges to the departments and individual officers:

☐ Officers were supposed to stay in one place long enough to develop partnerships with and trust among community residents.

☐ The community focus meant that officers need to spend more time working with the community and less time answering radio dispatches.

☐ To give careful attention to residents and to neighborhood-specific problems, officers were required to know their beats—including hot spots, crime trends, and community resources. (p. 5)

Early on, community policing was equated with foot patrol. The concept had nostalgic connotations, evoking images of ruddy beat cops (usually with brogues) giving homespun and salubrious advice.[1] The term also evoked a view of lighted windows of hospitable police storefronts in deteriorated neighborhoods.

In looking for common themes among wildly divergent definitions of community policing, Wycoff (1988) concluded the following:

> Philosophically, the programs tend to have in common the belief that police and citizens should experience a larger number of nonthreatening, supportive interactions that should include efforts by police to
>
> 1. Listen to citizens, including those who are neither victims nor perpetrators of crimes;
> 2. Take seriously citizens' definitions of their problems, even when the problems they define might differ from ones the police would identify for them;
> 3. Solve the problems that have been identified.
> 4. Some programs go even further to incorporate the idea that police and citizens should work together to solve problems. (p. 105)

Skolnick and Bayley (1986) alluded to the same process as "police–citizen reciprocity." Reciprocity "means that police must genuinely feel, and genuinely communicate a feeling, that the public they are serving has something to contribute to the enterprise of policing" (p. 212).

Mastrofski (1988), among others, has alleged that this requisite has been rarely met in practice. He wrote,

> Anyone who has observed a variety of community crime prevention programs readily ascertains that the bulk of the communication is from the police to the citizen, explaining and selling prepackaged strategies devised without the particular neighborhood and its residents' preferences in mind. (p. 52)

An excellent contemporary illustration is provided by the experience accumulated in Chicago's Alternative Police Strategy (CAPS), which is an ambitious community policing venture. The city trained both officers and citizens in joint problem-solving strategies. These strategies were exercised in beat meetings conducted throughout the city in church basements and public buildings during off hours. Advisory committees were also attached to police districts to guide precinct commanders in making policy decisions. Skogan et al. (2002) summarized the experience by noting the following:

> Beat meetings were good for disseminating information and promoting a sense of community involvement, but often did not provide an effective venue for creative problem solving by residents or police. . . . Although residents always brought up problems, many meetings did not discuss solutions; when they did, solutions were proposed most often by police. (p. 8)

Not only did officers preempt the citizens in considering courses of action, but the results of meetings tended to be generic resolves or promises to intensify traditional patrol activities. According to Skogan and Hartnett (1997), about half the conclusions reached at beat meetings fell under roughly two headings:

- ☐ Let's talk: The most common suggested solutions entailed improvements in how residents and police communicate with one another; this category made up one-quarter of all proposed solutions.
- ☐ We're working on it: The second most common solution (21%) was an announcement by police or agency repre-

sentatives that they were working on a problem. This served to end the discussion, and there was almost never any other feedback on their efforts. (p. 125)

The district advisory committees (DACS) in Chicago also managed to deviate from their prescription. The citizens appointed to the DACS often voiced parochial or private concerns, and police used the opportunity to deliver academic lectures featuring crime statistics. Skogan et al. (2002) reported,

> In most districts, the police set the agenda for DAC meetings, controlled all information about police operations, supervised the efforts of active subcommittees, and approved—if not actually initiated—significant DAC activities. Rather than being able to press the community's interests, their anomalous position is clear: As appointed creatures of the police department, DACs . . . receive more advice than they give. (p. 12)

It is of course possible that the denizens of some neighborhoods may be disinterested in crime and disorder problems and indifferent to what the police may do. Elsewhere, citizens may actively distrust the police. Such hostility is arguably worse than apathy, but at least it can motivate citizens to take an interest in trying to influence policing. Berkeley, California, residents, for example, have at times been vociferously hostile to police, but they have involved themselves in the smallest details of police work. By contrast, in observing eight neighborhood-oriented police projects, Randolph Grinc found that the officers were often disgusted with citizens who they felt were disinterested or apathetic. He reported the following:

> It became apparent that many police officers had become increasingly hostile toward community residents who, because of apathy or lack of interest in "bettering their own lives," refused to get involved in community policing efforts. . . . Police officers, many of who were extremely enthusiastic at the beginning of the INOP projects, often found themselves demoralized because of the lack of community enthusiasm and involvement. (Grinc, 1994, pp. 450–451)

Police cannot claim community input where there is neither community nor input. Weisburd and McElroy concluded that "perhaps scholars have romanticized the concept of community in their effort to develop a more community-oriented policing strategy" (1988, p. 100). The same charge about romanticized community conceptions has been lodged by other observers (such as Mastrofski, 1988). But one must keep in mind that if police insist on setting the agenda for joint activities, they cannot blame citizens for not buying into it.

Empowering Officers to Empower Citizens

The Chicago Police Department's community-policing mission statement was titled "Together We Can" (Rodriguez, 1993). In subservience to this theme, the document pointed out the following:

> At the same time it is working to empower the community, the Department must do more to empower its own employees. Officers at the beat level should have the opportunity and the power to identify and prioritize problems and to make decisions about how to solve them. Department supervisors should have the chance to be the mentors and motivators they were hired to be. The Department should develop organizational values that emphasize individual creativity, initiative, and ingenuity among Department members at all levels. Recognizing that these qualities do not just happen, the Department must nurture and reward them in its members. New approaches to training; new ways of measuring individual performance based on results, not activities; better and more regular career development opportunities; and improved and ongoing communications among Department management and employees are all critical to boosting productivity and morale. (p. 16)

Citizen-empowerment through officer-empowerment is called for if the goal is to achieve conjoint problem-solving, as in Chicago. But community policing is frequently imposed from above by enlightened chief executives, with limited concern for inducting officers as participants. And even where officer involvement is ostensibly a cherished objective, it can be neutralized through careless or insensitive implementation.

Sadd and Grinc (1996), the authors of the eight-city Innovative Neighborhood Oriented Policing (INOP) study, picked up on this problem. They reported considerable resentment of community police (COP) officers, who felt used and imposed on:

> Most of the officers interviewed felt that community policing was happening to them rather than with them and that there was no attempt to involve the rank and file in decision making. . . . While officers throughout the sites expressed distaste for specific aspects of community policing, they were almost unanimous in criticizing what they saw as heavy-handed implementation by management. Community policing emphasizes community empowerment and involving citizens in decision making. Rank-and-file patrol officers, however, generally argued that administrators had excluded them from decision making. (p. 11)

Such resentments can be exacerbated by the prevailing assumption among many officers that anything police executives do is liable to be politically motivated (Toch, 2002). As Sadd and Grinc (1996) pointed out, the inception of community policing especially invited the contention "that all new projects are driven by political pressures on police and city managers and are thus inherently of dubious value" (Sadd & Grinc, 1996, p. 77).

Being One's Own Police Chief

Skolnick and Bayley (1986) have written that "a reciprocal understanding of crime prevention will ordinarily be linked closely with a strategy of a real decentralization of command" (p. 214). A sense of what this means when carried to its logical conclusion can be gleaned from the neighborhood police teams we mentioned in chapter 2 in which the decentralization movement had its inception in the 1970s. The policy and procedures manual for a team in Holyoke, Massachusetts (Holyoke Police Department, 1970), for example, which was drafted by team members, provided that "questions concerning decision-making authority should normally be decided in favor of the most decentralized level consistent with the achievement of the objective of effective policing for the Team's jurisdiction." In case the import of this were not clear, the following sentence read, "in cases where provisions of this manual conflict with the general policies and procedures of the Holyoke Police Department, the provisions of this manual will be followed by Team members except in emergencies when the Team control is returned to the regular departmental chain of command."

The Holyoke team consisted of 15 members, including the director, who held the rank of captain. All 15 members had a vote in the Committee of the Whole, which was responsible for "Team organization and management matters." Specific topics were to be dealt with by standing and ad hoc committees of officers.

A Police–Community Relations Council, chaired by the team director, was made up of six neighborhood residents and two officers. The team director was officer in charge, but the manual said that "generally, the team's activities will be carried out as a group effort extensively employing the techniques of participating (sic) management." As an example, "in any instance where two-thirds of the Team members recommend dismissal of a Team member the Project Director shall respect their judgment and the officer shall be dropped from the team." The officers provided that they were not to be dispatched outside their turf (they had their own dispatcher) and the team's turf was to be off-limits to department members, except by request. The team headquarters was to be open "for community members' use and service," and the team was instructed to "concentrate on a philosophy of service and prevention rather than suppression of crime and disorder." The team proposed to evaluate its own performance and that of its members. It felt entitled to set its own goals, and team members were to "wear a variety of uniform and nonuniform clothing" to symbolize their autonomy.

Does decentralization require a high degree of autonomy? Probably not, but groups of individuals who work at a distance from headquarters tend to develop their own loyalties and *esprit de corps*. Moreover, those who work closely with a problem may resist instructions by central office executives who they feel are ignorant of local conditions. The executives, in turn, may fear that disengagement or distance can increase the incidence of police running amok (Kelling, 1988, p. 7).

Autonomy and Morale

We have noted that problem-oriented officers often show high morale and motivation; the same holds true of community-oriented officers who are accorded autonomy. Geographical decentralization is one reason community police program participants tend to feel liberated and demonstrate high levels of morale. The Flint, Michigan, foot patrol program, an exemplar early community policing venture, boasted about the fact that officers turned down promotions to remain on their job. A questionnaire administered to the officers showed that

> Many of the foot officers saw themselves as the "chief of police" of their beat areas. Their expertise ranged from helping residents install burglar alarms to conducting meetings in order to determine the priorities on which to focus crime fighting activities. Some foot officers emphasized activities and programs for the elderly, while other officers worked with juveniles or spent much of their time in public education forums. They viewed themselves as "professionals" writing articles for community newsletters, interacting with other community agency professionals, both in their uniforms and out, and making statements and presentations to the media. . . .
>
> The program promoted the development of a clear role identity among foot patrol officers legitimized by both the police department and the community. It also permitted a degree of autonomy in exercising the role. (Trojanowicz & Banas, 1985, pp. 11–12)

Goldstein (1987) painted a similar picture, speaking of community–policing programs across the country:

Most striking, for me, have been my observations of the impact that community policing has had on the police officers involved in these programs. The officers with whom I have walked and talked express immense satisfaction in getting to know citizens more intimately, in following up on their initial contact, and in seeing the results of their efforts. They like being helpful. They enjoy the freedom and independence they are given to be creative and imaginative, and to take the initiative in dealing with problems. And perhaps most important, they appreciate the trust that the programs place in them. (p. 28)

Freedom, of course, has a downside if it brings loss of support. Some community police officers have tried to retain the admiration of peers by playing the supercop (enforcement-oriented) role. But where service goals are salient, peer support may become irrevocably lost, and the "community connection" may have to make up for attenuation of the "police connection." Citizen esteem may have to partly substitute for departmental and peer support relinquished by involvement in service-oriented community-centered policing. Trojanowicz and Banas (1985) pointed out that the officers may become increasingly less dependent on peer approval and more sure of themselves:

The foot officers began to view the community as the reference point for job enrichment and satisfaction rather then depending on the police subculture. Their sometimes cynical motor colleagues became less and less important as a necessary support group. The foot officers could be innovative and did not need to worry about bearing the brunt of criticism or ridicule from either their supervisors or community residents. (p. 12)

Wycoff, who studied several community-oriented programs, wrote that officers can progress through a process that includes

☐ officer recognition (to their surprise) that most citizens welcome the opportunity to interact with police;
☐ a feeling that patrol work could be more interesting than they had realized;

□   a sense of pride in their work;

□   a growth in their sense of efficacy and personal compe-
    tence (an example of this being the officer who, over the
    course of the project, ceased referring to himself as a
    "plain ole, dumb ole cop" and began instead to think of
    himself as a leader in the neighborhood he served);

□   a recognition that there are many ways to approach polic-
    ing; and

□   an identification with the profession of policing, which
    extended beyond the officers' own organization, as they
    become aware of officers in other departments attempting
    to conduct similar programs. (p. 111)

The list of rewards can vary, but the principle is the same:
Autonomy permits officers to shape the work to maximize goals
they feel matter because of the results that are achieved.

But What of Quality Control?

Some police administrators find this picture enticing, but others
recall that freedom to do good is also freedom to do harm. As
for community input, they might ask, "Have you ever heard of
corruption? And what of local prejudice? Should cops arrest
neighborhood misfits, use shortcuts and clobber people? Protect
lawbreakers who are held in esteem? Community input is no
substitute for principled supervision." The administrators would
point out that the police are a unique profession. Officers have
the right to use force and can invoke or not invoke the law at
their pleasure. Police actions can therefore have tragic consequences. "If that team screws up," the experienced chief asks,
"Who do you think takes the heat?" It is also alleged that autonomy can be regressive: "The nostalgia bit is apt," the chief might
say, "It took 60 years to get professional police. Why turn the
clock back?"

We are reminded of the police reform movements at the
turn of the century. Taylor's concern (chap. 3, this volume)
was with getting lazy people to work. Police management
nowadays has a different worry, which has to do with honesty,
integrity, law-abidingness, evenhandedness, self-control, and

legality.[2] Chiefs will never relinquish their concern with enhancing the quantity of police product (incident accounting) but stand even less ready to abrogate supervision of quality (monitoring of misbehavior).

The Oakland project we have reviewed in detail is relevant and instructive in this regard, because it showed that peer pressure can be mobilized to reduce misconduct and that a peer-run quality-control entity can modify behavior. This is doubly important because the officer subculture left to its own devices can protect deviants to spite management (Westley, 1970). The subculture may not always succeed in this effort (it often has not), and individual officers may agree with managers and disapprove of the behavior the manager has sanctioned (they often do), but morale suffers with interventions that come unilaterally from above.

Experience in industry (Deming, 1986; Dobyns & Crawford-Mason, 1991; Ouichi, 1981) has increasingly confirmed that the control of work quality can be exercised in effective organizations if responsibility for quality control is relegated to workers. Such transfer of responsibility does not involve an abrogation of power, because managers continue to have overall jurisdiction over the production process. But workers who are trusted to concentrate on improving the quality of their own work avoid becoming alienated and stressed, as do workers who feel mistrusted and who feel that they are stereotyped as sloppy and corruptible.

Experiments in community policing especially require trust from above and arrangements in which quality control is left to officers with input from citizens. Officers must be assumed to care about quality policing, and this trust may be furthered by selecting the officers carefully and by preintervention training in which quality goals and methods are defined by groups of managers and officers. Subsequent redefining (possibly in joint groups) can cement trust over time.

Citizens must also be presumed to value the quality of police service. Where they do not show such concern, the hope must be that they are educable. However, where citizens continue to make demands that would lower quality of service, they must be resoundingly but politely rebuffed.

Composite Strategies

Can problem-oriented policing be community-oriented policing, and vice versa? This question has been answered frequently in the affirmative. An early program—the Community Patrol Officer Program (CPOP) in New York City—self-consciously and consistently saw itself as in the community-policing and problem-solving business. The program was envisaged as a hybrid by those who provided its technical support (the Vera Foundation) and was researched to see whether it lived up to the model. It was, moreover, a large-scale program, involving nine (sometimes 10) officers in each of 75 police precincts in the city of New York.

An official manual of the CPO program proclaimed that "of all functions of Community Patrol Officers, the most important, and the one that makes the CPOP different from other Department deployment strategies, is problem solving. Without problem solving as its foundation, CPOP makes little sense" (Vera Institute of Justice, 1988, p. 4). Community police officers were instructed to follow a sequential process in which they were to (a) discover and identify a problem, (b) analyze the problem, (c) design a tailor-made response, (d) get support for the response, (e) implement the solution, (f) evaluate its effectiveness, and (g) repeat the sequence if necessary.

The participating officers were provided with a community-oriented definition of "problem" to help them know a problem when they saw one:

> Sometimes problems come right up and bite you. Other times you have to sneak up on them before you can realize that it is a real problem that you're dealing with. In the simplest terms, a problem is anything that can have a negative effect on the community you are working in—something that causes harm to members of the community or is a potential source of disorder. Problems are generally a source of great concern to residents of the community, and they are not likely to go away unless something is done to correct them. (Vera Institute of Justice, 1988, p. 5)

Community police officer team members were instructed to use citizens on their beats as a source of problem definition.

They were also trained to use their powers of observation and to rely on other sources, such as fellow officers, departmental records, agency representatives, and the press. They were told to do serious, formal pattern analyses and to "look for similarities in crime patterns, time distributions of crimes, locations, etc." (Vera Institute of Justice, 1988, p. 5). In tackling a pattern thus analyzed, the officers were told that "the strategy chosen must go beyond the incident and address the underlying problem" and that "the solution should provide a substantial improvement for the residents of the community, reducing both harm to them, and fear of future harm" (p. 13). As for the range of solutions, they were told that combinatory solutions are better than simple solutions. Moreover, the officers were told, "Don't be limited by traditional police responses. There is nothing wrong with enforcement as a tactic, but it has its limitations, and on some problems it just doesn't work" (p. 21).

The officers in the program were told that "the solutions to some problems are within the capacity of the community to carry out themselves. Community police officers can play a critical role in helping citizens join together to work on a problem and in guiding them through the necessary steps" (Vera Institute of Justice, 1988, p. 17). But officers were also enjoined to "reach out and network" (p. 20), to collaborate with other police and public and private agencies in solving problems:

> Don't be afraid of calling another agency. Begin at the level of execution (the workers) or their supervisors, and work your way up. Find out if they can do what it is you need done. Whose approval do they need? What's the process? Who has to be asked? Does it have to be in writing? Who has to sign the request? After you find all of this out, run it past the CPOP supervisor for his or her approval. (Vera Institute of Justice, 1988, p. 24)

How Did It Work?

The CPO program began on a limited scale and was assessed by outside observers. Two of the observers (Weisburd &

McElroy, 1988) noted a difference in the problems the officers faced over time. When the officers first arrived, residents made suggestions that the officers found helpful, and during this phase "most of the problems the CPOs focused upon were quality of life concerns that were seldom addressed by regular patrol officers" (p. 91). At this juncture, "residents often told CPOs that they were more disturbed by these problems than by crimes, because the former represented constant annoyances" (p. 92).

Over time, the officers found the residents less discriminating in their suggestions and less helpful in setting priorities. One officer put it this way:

> When you've solved a problem or addressed a problem and the community sees that it's addressed, they give you something else. I went from drug selling to beer drinking and loud radios down to the stupidest thing. Yesterday, a lady told me a Sanitation guy didn't pick up her trash. (Weisburd & McElroy, 1988, pp. 92–93)

The proliferation of parochial requests led officers to use other data sources (such as crime statistics) or to selectively address specialized concerns, such as those of senior citizens or teenagers. By this time, some officers had decided to become crime fighters. Drug-dealing emporia came to particularly engage their attention. Weisburd and McElroy (1988) observed that "officers devoted significant portions of patrol time to individual locations, during which they would use a series of aggressive patrol tactics against those they believed were involved in the drug trade" (p. 94). Although community police officers had been strongly enjoined to use a broad array of problem-solving strategies, they became extraordinarily enforcement-oriented and made many arrests. One reason for this special focus was that, "in the view of the CPOs, these enforcement actions gained them respect and status from patrol officers and precinct supervisors" (p. 94).

The officers showed enthusiasm, ingenuity, and initiative in their newfound campaigns of rousting small-time hoodlums. They "might surprise those involved by, for example, jumping out of the van after coming down a one-way street in the wrong direction" (Weisburd & McElroy, 1988, p. 95). Such routines were immensely satisfying to the officers and created discomfort to some miscreants, who were forced to change their work schedules and locations. But it would probably be hard to argue that neighborhood drug problems were being solved, except in the short-run.

On the positive side, officers did manage to enlist help and often received support from citizens. In one case, for example,

> CPOs utilized beer drinkers in a local park to alleviate an ongoing drug problem there. They told a group of young men that they could continue to drink beer in the park only if they were neat and threw away the bottles after they were done. The CPOs added another condition to their bargain; that the beer drinkers get rid of the drug sellers in the park. The latter group was, in fact, convinced by the former to cease sales in that public area. (Weisburd & McElroy, 1988, p. 97)

More prevalently, officers in the project complained about citizen passivity and confessed that they could not inspire much citizen action. It has been repeatedly found that community organizing is a difficult task for police, and the same holds true for problem analysis in problem-oriented policing.

Studying Problems

To be problem-oriented, a CPO program must involve officers in research; to be community-oriented, a problem-solving program must involve citizens and be neighborhood-based. Most programs do not meet both of these requisites, although the Baltimore County (COPE) program (chap. 2, this volume) approximated the model, as did New York's CPO program and CAPS in Chicago.

One point of slippage elsewhere is in the way police problems have been studied. Most police officers tend to be Men and Women of Action, and action does not mean perusing tables. A modest survey (say, on fear) may be seen as fun for a time (Brown & Wycoff, 1987), but a mandate to do academic-sounding research, such as "study demographic profiles," could strain officers' patience and lower their morale. Chief Robert Burgreen of the San Diego police made this point about a community problem-oriented experience he attempted to promote:

> What it did was take beat officers and have them do their jobs a little differently—have them become students of their community rather than just climb in a car and go police every day. They were to study the ethnicity, the demographics of the community, the crime problems, the social service and referral agencies available, the community leaders, community organizations, and to literally know everything that was on that beat, and then to attempt to interact with the community and community leaders to impact neighborhood problems. . . . A year later we attempted to implement it department-wide, calling it Community-Oriented Policing. . . . We had some problems, which primarily revolved around the inability or the lack of desire of a lot of officers to become students. In a focused, grant-type environment, we were able to generally gain the compliance and support of officers to become that really tough student of the beat, and do the homework required. But department-wide, we found there were some officers who enjoyed it and some who thought that they quit doing homework when they left high school. . . . Now we are literally doing the work for them in providing them with the material so that they don't have to go out and develop it. We're also using videotapes to introduce the officers to their areas. (Burgreen, 1989, p. 12)

The San Diego police at the time of this comment opted for a compromise solution in which some officers continued to do community policing and others (whom the chief called the "homework squad") gathered and analyzed data:

> We have a staff of officers and analysts who work in our Operations Support Unit. Instead of everybody doing a little, we decided that we're going to take some people who are real good at this, and who understand what we're trying to do, and that's going to be their job. They're going to do it for everyone. Then we're going to have a training program

where people are taught how to use this material. (Burgreen, 1989, p. 12)

The San Diego model was a defensible one, but it deprived most of its participants of certain benefits.[3] The operations support staff were charged with feeding information to others but would not know how (or if) it was used. The officers who received the information had no strong incentive to take it seriously, because the input did not respond to questions the officers had asked. The applicability of demographics, for example, may not be immediately obvious, although the chief had argued eloquently for the relevance of statistics:

> People say, "What's this got to do with police work?" Well, it's got a lot to do with it. People who are poor, people who live in densely crowded housing, are much more likely to engage in certain kinds of conduct than other people are. People who live in upper-class neighborhoods are much more concerned about different issues. That gives you a basis from which to start understanding your community and work with them. (Burgreen, 1989, p. 14)

The word *problem* has frequently become ambiguous and adaptable to predilections. Crack dealers in a building can be seen as a "problem" and the responses to a problem thus defined may be indistinguishable from those of incident-driven policing. A stakeout does not by transmutation become "the exploration of a problem" because the responding officers happen to be CPOs. For officers to poll citizens to obtain rubber-stamp confirmation of such incident-related moves is to belabor the obvious.

A more defensible sequence is to invoke or deploy problem-oriented policing in tandem with incident-driven policing. According to Trojanowicz and Bucqueroux (1989), drug crime fighting lends itself to a sequential approach, which moves from an incident-driven to a problem-centered approach:

> Most often, the first priority in many areas is to reduce open dealing, to stabilize the neighborhood, then focus on indis-

creet dealing to maintain the pressure. As the area begins to improve, the CPO can brainstorm with people in the community about new ways to address the broader spectrum of drug problems. This might mean linking addicts to proper treatment. Or it could include working with area businesses to provide jobs for recovering addicts. (p. 5)

The activity in the example ends up problem-oriented because it tackles underlying conditions, addressing employment issues and linking addicts to treatment. It is community-oriented because it involves joint thinking by officers and citizens. It is also both in that what the officers and citizens brainstorm about are ways of dealing with underlying conditions (such as "the broad spectrum of drug problems"). The issue does not lie in the distinction between enforcement versus nonenforcement options, although incident-driven goals are always short-term enforcement goals achievable through acts such as arresting dealers. Problem-oriented approaches have a wider range of goals (for example, reducing addiction rates), which become much easier to pursue when shorter-term goals have been met.

Invoking citizens is always desirable but becomes especially profitable with longer term goals. In incident-driven community policing, citizens may be supportive (and sometimes bloodthirsty) cheerleaders, as is the chorus in a Greek play. This contribution cements relations and advances good will. It does not go far beyond these benefits, and no one is likely to learn to solve problems by being a cheerleader or being indiscriminately supported. Learning only occurs if citizens ask questions, such as, "How does one address the crack problem in this neighborhood, other than by inducing crack dealers to take unscheduled vacations?"

Such questions require an emphasis on the acquisition of knowledge, the drawing of inferences, the planning of action, and the monitoring of results. These activities require at least minimal involvement in research (such as interviewing drug users) or the using of social science data to the extent to which data are available. Citizen–officer study groups involved in interventions can request data from supportive planning and research units. They can also invite experts to whom they can pose grounded questions. The experts can be creditable academics (such as the authors of this book) but would have to be down to earth (congruent with the officers and citizens' experience) in their analysis of problems. Should the experts have credibility, they could learn a lot themselves and gain the benefit of having their knowledge used.

Linking Backyards

Community policing is by definition local because that is what communities are. Although neighborhood boundaries may be evanescent or arbitrary, they exist psychologically. Citizens become most upset or angry about threats, such as crimes, that occur in their neighborhoods. Events on one's own side of one's border impinge on "us" or "the community"; events on the other side have less intimate significance.

Problems are often defined ethnocentrically or parochially, and so are solutions. In many communities, the winning of the drug war means chasing drug dealers out of the neighborhood into the next one. This delightful outcome becomes a cause for celebration, no matter what it may do to folks who live outside the community. Police who are assigned to a neighborhood can come to share this sort of perspective. But police agency responsibility straddles neighborhoods, and this can lead to ambivalence where a community "solution" poses problems for other areas served by the police. The same dilemma faces service providers who serve broad categories of clients, including problem individuals who can be chased across neighborhood frontiers.

The nature of the issue becomes clearest with "sun-downing" (buying one-way bus tickets for undesirables) but transcends the effect of shifting a problem from one location to another. Any time a group is concerned with only its own share of a problem, it generates a psychology of indifference to those who have the problem elsewhere. NIMBY (not in my backyard) ultimately implies IABYBM (in anyone's backyard but mine). Such parochialism may be mostly inevitable in the short-run, but it must be counteracted with a more cosmopolitan perspective.

As community policing has spread across neighborhoods and localities, its sponsors have built bridges from one experiment to another to enlarge the perspectives of officers and citizens. One means of doing this is to arrange for cluster conferences (chap. 4, this volume) or annual award ceremonies (chap. 12, this volume) that link groups with each other. Local police departments thus discover that their problems are not unique and that it is possible for communities with the same problem to assist and support each other. If a solution that has been adopted in one city or neighborhood seems applicable to another, one can offer collegial assistance to speed the second intervention and enhance its effectiveness. This process can gain momentum if it is cumulatively used over time. A knowledgeable officer with expertise in homelessness or accident causation or family disturbances can serve as a consultant to assist a community that faces the problem by putting the local pattern in broader context, without short-changing its unique character.

The networking process among police departments can carry two connotations. The first connotation (dramatized in *The Music Man* number about the hazards of pool playing) has to do with defining the problem in such a way that local concerns become part of something larger than themselves. The Music Man's invitation to a transcendent definition says, "River City's problem can best be appreciated if we take a look at the outside world. When we do, we can notice that billiard halls elsewhere have led to a proliferation of massage parlors and other manifestations of moral decay. Far from being alone, River City can fight shoulder to shoulder with other communities that are concerned about unsavory trends in the use of leisure time." The other connotation has to do with the contribution of local achievements (such as the advent of the River City Marching Band), given the needs of other communities, who are hungry for ingenious ideas, such as the potential of musicianship as an antidote to licentiousness.

The second challenge, which is harder, is to make communities who feel part of the problem also feel that they are contributors to solving the problem. This cannot be done by leaving problem solving to elites (by disseminating the solutions devised by planners and strategists) but must involve grassroots exchange of information about local achievements adjudged to be exemplary, such as those we discuss in the next chapter.

Notes

1. The nostalgia has a basis in fact. Historians have shown that "the urban police acquired welfare responsibilities as the (nineteenth) century progressed, and then lost them to specialist agencies around the beginning of the twentieth century" (Emsley, 1983, p. 109). Monkkonen (1981) reported the following:

> Almost from their inception in the middle of the nineteenth century until the beginning of the twentieth, American police departments regularly provided a social service that from our perspective seems bizarrely out of character—they provided bed and, sometimes, board for homeless poor people, tramps. Year after year these "lodgers," as the police referred to them, swarmed to the police stations in most large cities, where they found accommodations ranging in quality from floors in hallways to clean bunkrooms. Often, especially in the winter or during depression years, there would be food, usually soup—nothing fancy, but something. During very bad depression years or harsh winters, the number of overnight lodgings provided by a police department exceeded all annual arrests. (pp. 86–87)

When social service agencies came into existence, the police helped them to perform former police functions. One service the police had been performing involved returning lost children to their parents. This task became the responsibility of child protective associations. According to Monkkonen (1981),

> A typical police–NYSPCC [child protection society] interaction involved the police discovering child abuse or neglect, or in some cases a child offender, after which the police asked the society to intervene and take the case. Often the society placed children in foster or orphan homes and actively aided in the criminal prosecution of parents. Concurrent with these forms of police–private cooperation, the police began more and more to use the society's assistance in dealing with lost children. In 1877, the society helped return only twenty-five lost children to their parents; twenty years later, the figure had leapt ten times to 2,810 lost children returned. Clearly, this private agency accounted for a substantial portion of the decline in the number of lost children returned by the police in New York. (p. 127)

2. Integrity-related concerns can lower morale among officers who feel themselves unfairly suspected. Typical of mistrust from above that invites resent-

ment was a New York City Police decision to subject officers to random drug tests. Under the rule, 10% of the force (2,600 officers at the time) would have been tested every year. (McKinley, 1989). In the long-run, actions such as this, which are designed to control deviance, often boomerang. They tend to cement solidarity and promote norms (like silence) that protect suspected deviants from scrutiny by management. Because this in turn limits information that management can get, it may inspire new surveillance efforts that escalate resistance.

3. The qualification applies to the officer-as-research-consumer model, not to the San Diego Police Department, which stands at the forefront of community policing and problem-oriented policing. The San Diego police over time have originated a plethora of ingenious solutions to problems encountered in their city and its vicinity.

Commitment and Community in Problem-Oriented Interventions

$\mathbf{A}$s we noted in chapter 11, most problem-oriented interventions these days are undertaken in police departments known to be community-oriented. This overlap is not coincidental. As we have seen, the definition of community-oriented policing is interwoven with that of problem-oriented policing in that the latter has come to be defined as a core component of the former.

It is of course possible to think of problem-oriented policing—as we have done in our earlier chapters—as a strategy for democratizing top-down police organizations. It is endlessly fascinating to review the large variety of problem-oriented police activities on record, attending to the opportunities they have afforded to rank-and-file officers to exercise ingenuity, to acquire knowledge and develop new bodies of expertise, to find a personally meaningful cause and feel that they are contributing to the world. But problem-oriented interventions also often provide rich opportunities for individuals and groups in the community to join police officers in problem-solving partnerships.

Such opportunities are surprisingly varied and can be appreciated best by examining superficially similar interventions that have addressed comparable problems in different jurisdictions. Where this occurs, one does expect to find some variation having to do with local conditions, because problems are apt to differ in scope and magnitude, as are the resources that may be available to the project participants. But other differences are apt to emerge when one focuses on the main protagonists, on their personal predilections and the contributions they have made. This sort of information can be gleaned by reading first-person accounts of problem-oriented officers, such as those submitted by some of the recent winners of the prestigious Herman Goldstein Award for Excellence in Problem-Oriented Policing.

Mending Broken Windows

We can begin by looking at two projects responding to the problem of graffiti, which is a minor quality-of-life improvement issue. Graffiti as a problem, however, has acquired considerable salience since the advent of the so-called broken windows theory, which could just as easily be called the "graffiti theory." As noted by LeDuff (2002), "the idea holds that . . . if graffiti and broken windows are tolerated, for instance, eventually prostitution and drug dealing and companion violence will find their ways to the street corners." Such thinking provides respectability to interventions that are concerned with targeting graffiti perpetrators and their creations.

An uncluttered example of such a project was initiated in Scottsdale, Arizona, in the summer of 1993. Detective Frank O'Halloran, a principal in this project, recalled that it "started out as a grass roots effort through Block Watch captains in our area, local paints merchants [two bicycle officers] and I" (O'Halloran, 1996, p. 561). The object of the initial concern of this group was "a large white colored building wall that faced a popular city park." This conspicuous edifice had been decorated years earlier by a local juvenile gang. Taking matters literally into their own hands, the officers repainted the wall with supplies that were donated to them by the merchants. To everyone's surprise, the newly painted wall remained graffiti-free for two subsequent years.

At the end of the summer, Detective O'Halloran found himself assigned to the department's Youth Intervention Unit, where he was charged with reviewing the city's graffiti reports. He recalled that such reviewing was done "for the free information provided by the gangs." This assertion presumes that gang graffiti are basically efforts at self-promotion and corporate advertising. The graffiti could thus be regarded as "the newspaper of the streets."

But this logic happened to be limited to gang graffiti, and O'Halloran reported that "soon after my new assignment commenced I began to witness a different style of graffiti and its sharp increase . . . at first, I did not recognize the new style of graffiti; and being schooled in the interpretation of gang graffiti, I also didn't understand it. It took some research and a lot of practice to begin to understand the differences" (O'Halloran, 1996, p. 563). The desire of O'Halloran and other detectives to understand the new, cryptic graffiti led them to speculations about the behavioral predilections of the graffiti perpetrators, with a view to frustrating or neutralizing them.

For O'Halloran and his group, addressing the evolving problem posed by lone-wolf graffiti artists (called "taggers") eventuated in a long-term campaign of attrition. Sergeant Mark Clark, a founding member of O'Halloran's unit who had become a dedicated expert on graffiti artists, explained that "one factor to consider when law enforcement and society decide to 'wage war' on graffiti vandalism, is that it can be taken as a challenge to taggers (enhancing the thrill they get). . . . Taggers will commit more graffiti, making an 'in your face' statement to society. . . . However, this must not be a deterrent to aggressive graffiti abatement. If a wall is tagged, painted and tagged over and over again, eventually the tagger will go somewhere else" (Clark, 1996, p. 568). Presumptively, the challenge experienced by the taggers was to be shared by his or her opponents.

In 1994, the Scottsdale City Council committed itself to a graffiti abatement campaign by funding a full-time graffiti paint-out person and setting up a graffiti hot line. The paint-out person's equipment, including his paint-out truck, was contributed by local merchants. Paint acquisition by the paint-out person proved to be no problem because it developed that "every paint merchant has paint that is improperly mixed or that has other problems for which special disposal is required" (O'Halloran, 1996, p. 561). Seed money that was required for the hotline had come from a realty company. O'Halloran observed that the realtors understand the broken windows theory better than anyone. To them, it's not a theory; it's a law. If a prospective home buyer sees graffiti in the neighborhood near the sale, there won't be a sale. Property values will have to come down to accommodate the apparently deteriorating neighborhood. (O'Halloran, 1996, p. 562)

Sergeant Clark had filed a successful grant proposal covering a digital camera, as well as assorted computer software and hardware for the unit. The paint-out person took pictures of the graffiti (presumably before and after paint-outs), and an incident file was generated containing color photographs. The unit also relied on qualitative approaches customarily used by detectives to understand the dynamics of incidents and the motives of perpetrators. Sergeant Clark recalled that "the Gang/Youth Unit has interviewed numerous graffiti vandals during the course of our investigations." Interviews were also routinely conducted with the parents of juvenile suspects.

O'Halloran observed that "law enforcement tends to measure success in arrests and convictions for crimes." Scottsdale pursued such outcomes but did not attain them in appreciable numbers. The Scottsdale hotline had been upstaged by a campaign in a neighboring city (Phoenix), and an ambitious graffiti-vandal sting that involved several police agencies reported "very limited success with less than a dozen arrests." Efforts of a nonenforcement nature were somewhat more successful. A regional Graffiti Task Force with business representation was organized, for instance, and produced several model ordinances, mostly concerned with restricting the sale of graffiti implements and supplies.

The Scottsdale intervention may be of limited import, but it illustrates several process-related issues about the intersection of officers and citizens. The content of the intervention responded directly to customer demands, which accounts for the unprecedented high level of citizen generosity and involvement. Neighborhood beautification concerns dovetailed with the financial interests of local business groups, guaranteeing expeditious action by the city council and the ready availability of funds. Sustained citizen interest also helped to ensure the longevity of the project. This mattered because the strategy used in this project was one of long-term containment, with success modestly defined as the ratio of painted-over graffiti to freshly produced replacements. The presumption was that the war on graffiti, like freedom, had to be won through indefatigable and tireless dedication.

The concept of graffiti was born in Italy, and Rome, the capital of the country, had created an Office of Urban Decorum to deal with the problem in its native habitat. The manager of the office described its concern not as one with "broken windows" but as "a question of civility" (Bruni, 2003). He and others in Rome said there were "distinctions between what they deemed acceptable graffiti, like a proclamation of romantic ardor, and unacceptable graffiti, like a swastika. They also indicated some respect for the vibrant, creative impulse that graffiti signaled" (Bruni, 2003).

An interesting issue is the nature of the relationship—other than that of bellicosity—between problem-oriented officers and offenders. Graffiti experts show a surprising measure of grudging respect for graffiti perpetrators, even though they pointedly call them "vandals." In a sense, the Scottsdale intervention could be defined as a competitive game, with superior information and staffing providing an edge to the city and the graffiti eradication experts. In the concluding words of Detective O'Halloran,

> it is too soon to call this a victory. . . . But our continual efforts to work in partnership with the citizens of Scottsdale and the business community along with the police department's willingness to refine our . . . reporting process, data base, hotline and investigations will reduce incidents of graffiti and help win the war of graffiti abatement. (O'Halloran, 1996, p. 562)

Using the Products of the Problem to Address the Problem

In 2000, a detective from the San Diego, California, police department recalled the following incident from the problem-oriented history of the department:

> The [Mid-City] division had already widely adopted prob-
> lem-solving techniques, including weekly community meet-
> ings. At a community meeting in March 1999, an officer pre-
> sented crime statistics for robberies, prostitution and drug
> offenses in Mid-City. After listening to the litany, a member of
> the community asked, "What about the graffiti problem?" . . .
> The officer was surprised, but had to concede that graffiti
> was an important quality-of-life concern for the community.
> From that point on, graffiti became a top priority for the San
> Diego Police Department's Mid-City Division. (San Diego,
> 2000a, p. 5)

The officers who attended the meeting followed up with an
informal eye-balling survey of their division, but "stopped counting at 300 [graffiti]" and decided the citizens had a case. Satisfied
that they had a legitimate problem, they constituted a team
(comprising one detective and two officers) to research the graffiti
problem and establish liaison with other city agencies. One of
the agencies they contacted was the juvenile probation department. The probation department in turn "convened a graffiti
focus group involving ten convicted taggers" (p. 5) to reminisce
about their tagging careers. Among the motives the members of
this focus group adduced for their illicit avocation, they listed
the thrill of risk-taking, the need for acceptance and attention,
and the incentive of competition.

The officers in the division then conducted their own motiva-
tional interviews with juveniles who had been arrested for tagging. Half of the 59 taggers in custody claimed that they had
been the innocent targets of false arrests, but the other offenders
decided to cooperate with the officers and designated "boredom,
desire for recognition and popularity, gang membership and
personal tag identification" as motives for originating graffiti
(San Diego, 2000a, p. 7).

In planning their problem-oriented response, the officers decided to intersect with the offender motives highlighted in their
inquiries and to aim their intervention at juveniles. The officers
did opt to use paint-outs, but in their version, "juveniles on
probation for tagging cleaned up [the] graffiti with bi-monthly
paint-outs at heavily tagged sites" (San Diego, 2000a, p. 8). A
more elaborate project involved students at the local junior high

school, who "painted murals on heavily tagged walls." The content of murals was to "reflect positive images of the community" (San Diego, 2000a, p. 8) and was designed in consultation with teachers and adult citizens. In another project enlisting juveniles, a youth bike team was constituted to serve as a monitoring force to patrol tagged sites. This team—called "kids in control"— was said by the officers to have located offenders previously unknown to the police.

The project officers discovered that the probation staff did not have the resources to work with graffiti perpetrators. A probation officer complained to the police officers that "we do not have enough case workers to handle the number of juvenile offenders. We need help if we are going to keep on top of the taggers." In response, the officers decided to act as ancillary probation staff members. In that capacity, "an officer, called a 'handler,' visited weekly with the tagger to monitor behavior. The handler checked on the juvenile's school, home and street contacts and updated the juvenile's file after each visit" (San Diego, 2000a, p. 8). Repeat offenders caught recidivating by the handlers "were sent back to the probation officer, ordered to perform paint-outs, or serve other community service time" (p. 8). This combination apparently worked fairly smoothly, because it achieved tenure and was formalized, with probation regularly assigning offenders to paint-outs and the police appointing additional officers as handlers.

Two features of the San Diego intervention were especially noteworthy. One was its focus on juveniles—the reliance on age-mates of the taggers to address elements of the problem. The other was the involving of the offenders themselves. Although for the offenders being forced to do paint-overs may have come across as punitive, and may even have been seen as a demeaning experience, it did earn adult attention, conveyed messages from the criminal justice system using the offender's own medium, and provided a restorative opportunity. There was also the obvious fact that being sent out with a paint brush or spray gun beats being placed on probation or being sentenced to a term of confinement.

Although the handler role was described by the San Diego officers in enforcement terms ("zero tolerance"), it obviously represented tough love, with a strategy that involved bending over backward to provide recidivistic offenders a fresh opportunity to shape up. Like it or not, the handler assignment was also a role with distinct social work overtones. This emphasis again emerges in a second feature of the intervention, which is that of blurring the boundaries between participating agencies, particularly between the police and juvenile probation departments. Although problem-oriented policing by definition calls for collaborative activities, those in the project were unprecedentedly symbiotic. Having discovered that probation lacked resources to adequately attend to a group of offenders who were of mutual concern, the police stepped in and created a hybrid role (that of handlers) to provide probation services to the offenders. It may have called for fast verbal footwork to define these services in enforcement terms. It may be similarly obvious in retrospect that buying bicycles for mini-cops and sponsoring wall-painting sessions are quasi-parental activities and thus placed the officers in surrogate parental roles.

Sampson and Scott (2000) pointed out that "cities have responded to graffiti and tagging in different ways, many incorporating multiple strategies" (p. 77). They noted that "some cities limit access to vandals' tools . . . some limit access to vandalized site . . . some incorporate aspects of restorative justice . . . some choose shaming . . . some encourage increased community vigilance . . . some try educational efforts . . . some offer more conventionally acceptable artistic endeavors. And some threaten to penalize victims to guarantee timely graffiti removal" (p. 77).

Evicting Undesirables

Both of the graffiti projects exemplified a number of attributes that we regularly encounter in problem-oriented activities that take place in community police organizations. Such interventions are often initiated in response to concerns raised by citizens or to address needs that have been prioritized by citizens. In researching the citizen-nominated problems, officers may consult experts and service providers in the area and may evolve solutions in consultation with citizens and officials. The prescriptions that emerge for ameliorating the problem tend to be framed so that they improve the quality of life in the community in some tangible way. Strategies used in solving problems that help improve the community vary, and might not prominently include enforcement tactics, such as arresting and punishing perpetrators. The Scottsdale intervention made a token effort to arrest offenders but was primarily designed to neutralize the destructive impact of their offenses. The focus of the San Diego project was on the prevention of offenses. The officers took a hand in the rehabilitation of repeat offenders and recruited juveniles to exert positive influence on their peers.

Problem-oriented interventions often deviate from this standard community-oriented formula and may do so in a number of ways. In many police projects, "getting the bad guys" becomes an overriding goal. Some problem-oriented cops-and-robbers interventions of this kind temporarily reduce incident rates but leave the sources of problems unaddressed. The focus on crime fighting can also lead to police actions that lower rather than raise the quality of life for some segment of the community.

To illustrate these interesting issues, we turn to a second project of the Mid-City Division in the San Diego Police Department involving a different group of officers (San Diego, 2000b). The problem of concern to these officers, on the face of it, was a human service problem, that of deinstitutionalized mental patients who had set up residence in the community. The course of action that the officers and citizens embarked on resulted in eviction of the patients, who were perceived as a source of trouble by their neighbors. Crime-related numbers in the neighborhood did show improvements, but the targeted mental patients were left painfully adrift.

The focus of concern in this project was a small apartment complex that had been converted into an "independent living" residence for mentally ill individuals. Such settings are frequently located in lower class neighborhoods, where they can exist relatively inconspicuously. In this case, however, the immediate vicinity of the residence included a gang turf, thriving drug bazaars, and "one of the city's most infamous prostitution strips"

(San Diego, 2000b, p. 32). It also included neighbors who volubly complained about the "lack of control and care" that was being exercised by those running the residence, as evidenced by an increase that the citizens and the beat officer recorded in disruptive incidents in the neighborhood. Supporting data that were collected by a problem-oriented team including members of the community documented this increase, which was clearly reflected in statistics related to radio calls and service requests. Less clear than this increase, however, was the role played by the mental patients in the incidents.

As is often the case, some of the disturbed residents were multiproblem patients, who were addicted to drugs or alcohol. The patients who transacted business with local drug merchants to sustain their drug habits "were frequently assaulted and robbed by the dealers" (San Diego, 2000b, p. 34). Given such incidents of victimization, "officers began to realize how vulnerable the residents of the independent living facility were to criminal predators in the neighborhood" (p. 34). The officers thus had reason to empathize with the patients. They also read up on "research nationwide on [police] problem solving for facilities for people with mental illness" (p. 35). This literature almost invariably describes partnership arrangements between police and mental health providers that are designed to assist patients.

Another line of research pursued by the officers also appeared patient-centered. The officers investigated service-delivery modalities in California and discovered that "independent living facilities were supposed to accept only those people capable of living on their own" (San Diego, 2000b, p. 35). This fact suggested a strategy or approach to the officers and citizens, who set about demonstrating that the concept of independent living "was a misnomer" for the residence of concern to them. Sympathetic clinicians were recruited to the cause, and they obligingly "concluded . . . that all 32 residents were mentally ill and incapable of independent living" (p. 38). Thus the stage was set for closure of the targeted facility, which "either had to evict all residents who needed care and supervision or had to qualify for a State license" (p. 39).

There was no question about which option was to be exercised. The police had long been unfavorably disposed to the manager, who had turned out to have a criminal record. The neighbors were equally sanguine and "raised the stakes by threatening the manager with a civil lawsuit under the Safe Streets Now Act, which provides that each resident can individually sue a business or resident for quality-of-life issues" (San Diego, 2000b, p. 39). The city helpfully announced (through the police) that it "planned to initiate an abatement process under the city's nuisance ordinance" (pp. 39–40). Faced with these unsubtle contingencies, the manager resigned, and "the owner evicted the residents and sold the property" (p. 40). Follow-up documentation collected by the team "disclosed that the residents of Elmwood Avenue felt safe again and were proud of their problem-solving partnership with the police" (p. 40). The team members appeared little troubled by the fact that their intervention had not touched on neighborhood problems that had victimized the mental patients, nor by the fact that the patients they themselves had certified as "incapable of independent living" had been relegated to homelessness.

Whereas in the Mid-City graffiti project some people who were sources of the problem were invoked in its solution, the mental health project resolved the problem on the backs of its repositories. Hypothetically, the certification of mental patients as in need of care could be a step to arranging for their care, but no one in the project evidenced interest in the patients. The concern for the "adequacy of service" for the patients was an arguably cynical subterfuge. The citizens were interested in finding a way to shut down a locus of neighborhood problems; the officers were concerned with helping the citizens, who were their community-policing constituents. The officers also appeared pleased because they were able to define their campaign as directed against "bad guys" in the shape of the ex-offender manager and a blood-sucking property owner. Moreover, everyone involved could regard the exercise as an exemplar of successful problem-oriented policing in that research, collaboration, and innovative action had resulted in a reduction of the problematic incidents that were of initial concern.

Because community policing requires responsiveness to a community, it can understandably lead to situations in which "respectable" citizens are carefully attended to when they demand action against disreputable citizens. This scenario represents a particularly welcome development where the disreputable citizens are offenders and community sentiments translate into support for crime-fighting goals of the police. But the demand for action can become problematic where the "disreputable" citizens are perennial underdogs or individuals facing mental or physical challenges, who could use support, protection, or advocacy. The police happen to be uniquely situated to spearhead any response to such needs because the police are the only public agency that is available 24 hours a day, seven days a week, and that can mobilize services from other public agencies. Where this opportunity is ignored, people who could benefit from constructive problem-solving moves can become targeted by offensive problem-solving moves, merely because their neighbors disapprove of them. The enforcement-oriented interventions that can thus ensue are apt to feature sun-downing approaches or the displacement of symptomatic behavior from one neighborhood to another. They can also result in the aggravation of the conditions from which the disadvantaged individuals suffer, making the group more disadvantaged and more of an eyesore to their "reputable" neighbors.

Combinatory Strategies

A more complex (and more challenging) set of pressures can be generated in neighborhoods or communities in which citizens and social service providers espouse values of philanthropy and compassion. This stance can occasion a force field in which some citizens' concerns for the amelioration of suffering among disruptively disadvantaged subpopulations compete with demands by other citizens for social control and public order.

An interesting example of such a force field is provided by an experience of the Los Angeles County Sheriff's Department, whose jurisdiction encompasses the affluent city of West Hollywood. During the period when this community was incorporated, the Sheriff's Department noted that "newly elected city officials were strong believers in taxpayer financed soup kitchen and feeding programs, and started many of them" (Los Angeles,

1996, p. 323). After a time, the city leaders were said to have experienced "compassion fatigue" as a result of the fact that more homeless individuals gravitated to West Hollywood. Services were consequently curtailed, but "public areas and parks remained inundated with hundreds of transients who loitered, slept, and drank, in full public view" (p. 323). Aggressive panhandling became a problem. The department also reported that "rummaging recycling thieves" emptied garbage containers and left "huge messes." Citizens complained to the police, and "the deputies decided to make this [homeless] issue a priority" (p. 324).

The deputies remained cognizant of the fact that the city's political climate was compassionate and civil rights-oriented:

> City officials specified that whatever new approach was to be taken, each transient was to be treated as an individual, and that no homeless "sweeps" should occur. Most City council members and City officials were members of the American Civil Liberties Union (ACLU) and did not want a perception that the City was "anti-homeless." Deputies also knew that many cities are embroiled in litigation for implementing perceived draconian measures to address the "homeless problem." (Los Angeles, 1996, p. 324)

The deputies discovered, on the other hand, that in some quarters there was a strongly articulated desire for draconian measures and that "there were hundreds of people who were so fed up, that they didn't care how [enforcement] was done" (Los Angeles, 1996, p. 324). Such constituents were generally well-disposed toward the department, whereas "open hostility between social service agencies and police were common denominators" (p. 324). The deputies decided to confront the latter problem and evolved a team approach in which officers worked shoulder-to-shoulder with agency staff. They started by inviting social workers to ride along with them "in what became known as 'Operation Outreach' " (p. 324). In Operation Outreach, the officers enforced the law against delinquent homeless offenders, and social workers offered services to other homeless individuals, who (if interested) were driven to shelters by the police. The overall goal of the intervention was to "positively impact the community's quality of life without a backlash" given that "had deputies conducted 'sweeps' without the outreach workers, it is highly probable there would have been major negative repercussions for operations averaging nearly 10 arrests of the 'homeless' each time" (p. 326). The deputies reported with satisfaction that under the new arrangement "there have been absolutely no negative repercussions" (p. 326). This result was achieved despite the fact that repeat violators had begun to serve serious sentences in local jails because the deputies had prepared "lengthy synopses" for the judges that detailed the careers of recidivistic homeless offenders.

The operation thus not only addressed an enforcement problem but effectively dealt with public relations problems, transmuting potential conflict situations into win–win resolutions. The social workers and the deputies had come to admire each other's humanity and professional skills, and their clients had expressed appreciation, although "a few confess they are more afraid of another long winded speech from a social worker than of getting arrested" (Los Angeles, 1996, p. 327). City stores welcomed the return of pilfered shopping carts, and in interviews, citizens reported that they felt safer after the operation was initiated. Several newspapers also published laudatory stories by reporters who had been taken on ride-alongs by the officers and described their "kinder, gentler approach to police work" and the innovative nature of their program.

In reporting on their activities, the deputies stressed the importance of institutionalizing any intervention. They wrote about their operation that "as with many successful ways of working towards solutions, if these methods were halted today, the success achieved would be quickly eroded" (Los Angeles, 1996, p. 328). This point is extraordinarily important. If one is to effectively address community problems, this frequently involves setting up new organizational structures and instituting new routines and practices. The "solution" one arrives at does not lie in the inception of this process but in its continuing implementation. That is one reason why substantial problem-oriented approaches almost always presuppose organizational reform. It is critical for a department to show an unreserved willingness to let its officers come up with ideas and try them out for size. The real test of commitment, however, is the readiness for making changes that allow for long-term implementation of new ideas.

Creating Services

East of West Hollywood and the Los Angeles area lies the city of Fontana, California, with a population of about 108,000. In Fontana, the police department recorded that over time it "became extremely proficient at developing strategies that would cause homeless [citizens] to relocate" (p. 2). These strategies, however, proved notoriously unsuccessful in that "by early 1996, any person driving down a major street in Fontana was likely to see large numbers of obviously homeless people sitting on the sidewalks, walking down the streets, or panhandling" (Fontana, 1998, p. 2).

Business representatives in Fontana had ranked the homeless issue as a priority problem, but the business establishment in Fontana was not the only significant constituency in town. The police department reported that they

> also found that there were a number of groups, mostly churches, in our city that were supplying meals and clothing to the homeless. These groups by helping the homeless were inadvertently making Fontana a more attractive place for the homeless. No other city in our area had the amount of resources devoted to helping people who were living on the street. (Fontana, 1998, p. 3)

The police department concluded that "of all the factors identified as contributing to the homeless problem, we felt that the only one we could have any serious impact on would be those organizations in the community" (Fontana, 1998, p. 3). The department, therefore (in the shape of a corporal who had been assigned to run the project), called for a planning group of assorted community representatives, including business people and members of the clergy. This task force munificently decided to "develop a plan with a goal of improving the individual condition of homeless subjects" (p. 3). On the face of it, the plan was an ambitious philanthropic undertaking, involving "a facility that will serve as a temporary processing center equipped to feed, bathe, clothe, and find housing for the homeless" and "a program to rehabilitate those individuals and integrate them back into society through training provided by local rehabilitation centers and churches" (p. 3). The members of the planning group called this two-stage operation the Transient Enrichment Network for Fontana, or TEN-4 for short (pp. 3–4).

No money had been budgeted for the intervention, which consequently needed to rely on existing service providers, voluntary contributions, and arm-twisting. According to the report, "members of the group led by Fontana Police Department personnel went to businesses, community groups, and individuals who were most affected by the homeless problem. They solicited donations of time, materials and money" (Fontana, 1998, p. 4). The screening center was to be opened in a mall under construction. Because there were no funds for the center, "the city worked out a creative financing plan, allowing for the owner of the strip mall to receive a significant discount on sewer fees, in exchange for 18 months free rent" (p. 4). A counselor and two ministers volunteered their time to staff the facility, and an army of drivers made themselves available to pick up homeless inductees and transport them to and from the center. The churches agreed to curtail the services they had heretofore provided to homeless individuals and to act as referral agents for the program. Suitable accommodations for homeless people were created or located, and rehabilitation and retraining facilities were mobilized. Several employers evolved part-time and full-time job opportunities for the graduating working homeless individuals. Concurrently, according to the report, "officers were encouraged to and became more aggressive in enforcing nuisance laws against sleeping on sidewalks . . . aggressive panhandling, and drinking in public" (p. 5).

The rehabilitative portion of the program was a notable success. Approximately 500 clients were resettled within a two-year period. There were others, to be sure, who were less receptive to the intervention, and may have found the city inhospitable, and left town. As a result of concurrent developments, according to the department's report, "the total number of homeless people actually living in Fontana has been reduced by more than 90 percent" (Fontana, 1998, p. 6). Moreover, "issues involving homeless people [were] simply no longer important to the business community in the city of Fontana" (p. 6).

The Fontana program has won a number of awards. It clearly stands out because of its grassroots, nonbureaucratic structure, its social service orientation, and its mobilization of citizen involvement. The planning group convoked by the police included representatives of religious groups. Such organizations are highly motivated to engage in charitable work, have experience in fielding volunteers, and were already invested in assisting homeless individuals. The planning exercise provided these groups with an opportunity to increase the effectiveness and scope of their humanitarian efforts by convincing others in the community to join their cause. Business representatives in the group were interested in getting homeless people off the streets, but they had no stake in having homeless people arrested and punitively dealt with. In fact, past experience had documented the fact that an enforcement approach could at best afford temporary respite or evanescent relief. The notion of changing unproductive individuals into contributing citizens would also tend to appeal to business representatives, combined with the prospect of an expanded labor pool. Moreover, there could be public-relations payoff for business in a joint project with churches that could be defined as an exercise in philanthropy, civic improvement, and citizenship.

The sponsorship of the proposed project by the police (who convoked the group) and, by extension, the support of city government, provided another key ingredient. In community policing, the police tend to become senior partners in collaborative problem solving. The role of the police is unique, because they are not only able to supply resources but also have clout in that they can invoke the law where required. A project that involves police participation also becomes a public rather than a private enterprise. The police legitimize interventions, because they are presumed to be disinterested, unsentimental, and concerned with promoting public order.

What ultimately most distinguished the Fontana project, however, was the range and number of voluntary contributions that were mobilized to bring it to fruition and ensure its continuance. The core of the intervention was a new entity staffed and sustained by volunteers, which exercised a new function—that of intake, reception, screening, and referral for an impressive network of services. Moreover, some of the services had to be created from scratch. This monumental achievement was accomplished without an organizational superstructure, by informally coordinating varied contributions of individuals, groups, organizations, and agencies that participated in the project. The project therefore stands out as exemplifying the power that can be unleashed by enlisting citizens in addressing a problem with an intervention of substance.

Creating an Institution

The *New York Times* described the contrasting fate of two immigrant job centers, one of which had opened with community support and another that was facing eviction (Gootman, 2002). Migratory laborers are a reliable source of acrimony in many communities, as are the locales in which day workers tend to congregate. Such settings can produce a variety of messy situations that call for responses from the police. But more fundamentally, they present the community with a humanitarian problem, consisting of temporary residents who are powerless, stigmatized, and susceptible to exploitation.

Day laborers can be defined as individuals with problems who may in turn create problems for others. This presents a compounded challenge to the police, although responding to the challenge is somewhat uninviting because the payoff looks unpromising, the subject invites controversy, and the long-term situation appears insoluble. These considerations make it even more impressive that a team of two officers, attached to the City of Glendale (California) Police Department, designed and implemented a comprehensive response to their city's migrant labor problem (Gillman & Ruiz, 1996). The officers did this acting in accord with their department's community-policing mission statement, which evolved out of a community police unit strategy meeting. In this meeting, the department's community police officers decided that their "targeted problems needed to be long term and recurring, [to] create blight in the community and negatively influence the quality of life in a given area" (Ruiz, 2002, p. 2). The migrant labor project handsomely qualified because "the problems associated with the congregation of day laborers had plagued the city for almost 25 years. It was a genuine community problem involving blight and quality of life issues for all concerned—residents, business owners, and even the laborers themselves" (p. 2).

To update themselves on the problems of the migrant workers, "officers met with the laborers routinely to learn more about their perspective and stay abreast of their needs and concerns" (Ruiz, 2002, p. 2). In drafting the proposal to their migrant labor project, the two officers—Ronald Gilman and Javier Ruiz—dealt in compassionate terms with the compounded travails of the laborers. They pointed out that

> like all of us, day laborers want to work in order to provide basic necessities for themselves and their families. When hired, the day laborers usually make less than minimum wages and may work one or two days a week, if at all. Often times they do not receive their promised wages. Many are fearful of government officials, especially immigration officers, and are reluctant to sign anything. (Gillman & Ruiz, 1996, p. 337)

The officers described their proposed intervention as a program to "develop, manage and operate a fixed hiring site where prospective day laborers could congregate to solicit temporary employment" and emphasized that the object would be to "offer a safe and clean environment for workers, away from streets and street corners" (Gillman & Ruiz, 1996, p. 339). With respect to more traditional police concerns, the benefits the officers envisaged would be to eliminate the undesirable consequences of workers milling about on city street corners, such as traffic obstruction, fights over job opportunities, littering, and public intoxication.

While working through the details of their problem-oriented proposal, the officers created an advisory group—the Day Labor Advisory Board—comprising key business and neighborhood representatives who served as a sounding board for their prospectus. They also embarked on a course of consultation with staff members of a day labor program that had been instituted in the city of Los Angeles. A lesson the officers said they derived from the Los Angeles project was "the serious drawbacks to not having a comprehensive program," so in promoting their own proposal, the officers insisted that "without each of the components in place, the program is likely to fail" (Gillman & Ruiz, 1996, p. 341).

Among the components that the officers listed as nonnegotiable was the establishment of a fully furnished, professionally staffed hiring center at a location of their choice, to be run at no cost to the city. The officers selected a large, strategically located lot, and set about inventorying the amenities their hiring hall would require, ranging from a covered waiting area, to benches, restroom facilities, drinking water, a pay phone, and "wrought iron or ornate iron fencing" to prevent accidents (p. 5).

Another core component of the proposal envisaged the introduction of municipal code sections to encourage laborers and employers to use the hiring center by setting up "no solicitation" zones elsewhere in the city, subject to strict code enforcement by the police. To preempt the need for wholesale arrests of violators (which was not part of the plan), an education program was also written into the proposal.

One of the functions envisaged for the center staff was that of regularizing and systematizing the procedures for hiring workers, to make these fair and equitable. A mini-civil service system was to be set up, to include a running roster of the laborers and their skills, with a mechanism for the monitoring of wage negotiations. (The officers noted that the workers would be able to count on "a commitment from the police that if employers do not pay them, there would be a criminal follow-up and/or prosecution.")

In the proposed center, workers were to be hired in strict random order within vocational categories, although provisions were to be made for special requests by employers. An outreach worker was to be attached to the center to solicit and administer donations of food, tools, and services and to arrange for social services that might be required by the workers. The officers also obligated themselves to locate sources of additional funds. In the interim, the Day Labor Advisory Board was to become the vehicle of implementation for the project. A report by the police department records that "Advisory Board meetings addressed the development of a long term, collaborative approach to the day labor issue. Prior to these meetings, the private sector [had] felt the problem was the responsibility of the City, and City officials felt it was a shared responsibility" (Ruiz, 2002, p. 6).

The private sector eventually came to shoulder a great deal of the project's burden. The Home Depot store—which stood to gain business from the center—made a very substantial investment in the project, including both construction material and a full-time staff position for five years. Catholic Charities agreed to administer the program. The officers secured supplementary funding, as they had anticipated, drawing on community block grant funds that had originally been earmarked "for the improvement of neighborhoods through the removal of blight" (Ruiz, 2002, p. 9).

The police department judged the project an unqualified success. They reported that "the Day Labor Program has dramatically improved the quality of life for day laborers, the surrounding community, local business and has reduced the demands placed on emergency services" (Ruiz, 2002, p. 8). This outcome was especially important to the officers because, "while [they] were determined to solve the problems related to the day laborers, their true incentive was a better quality of life for everyone involved, including the laborers themselves" (p. 9). Statistics had also shown that in the past, workers had spent most of their time waiting at curbsides for work that did not materialize. With the inception of the program, "on the average day the hiring rate of laborers has risen from 10% to approximately 80–100%" (p. 8). Moreover, "laborers have taken advantage of social services offered at the center, including English language instruction, computer classes and classes related to immigration" (p. 8).

A final outcome alluded to by the department was that of the organizational links that had been generated, "the partnerships created with the various entities throughout the community to ensure that their commitment to the success of the project continues" (Ruiz, 2002, p. 8). Task forces and interorganizational arrangements such as those instituted for the project can survive and mutate, transcend their original mission, and lend themselves to other problem-oriented planning efforts.

The organizational links forged for the center project did not include the U.S. Immigration and Naturalization Service, whose representatives might have had mixed feelings about the clients of the center. The Glendale officers explicitly addressed this delicate issue by noting that, "as conceived, the Day Labor Program would operate without bias regarding immigration status. The program is designed to solve problems, and focusing on a lesser included problem would be of no benefit" (Gillman & Ruiz, 1996, p. 349).

In relation to any problem, there are always variables an intervention cannot address, to be relegated to "lesser included" status or to be regarded as constants. Some such variables can be addressed at higher levels of governance, as matters of state or national policy. They can also be subjects of problem-solving efforts through local applications of public policy. For instance, a problem-oriented activity related to the immigration status of day laborers would have to be based on knowledge of prevailing types of immigrants and work opportunities and entail consultation with employers and service providers. Obviously, national policies about immigration would have to be taken into consideration. But a problem-oriented strategy rests on the presumption that uniform, across-the-board enforcement needs tempering through thoughtful accommodations by individuals familiar with local problems and their attributes.

Problem-oriented policing is necessarily local even when it is practiced by police agencies whose jurisdiction covers many localities. By encouraging local problem solving, agencies add credibility and relevance to their practices. They can also thereby close the experiential distance said to exist between headquarters and the field. But in problem-oriented efforts wheels do have to be reinvented. Each project we have summarized, for example, can claim sister projects in other police agencies across the country. Precedents may be emulated in designing a project but can never result in precise replication. This is not merely because configurations of problems will vary in detail but because the commitment of key participants must always be secured, and this can only be done by starting the process from scratch to engender genuine participation.

Problem-oriented policing is a national movement, in the sense that experiences of participants can be profitably pooled and success stories disseminated. A sense of community can be fostered among police departments who have experimented with problem-oriented approaches. The Goldstein award competition—on which this chapter is based—exemplifies the networking activities instituted to support and reinforce pioneering efforts and to make participants feel less lonely and out of step. This is especially critical for the type of projects we have reviewed, which emphasize humanitarian goals, quality-of-life concerns, and collaborative involvements.

It is axiomatic that the profession of policing today is undergoing changes. The transformation comprises divergent developments. The challenge is for activities with varying emphases to accommodate each other. Community policing has to learn to survive in agencies in which "social work" remains a pejorative designation, success is equated with a "good bust," and crime fighting is a widely advertised goal. By the same token, the need for cohabitation extends to the enforcement-oriented officers. It is not surprising that sometimes all factions involved are apt to feel shortchanged, concluding that history, and their superiors, favor the other factions. Those who run police departments may in turn feel as if they are conducting a discordant ensemble, concurrently playing different tunes.

This picture reflects the ineluctable fact that policing is many things to many people. But policing has always had manifold missions. Police have been charged with fighting crime, preserving public order and civility, resolving conflicts and disputes, and reducing or ameliorating fear. The roster of public mandates has now been expanded: Community policing presents the police with a new set of goals to be achieved and a new set of approaches for achieving them. This development does not invite zero-sum games. Problem-oriented, community-oriented policing merely adds to what there is, providing expanded opportunities for police officers and new ways for police departments to relate to their constituents. As success stories such as those we have reviewed multiply, more police officers and more communities are apt to become involved in innovative problem-oriented activities.

Herman Goldstein, the originator of the trend, has thought of it prospectively, with understandable pride and a measure of trepidation. He has written the following:

> The best cases that have emerged from the work of police officers . . . [who] take creative approaches to old problems, using non-traditional strategies, and go on, within the limits of the officers involved, to demonstrate what they were able to achieve. The cases clearly confirm that there is indeed an enormous reservoir of talent, resourcefulness and commitment in street-level officers that has not been tapped. (Goldstein, in press, p. 5)

On the other hand, Goldstein also pointed out that the need for the rethinking of police work is such that "spectacular as the results of some officer-led projects have been, it is unrealistic to expect that these efforts alone carry sufficient force to meet the larger need" (Goldstein, in press, p. 5). Hence, he has concluded that local projects require help in the form of added research expertise:

> To energize and hasten the development of problem-oriented policing, the greatest current need, in my opinion, is to invest heavily in building a capacity into local policing to analyze discrete pieces of police business in depth and to carefully evaluate the effectiveness of alternative strategies for responding to them. Such an investment should continue to draw on the knowledge and experience of all police employees, but it will depend heavily, for its success, on the full engagement of the chief executive and management. And it will require in one form or another, the acquisition of research skills that are not currently available within police agencies. (Goldstein, in press, p. 6)

Chapter

13

Extending the Approach to Interagency Problem Solving

O ne of our key assumptions is that no organization that serves the public can be an island unto itself. Once one digs beyond symptoms of any problem that distresses the community, one finds that the needs that must be addressed do not neatly correspond to categories of service delivery and are not the purview of any single agency that does service delivering.

The only legitimately insular problem-solving activities may be those that have to do with problems that are internal to an organization and call for improvements in its functioning. But even internal reforms must keep external constituencies in mind. In Oakland, for example, citizen complaints were our obvious outcome measure. Moreover, the Oakland project yielded ideas for partnerships to prevent citizen conflicts from escalating. New arrangements (for instance, a family crisis referral network and a unit to resolve landlord–tenant disputes) were experimentally instituted. Even entities customarily kept at a distance—such as the public defender's office—were enlisted in collaborative arrangements (Toch et al., 1975). In new policing strategies, the police are often instigators of coalitions and function as their coordinators. Multiple initiatives involving different partners can be organized, with police as the linchpins.

An award-winning British project (Cleveland Police, 1998) is of interest in this connection because of its unusual complexity, encompassing approaches to constituencies that included administrators of a housing complex, neighborhood schools, elderly residents living in fear, alienated delinquents, and their families.

A police team composed of six officers and a sergeant had concluded that enforcement activities aimed at the control of delinquency and disruptiveness among resident youths in a housing complex allocated to the team had not only been ineffectual but had resulted in hostility to the police by all parties concerned. The officers said they had discovered that the

> response in addressing [the problem] was of a typical "Fire Brigade" approach. This manifested itself in Police Officers simply papering over the cracks. There was no attempt to understand the full extent of the problem or consideration of any partnership work to alleviate it. Communications with the local community had been non-existent, giving the impression that the Police did not want to understand the community concerns. (Cleveland Police, 1998)

At the inception of their work, the officers reported that they were achieving uneven results. These included discouraging encounters with senior citizen residents, such as

> public meetings, which were initially poorly attended. Those who did attend expressed a sense of helplessness and nowhere to turn. The meetings identified that the problems had been getting progressively worse over the last two years. (Cleveland Police, 1998, p. 3)

The next steps required reassuring the disgruntled citizens that their concerns were being seriously attended to and enlisting the cooperation of Housing Unit officials who had also become discouraged and apathetic. Neighborhood schools were approached at this time and they offered the use of their facilities, but they initially were reluctant to play a more active role. The officers then persuaded local governance representatives to allocate some funds and to appoint a project coordinator who "had tremendous drive and ability with young people and was determined to make the project a success" (Cleveland Police, 1998,

p. 4). More help was also obtained from the staff of a youth service agency.

The core of the project was to be a "positive policing approach toward the youths," who the officers found were not only delinquent but "bored and disillusioned with life" (Cleveland Police, 1998, p. 4). The problem-oriented coalition initiated and spearheaded by the police decided to try a unique response to the problem, in which the offending youths were to be enlisted as active participants. As in Oakland, the individuals who were the source of the problem were thus drafted to be the vehicle to its solution. The youth workers and the police approached the offending delinquents, and they offered them membership in a gang-equivalent organization. As described by the team members,

> Building on the relationship that was starting to develop between the Police and the youth, the Police identified the "potential ringleaders and trouble-makers" and invited them and their friends from the estate to a meeting . . . the Police and Youth Workers listened to the 20 young people and some of the parents who attended. A series of meetings were held and the "Raby Rebels" was formed. It was a group of young people, run by the young people, policed by the young people and organised by them. The first few meetings were undisciplined and would have ended in "free for alls" had it not been for the Youth Workers and Police. Slowly, however, the group learned how to behave so that everyone had their say and progress was made.
>
> The Youth Workers initially put in hours of work putting together a summer programme that the "Raby Rebels" wanted to do. However, gradually the young people were given tasks and responsibilities and had to report back to the meetings.
>
> The "Raby Rebels" formulated a set of rules which included behaviour boundaries while on group activities, as well as while on the estate. Anyone breaching these would be excluded from the group for a period of time. (Cleveland Police, 1998, p. 5)

The previously described transmutation of the young offenders into a prosocial group made a reassuring impression on the housing unit residents. Eventually, the elderly tenants who had been thoroughly intimidated by the youths came to actively lend their support to the project:

> the most significant breakthrough for the Police came on 16th July, 1997. At one of the Raby Rebels' meetings where the youths, some parents, Police Officers and Youth Workers were in attendance, the main complainers arrived. They spoke to the group, explaining their side of things in a positive, not negative way. They offered their support for the group in the form of fund raising so the group would be able to continue after the summer holidays had finished. This signaled the beginning of the new community spirit. (Cleveland Police, 1998, p. 5)

The youths in turn arranged entertainment events for the community, including a street party and a Teddy Bears picnic for the children. Their truancy problem in the schools appeared to have been addressed as a byproduct, making the schools a more enthusiastic part of the project. Finally, the youths with delinquency records largely discontinued offending, and a survey among housing unit residents yielded nondisgruntled responses.

Beyond Problem-Oriented Policing

In considering the status of their completed project the problem-oriented constables and their sergeant concluded that "due to the community involvement it is unlikely that any continued Police effort will be likely, but due to the commitment of local officers monitoring will continue" (Cleveland Police, 1998, p. 9). This statement is revealing: The officers recognized that their catalytic function had been discharged and that success had put them out of business. This left them feeling understandably ambivalent. On the one hand, the goal in the change business is to promote the autonomy of one's clients. On the other hand, one becomes invested in a process that one has nurtured and in the relationships one has developed. An assessment stage mitigates the pains of separation and is part of the problem-oriented process.

Problem-oriented interventions vary in the amount of police involvement they require. In theory, any agency can take the lead in coalition building. The Raby Rebels could thus have originated with the housing complex staff, the mayor's office, a youth service agency, or the schools, even if delinquency reduction were retained as the objective. In the United States, public order-related activities have frequently originated in schools. The initiatives on occasion have followed the same logic as the Raby Rebels Project in that young people have been mobilized. Students have addressed a local delinquency problem in a number of schools by designing and implementing a peer-centered solution.

A Student–Teacher–Police Partnership

One of the best-documented problem-oriented projects in an educational setting is the Charlotte School Safety Project, studied and described by Kenney and Watson (1996). This project was intended to "implement community policing and problem-solving techniques in a high school setting . . . to create an environment in which students, working in cooperation with teachers, administrators and police officers, could identify and attempt to reduce problems of crime, delinquency, and disorder in a Charlotte public high school" (p. 437). The police were involved in the project but were relegated to a supporting role.

According to Kenney and Watson (1996), project details were shaped by teachers, "though the heart of the project required student participation in the problem-solving process" (p. 437). The teachers acted as facilitators, and police largely became legitimators of the activity:

> As the first week of classes got underway, the school's police resource officer attended each of the 11th grade history classes to give a brief presentation on community policing and its relationship to civic responsibility and the problem-solving model that had been added to the course curriculum. Observing that the community policing concept was nearly 4 years under way in Charlotte, the officer advised that his

department was attempting to re-create an earlier, more small-town feeling in the city "by sending police officers out to talk to the public to find out what kinds of concerns they have and what kind of changes they want." Challenging the students to do likewise in their own school, he went on to ask each class to "work together to make your community a better one to be in." (Kenney & Watson, 1996, pp. 444–445)

The police resource officer in the school acted as a consultant to the problem-centered classroom sessions. According to Kenney and Watson (1996), "the police resource officer assigned to the experimental school regularly attended the problem-solving classes and participated as fully as requested" (p. 438). However, Kenney and Watson noted that "although police–student relations appeared strong, we were surprised at how little police involvement was actually required" (p. 438). The police sometimes became an outside resource to the students by supplying materials such as statistical compilations and making themselves available to support solutions the students might devise. Organizationally, the project also enjoyed the backing of the top police administrators, who participated in the planning and request for federal support.

The experiment was based on the proposition that students who have been empowered and enabled to address school-related public disorder problems would do so constructively and effectively. The students were thus accorded a great deal of autonomy. It was assumed that "whatever problems students identified would be pursued; teachers . . . would allow each student group to discover for itself if a particular problem existed and the constraints that might prevent a satisfactory solution" (Kenney & Watson, 1996, p. 445). The students worked in small groups, who reported to their classmates, "after which a problem designated as 'class project' was selected by class vote" (Kenney & Watson, 1996, p. 445).

One hot spot located by the students was the lunchroom, which had been a frequent site of conflict and fighting. The students suspected that some of the procedures and routines followed during mealtimes contributed to the violence by generating frustration and tension. After consultation with lunchroom workers, they suggested solutions involving additional serving lines and an expanded menu.

One of the interesting discoveries that was made by some students was that attendance and tardiness policies that they assumed were unnecessarily strict were welcomed by their peers. They also discovered that they had themselves engaged in behavior that was of concern to other students, "leaving them to conclude that they had, in fact, been part of the problem" (Kenney & Watson, 1996, p. 447).

Another group of students made unsettling discoveries when they "became immersed in the more general problem of teen pregnancy" (Kenney & Watson, 1996, p. 447). In designing a proposed program, the students found that there were issues relating to content and emphasis (sex education versus abstinence) that could not be resolved. Rather than becoming discouraged, the groups of students thrived on the controversy, and "discussions about the significance of social problems and the positive view that 'city hall' can be fought occupied much of this group's remaining class time" (p. 447).

In the outcome study that was reported by Kenney and Watson (1996), fear levels (such as fear of being harmed or bothered) were shown to have declined appreciably in the experimental school, with no declines registered in a control school. Simultaneously,

> the school's administration reported a 29% school wide reduction in incidents requiring student suspension, including 70% fewer "student–student conflict" and 46% fewer "student–teacher conflict" suspensions. Unfortunately, similar disciplinary data were not available from the control school for comparison. (Kenney & Watson, 1996, p. 450)

One benefit of relegating the nomination and studying of problems to those who are close to the problem is that they are familiar with the forces that impinge on the protagonists. Thus, according to Kenney and Watson (1996), "the conflicts that surfaced during this project were related to everyday school interactions" (p. 453). This meant that "as we have often found in other community settings, taking care of the little things will often satisfy the bigger ones" (p. 453).

The Charlotte project is one of a line of experiments extending over several decades, in which schools have attempted to address problems of crime, vandalism, and disorder. The project, however, differs from others in its explicit linkage to the concept of problem-oriented policing. The intervention marks a confluence of two compatible strategies of organizational change. It also illustrates the variety of approaches that are subsumable under problem-oriented policing, including some in which police can take a backseat in interagency coalitions and support the problem-solving efforts of others.

Problem-Solving Activities
as Learning Experiences

Organizational psychologists have long known that learning and organizational change are related to each other and that in the absence of learning opportunities, stultification is likely to occur (Argyris & Schon, 1976). Organizations that do not provide learning experiences for their members are apt to have trouble adapting to changing conditions in turbulent environments. Such organizations are also likely to become hotbeds of routinization and boredom, with consequent lowering of motivation and morale.

There are many ways of fostering learning, but problem-solving carries advantages because (a) it occurs in response to a need or challenge that provides justification to the exercise, (b) it generally starts with brainstorming and unimpeded exploration, (c) but it requires the disciplined collection of information (d) that gives focus to one's thinking, and (e) informs the action implications that one draws from one's review. Once proposals get enacted and implemented, (f) the process further yields experiences that ratify one's inferences or may require their modification.

In practice, it is of course possible for some of these steps to be short-circuited or taken lightly. The Raby Rebels constables, for example, were forced to confess that "the officers identified there was a danger of jumping straight to the response stage before completing thorough analysis. It is also felt it can be difficult evidencing tangible results in the assessment stage" (Cleveland Police, 1998, p. 9).

Although problem-solving often involves formal research, it is not by virtue of this fact an off-putting "academic" modality. In the Safe School Project, problem-solving took place in the classroom, but it was clearly separated from conventional instruction and involved "a task that many students told us was more interesting than they had initially imagined" (Kenny & Watson, 1996, p. 437). Such excitement derives from the fact that problem solving deals with real-life material, has real-life consequences, and focuses on conditions of real people with whom one intersects. In problem solving (unlike academia), living and learning are linked.

The same holds for the contrast between problem solving and standard training, which at best relies on simulation and remote or hypothetical scenarios. Problem solving not only links learning and action but requires a mindful approach to action that is presumptively habit-forming. Members of organizations who are assigned to solve problems not only learn a lot about the problem they are solving but also (a) become sensitive to the existence of other problems, (b) learn to analyze data, and (c) learn to deal with resistances to the implementation of change.

Problem solving hones interpersonal skills. This is so because one cannot address a problem without intersecting with others, whose needs must be accommodated. For one, most problem solving occurs in teams, and one must learn to work with members of one's group. Data collection usually calls for inquiries, such as interviewing that may be different from one's customary approach to the task (such as interrogation by police). Offenders may thus usually come to serve as data sources, with their concerns empathetically responded to by police. Solutions must also be sold, linkages with collaborators must be forged, and partnerships sustained. Finally, diplomacy is required to keep one's show on the road.

The extent to which consultants may be needed in problem-solving efforts varies with the nature and scope of the activity. Where substantial data collection occurs, it is generally helpful to have research assistance, such as that provided to our Oakland officers. Facilitation may also be helpful, both within a group or organization or in relation to external constituencies. (Such assistance ought to be made available rather than imposed. In the Chicago CAPS program, for example, when officers felt overwhelmed by the challenges of running community meetings, they welcomed the contribution of facilitators.)

Supporting Problem-Oriented Activities

Where partnerships of social scientists and organizational problem solvers are forged, they are enriching to both parties. This was intuited by Kurt Lewin, who invented the concept of action research. Lewin has been called the progenitor of social psychology. He was unquestionably the founder of applied social psychology, and action research lies at the heart of this discipline and of applied social science in general. Action research is mostly organizational problem-solving, done by closely collaborating social scientists and members of organizations. The social scientists who become involved in these collaborations are researchers who want to effect social improvements. Their organization partners are practitioners who are sold on the need for valid and reliable documentation.

There are, of course, individuals who may wear both hats, usually interchangeably. This fact has historical precedent. A famous early action researcher attained a doctorate in psychology under Lewin and then headed an innovative pajama factory (Marrow, 1969). Another pioneer (McGregor, 1960) presided over a problem-oriented liberal arts college.

Police do have a widespread reputation for being suspicious of outsiders, which is partly deserved. The stance may have something to do with the fact that police actions have at times been prejudged and unfairly characterized by unfriendly observers. But a measure of defensiveness can be expected in working with any organization, and experience shows that it can usually be surmounted. One reliable ingredient in overcoming resistances and cementing rapport is a willingness to learn and a desire to contribute by both parties. Beyond this, personal relationships are usually forged, which are strengthened by a mutual recognition of interdependence.

It is in the nature of teams that they are more than the sum of their individual contributions. Although roles are separable (into research and action), intimacy breeds cross-fertilization. Satisfactions attained in researcher–practitioner teams derive from the subtle merger and overlap of roles. Academics are liable to describe problem-oriented projects with a proprietary air that reflects their personal investment. Practitioners may come to think and talk about their work in terms contaminated by social science concepts.

There is the joint sense of common cause and shared satisfaction of making a difference. There is the awareness of the campaign jointly waged—often against discouraging odds and inhospitable circumstance. Out of such experiences, emotional links are invariably forged. There is thus little doubt, in retrospect, that the participants in our Oakland Project will recall fondly the words "we'll miss you sons of bitches," commemorating the first phase of the project. No comparable feedback has ever yielded similar fulfillment.

Postscript

This book has focused on the role of participants in problem-oriented policing. We have not dealt with currently evolving developments in the field or with its present status. As noted by John Eck (personal communication, 2003), among others, there is a great deal of ferment and effervescence in the area. As examples, Eck alludes to

> advances in the knowledge base and processes of problem-oriented policing. These include the development of a set of problem-solving awards in the U.S. and Britain, an annual conference in San Diego, problem-specific guides, a framework for the analysis of problems based on Routine Activity Theory . . . [a] Center for Problem Oriented Policing in Madison (with Web site), a step by step guide for problem analysts in the UK on problem solving . . . a classification scheme for problems, the beginning of a theory of problems, and a number of other advances.

Eck (personal communication, 2003) speculated that we may be "on the verge of creating a technology (if not a science) of problem solving." And there is no doubt that many participants in problem-oriented ventures will avail themselves of new developments in technology and science. Other police participants, however, will no doubt continue to operate more informally or intuitively, substituting vigor for rigor, but making useful contributions. As observed by Cordner and Biebel (2003),

> when they do problem solving, [such] officers take a thought-
> ful approach, try to gather some information before pro-
> ceeding, and often implement a multi-pronged response to
> problems. This is better than not thinking, not gathering infor-
> mation, and relying on only one response. Modest though it
> is, problem solving is probably more effective than reactive
> policing. (p. 18)

We have said that problem-oriented efforts must limit their targets to what is possible. A police department cannot reduce poverty but it can persuade a slum landlord to repair his or her building. It can usually not reach drug overlords, but it can get rid of the drug dealers who are making life impossible for the tenants living in an infested housing project. You change what you can and challenge what you cannot.

We have also said that problem-oriented interventions have become linked to community-oriented policing, which must start with where the public is, with its perception of the problem. But it is worth noting that the process of participating in change efforts may well change the public's perception of a problem from one that bureaucracy must solve to one that offers room for participatory action.

It is plausible that grassroots problem solving will not only bring serious thinking to bear on local problems but will also develop understanding, confidence, and competence in the participants in these efforts. This may help counteract the growing apathy, cynicism, and nonparticipation that keeps the consumers of public services from having any real impact on the decisions being made at all levels of government.

I think that it may be particularly fortunate that police departments are now involved in a more self-conscious approach to the enforcement problems that they face. Recent changes in the world have raised questions about whether the effectiveness of a community or of a culture can be enhanced or impaired by the nature of its security arrangements: The less repressive we can be about the business of ensuring our security, the safer the preservation of our culture. Local police have untapped expertise and unquestioned clout that can help modulate unreasonable demands from politicians who may be inspired by unreflective hysteria and paranoid thinking. To this end, problem-oriented analysis may help to define proportionate responses to threats, which can contribute to the survival of enlightened democratic institutions.

Appendix

SESSION RATING FORM

Check (✔) the appropriate box

	Very high	High	Average	Low	Very low
Productivity					
Interest					
Group participation					
My own participation					
Group morale					
My own morale					

CIRCLE THE ADJECTIVES THAT DESCRIBE TODAY'S SESSION:

Academic	Fun	Promising	Instructive
Enjoyable	Torture	Thought-provoking	Bland
Sick	Monotonous	Critical	Silly
Sensible	Relevant	Creative	Helpful
Beautiful	Wasteful	Phony	Informative
Constructive	Pleasant	Puzzling	Frustrating
Challenging	Painful	Aimless	Damaging
Inconclusive	Unfair	Enlightening	Confusing
Slow	Immoral	Great	Encouraging
Purposeful	Subversive	Nonsense	Pointless
Uninformative	Strange	Weakening	
Valuable	Practical	Sane	
Hopeless	Sad	Weird	
Rambling	Honest		

References

Alvarez, L. (2003, October). U.S. gift to Britain: The model of a modern cop. *New York Times.*

Angell, J. E. (1971). Toward an alternative to the classic police organizational arrangements: A democratic model. *Criminology, 19,* 185–206.

Argyris, C. (1957). *Personality and organization.* New York: Harper & Row.

Argyris, C., & Schon, D. (1976). *Organizational learning.* Reading, MA: Addison-Wesley.

Armacost, B. E. (2004). Organizational culture and police misconduct. *George Washington Law Review, 72,* 453–546.

Barclay, D. (1989, April 23). Black Panthers' rise shocked America. *Albany Times Union.*

Bard, M. (1969). Family intervention police teams as a community mental health resource. *Journal of Criminal Law, Criminology and Police Science, 60,* 247–250.

Berman, I. S. (1987). *Police administration and effective reform: Theodore Roosevelt as police commissioner of New York.* New York: Greenwood Press.

Bittner, E. (1967). The police on skid-row: A study of peace keeping. *American Sociological Review, 32,* 699–715.

Bopp, W. J. (1977). *"O.W.": O.W. Wilson and the search for a police profession.* Port Washington, NY: Kennikat Press.

Bowling, B. (1999). Rise and fall of New York murder: Zero tolerance or crack's decline? *British Journal of Criminology, 39,* 531.

Brown, L., & Wycoff, M. A. (1987). Policing Houston: Reducing fear and improving service. *Crime and Delinquency, 33,* 71–89.

Bruni, F. (2003, February 14). Every stone has a story, and graffitisti to tell it. *New York Times.*

Burgreen, R. W. (1989, April 30). Interview. *Law Enforcement News, 15.*

Carr, D. K., & Litman, I. D. (1990). *Excellence in government: Total Quality Management in the 1990s.* Arlington, VA: Coopers & Lybrand.

Clark, M. (1996). A few thoughts on graffiti vandalism in Scottsdale. In *Conference resource book, seventh annual Problem-Oriented Policing Conference* (pp. 567–569). Washington, DC: Police Executive Research Forum.

Cartwright, D., & Zander, A. F. (Eds.). (1968). *Group dynamics: Research and theory* (3rd ed.). New York: Harper & Row.

Cleveland Police, England. (1998). *Baby Rebels Youth Project: Proactively dealing with juvenile crime in a housing project.* Washington, DC: Police Executive Research Council, Submission to Herman Goldstein Award Competition.

Cordner, G. W. (1986). Fear of crime and the police: An evaluation of a fear-reduction strategy. *Journal of Police Science and Administration, 14,* 223–233.

Cordner, G., & Biebel, E. P. (2003, March). *Problem-oriented policing in practice.* Paper presented at the annual meeting of the Academy of Criminal Justice Sciences, Boston.

Couper, D. C., & Lobitz, S. H. (1991). *Quality policing: The Madison experience.* Washington, DC: Police Executive Research Forum.

Cumming, E., Cumming, I., & Edell, L. (1965). Policeman as philosopher, guide and friend. *Social Problems, 12,* 276–286.

Davis, K. C. (1975). *Police discretion.* St. Paul, MN: West.

Deakin, T. J. (1988). *Police professionalism: The renaissance of American law enforcement.* Springfield, IL: Charles C. Thomas.

Deming, S. K. (2004, April 28). New York gospel of policing by data spreads across U.S. *New York Times,* pp. B1, B6.

Dixon, D., & Coffin, P. (1999, December). Zero tolerance policing of illegal drug markets. *Drug and Alcohol Review, 18,* 477.

Dobyns, L., & Crawford-Mason, C. (1991). *Quality or else.* Boston: Houghton-Mifflin.

Duckles, M. M., Duckles, R., & Maccoby, M. (1977). The process of change at Bolivar. *Journal of Applied Behavioral Science, 13,* 387–399.

Eck, J. E., & Maguire, E. (2000). Have changes in policing reduced violent crime? An assessment of the evidence. In A. Blumstein & J. Wallman (Eds.), *The crime drop in America* (pp. 207–265). New York: Cambridge University Press.

Eck, J. E., & Spelman, W. (1987a). *Solving problems: Problem-oriented policing in Newport News.* Washington, DC: Police Executive Research Forum.

Eck, J. E., & Spelman, W. (1987b). Who ya gonna call? The police as problem-busters. *Crime and Delinquency, 33,* 31–52.

Emsley, C. (1983). *Policing and its context, 1750–1870.* London: MacMillan.

Federal Bureau of Investigation. (1976). *Uniform crime reports, 1971–1975.* Washington, DC: U.S. Government Printing Office.

Fontana Police Department. (1998). *"Ten-4": The transient enrichment network: A community collaboration to reduce homelessness.* Fontana, CA: Fontana Police Department.

French, W. L., & Bell, C. H., Jr. (1999). *Organization development: Behavioral science interventions for organization improvement* (6th ed.). Upper Saddle River, NJ: Prentice-Hall.

Gain, C. R. (1972). *The state of the art. (The police: What we know).* Paper presented at California Justice Research Conference, San Francisco.

Geller, W. A., & Toch, H. (1996). *Police violence: Understanding and controlling police abuse of force.* New Haven, CT: Yale University Press.

Gillman, R. D., & Ruiz, J. H. (1996). City of Glendale, Community Police Partnership (COPPS), Proposal for day labor program. In *Conference resource book, seventh annual Problem-Oriented Policing Conference* (pp. 335–366). Washington, DC: Police Executive Research Forum.

Goldstein, H. (1979). Improving policing: A problem-oriented approach. *Crime and Delinquency, 25,* 236–258.

Goldstein, H. (1987). Toward community-oriented policing: Potential, basic requirements and threshold questions. *Crime and Delinquency, 33,* 6–30

Goldstein, H. (1990). *Problem-oriented policing.* New York: McGraw-Hill.

Goldstein, H. (in press). On further developing problem-oriented policing: The most critical need, the major impediments, and a proposal. In J. Knutsson (Ed.), *Mainstreaming problem-oriented policing.* Monsey, NY: Criminal Justice Press.

Goodenough, A. (2001, July 23). School chief resists push to copy police. *New York Times,* pp. B1, B4.

Gootman, E. (2002, September 19). Battling on two fronts in L.I. over immigrant job centers. *New York Times,* p. B5.

Grant, J. D., Grant, J., & Toch, H. (1982). Police–citizen conflict and decisions to arrest. In V. J. Konecni & E. B. Ebbesen (Eds.), *The criminal justice system: Social–psychological analysis* (pp. 133–158). San Francisco: W. H. Freeman.

Graper, E. D. (1969). *American police administration: A handbook on police organization and methods of administration in American cities.* Montclair, NJ: Patterson Smith. (Original work published 1921)

Greene, J. A. (1999, April). Zero tolerance: A case study of police policies and practices in New York City. *Crime and Delinquency, 45,* 171.

Grinc, R. (1994). "Angels in marble": Problems in stimulating community involvement in community policing. *Crime and Delinquency, 40,* 437–468.

Guest, R. H. (1979). Quality of work life—Learning from Tarrytown. *Harvard Business Review, 57,* 76–87.

Hackman, J. R., & Oldham, G. R. (1976). Motivation through design of work: Test of a theory. *Organizational Behavior and Human Performance, 16,* 250–279.

Hackman, J. R., & Oldham, G. R. (1980). *Work redesign.* Reading, MA: Addison-Wesley.

Herzberg, F. (1966). *Work and the nature of man.* Cleveland, OH: World.

Hevesy, D. (1989, August 23). Huey Newton symbolized the rising Black anger of a generation. *New York Times.*

Holyoke Police Department. (1970). *Policy and procedure manual, Model Cities Police Team Project, Holyoke, Massachusetts.* Holyoke, MA: Author.

Kansas City Police Department. (1980). *Response time analysis.* Washington, DC: U.S. Government Printing Office.

Kelling, G. L. (1988). Police and communities: The quiet revolution. *Perspectives on Policing* (No. 1). Washington, DC: National Institute of Justice.

Kelling, G. L., & Kliesmet. R. B. (1996). Police unions, police culture, and police use of force. In W. A. Geller & H. Toch (Eds.), *Police violence: Understanding and controlling police. Use of force* (pp. 191–212). New Haven, CT: Yale University Press.

Kelling, G. L., Pate, T., Dieckman, D., & Brown, C. E. (1974). *The Kansas City Preventive Patrol Experiment: A technical report.* Washington, DC: Police Foundation.

Kelling, G. L., Wasserman, R., & Williams, H. (1988). Police accountability and community policing. In *Perspectives on Policing* (Whole No. 7). Washington, DC: National Institute of Justice.

Kenney, D. J., & Watson, T. S. (1996). Reducing fear in the schools: Managing conflict through student problem solving. *Education and Urban Society, 28,* 436–455.

LeDuff, C. (2002, October 24). Los Angeles police chief faces a huge challenge. *New York Times,* p. A22.

Los Angeles County Sheriff's Department, West Hollywood Station. (1996). Operation Outreach. In *Conference resource book, seventh annual Problem-Oriented Policing Conference* (pp. 557–566). Washington, DC: Police Executive Research Forum.

Louisiana: Firings in crime-rate investigation. (2003, October 24). *New York Times.*

MacNamara, D. E. J. (1977). August Vollmer: The vision of police professionalism. In P. J. Stead (Ed.), *Pioneers in policing* (pp. 178–190). Montclair, NJ: Patterson Smith.

Marrow, A. J. (1969). *The practical theorist: The life and work of Kurt Lewin.* New York: Basic Books.

Marshall, J. (1999). *Zero tolerance policing.* Adelaide: South Australia Office of Crime Statistics.

Maslow, A. H. (1954). *Motivation and personality.* New York: Harper.

Mastrofski, S. D. (1988). Community policing as reform: A cautionary tale. In J. R. Greene & S. D. Mastrofski (Eds.), *Community policing: Rhetoric or reality.* New York: Praeger.

McArdle, A., & Erzen, T. (Eds.). (2001). *Zero tolerance: Quality of life and the new police brutality in New York City.* New York: New York University Press.

McGregor, D. (1944). Conditions of effective leadership in the industrial organization. *Journal of Consulting Psychology, 8,* 55–63.

McGregor, D. (1960). *The human side of enterprise.* New York: McGraw-Hill.

McKinley, J. C. (1989, September 6). Police face drug tests in New York. *New York Times.*

Monkkonen, E. H. (1981). *Police in urban America, 1860–1920.* Cambridge: Cambridge University Press.

Moore, M. H. (2003). Sizing up Compstat: An important administrative innovation in policing. *Criminology and Public Policy, 2,* 469–493.

Muir, W. K. (1977). *Police: Streetcorner politicians.* Chicago: University of Chicago Press.

National Advisory Commission on Civil Disorders. (1968). *Report of the National Advisory Commission on Civil Disorder*. New York: Bantam Books.

National Advisory Commission on Criminal Justice Standards and Goals. (1973). *Police*. Washington, DC: U.S. Government Printing Office.

National Research Council of the National Academies. (2003). *Fairness and effectiveness in policing: The evidence*. Washington, DC: National Academies Press.

New York State Police. (1989). *Mission statement to NYSP members manual and civilian employee manual*. Albany, NY: Author.

New York Times. (1990, September 24).

Northeast Patrol Division Task Force. (1974). *Conflict management: Analysis/ resolution report*. Kansas City, MO: Kansas City Police Department.

O'Halloran, F. (1996). Strategies for graffiti abatement. In *Conference resource book, seventh annual Problem-Oriented Policing Conference* (pp. 557–566). Washington, DC: Police Executive Research Forum.

Ouichi, W. (1981). *Theory Z: How American business can meet the Japanese challenge*. Reading, MA: Addison-Wesley.

Pate, T., McCullough, J. W., Bowers, R. A., & Ferrara, A. (1976). *Kansas City Peer Review Panel: An evaluation report*. Washington, DC: Police Foundation.

Pearlmuter, L. C., & Monty, R. A. (1979). *Choice and perceived control*. Hillsdale, NJ: Erlbaum.

Peters, T. (1988). *Thriving on Chaos: Handbook for a management revolution*. New York: Knopf.

Police Assessment Resource Center. (2003). Oakland PD issues "riders" reform report. *Best Practices Review, 2*, 1.

Police Executive Research Forum. (1989a). Down it comes. *Problem Solving Quarterly, 2*(1), 6.

Police Executive Research Forum. (1990). *The key elements of problem-oriented policing*. Washington, DC: Author.

President's Commission on Law Enforcement and Administration of Justice. (1967a). *The challenge of crime in a free society*. Washington, DC: U.S. Government Printing Office.

President's Commission on Law Enforcement and the Administration of Justice. (1967b). *Task force report: The police*. Washington, DC: U.S. Government Printing Office.

Rashbaum, W. K. (2003, June 20). West side crime statistics were softened, police say. *New York Times*, p. B3.

Reuss-Ianni, E. (1983). *Two cultures of policing: Street cops and management cops*. New Brunswick, NJ: Transaction.

Rodriguez, M. L. (1993). *Together we can: A strategic plan for reinventing the Chicago police department*. Chicago: Chicago Police Department.

Roethlisberger, F. J., & Dickson, W. J. (1961). *Management and the worker*. Cambridge, MA: Harvard University Press.

Rothman, D. J. (1980). *Conscience and convenience: The asylum and its alternatives in progressive America.* Boston: Little, Brown.

Ruiz, J. R. (2002). *Glendale Police Department Labor Day Project.* Glendale, CA: City of Glendale Police Department.

Sadd, S., & Grinc, R. M. (1996). *Implementing challenges in community policing: Innovative neighborhood-oriented policing in eight cities (Research in brief).* Washington, DC: National Institute of Justice.

Sampson, R., & Scott, M. S. (2000). *Tackling crime and other public-safety problems: Case studies in problem solving.* Washington, DC: U.S. Department of Justice, Office of Community Oriented Policing Services.

San Diego Police Department, Mid-City Division. (2000a). Graffiti prevention and suppression. In *Excellence in problem-oriented policing: The 2000 Herman Goldstein Award Winners* (pp. 4–9). Washington, DC: National Institute of Justice.

San Diego Police Department, Mid-City Division. (2000b). Reclassifying a home for people with mental illness. In *Excellence in problem-oriented policing: The 2000 Herman Goldstein Award Winners* (pp. 31–39). Washington, DC: National Institute of Justice.

Sherman, L. W. (1974). The sociology and social reform of the American police: 1950–1973. *Journal of Police Science and Administration, 2,* 255–262.

Sherman, L. W. (1975). Middle management and police democratization: A reply to John E. Angell. *Criminology, 12,* 363–377.

Sherman, L. W., Milton, C. H., & Kelly, T. V. (1973). *Team policing: Seven case studies.* Washington, DC: Police Foundation.

Silverman, E. B. (1999). *NYPD battles crime: Innovative strategies in policing.* Boston: Northeastern University Press.

Skogan, W. G., & Antunes, G. E. (1979). Information, apprehension and deterrence: Exploring the limits of police productivity. *Journal of Criminal Justice, 7,* 217–242.

Skogan, W. G., & Hartnett, S. (1997). *Community policing Chicago style.* New York: Oxford University Press.

Skogan, W. G., Steiner, L., Dubois, J., Gudell, J. E., & Fagan, A. (2002). *Taking stock: Community policing in Chicago.* Washington, DC: National Institute of Justice.

Skolnick, J. H., & Bayley, D. (1986). *The new blue line: Police innovation in six American cities.* New York: Free Press.

Smith, B. (1960). *Police systems in the United States* (2nd rev. ed.). New York: Harper & Row.

St. Louis Police Department. (1970). *The St. Louis Detoxification and Diagnostic Evaluation Center.* Washington, DC: U.S. Government Printing Office.

Swope, C. (1999, September). The Compstat craze. *Governing,* 40–43.

Taft, P. B. (1986). *Fighting fear: The Baltimore County C.O.P.E. Project.* Washington, DC: Police Executive Research Forum.

Taylor, F. W. (1911). *Principles of scientific management*. New York: Harper & Brothers.

Time. (1969, December 19).

Toch, H. (1992). *Violent men: An inquiry into the psychology of violence*. Washington, DC: American Psychological Association.

Toch, H. (1997). The democratization of policing in the U.S., 1895–1973. *Police Forum, 7*.

Toch, H. (2002). *Stress in policing*. Washington, DC: American Psychological Association.

Toch, H., Grant, J. D., & Galvin, R. T. (1975). *Agents of change: A study in police reform*. Cambridge, MA: Schenkman.

Trojanowicz, R. C., & Banas, D. W. (1985). *Job satisfaction: A comparison of foot patrol versus motor patrol officers*. East Lansing, MI: Neighborhood Foot Patrol Center.

Trojanowicz, R., & Bucqueroux, B. (1989). What community policing can do to help. *Footprints, 2*, 1–8.

Trojanowicz, R., & Bucqueroux, B. (1990). *Community policing: A contemporary perspective*. Cincinnati, OH: Anderson.

Union leaders allege fudging of statistics in New York Crime. (2004, March 24). *New York Times*, pp. B1, B3.

Vera Institute of Justice. (1988). *Community Patrol Officer Program: Problem-solving guide*. New York: Vera Institute.

Walker, S. A. (1977). *A critical history of police reform: The emergence of professionalism*. Lexington, MA: Lexington.

Washington Post. (1980, July 25).

Watts, G. (1983). QWL: CWA's position. *QWL Review, 1*(4), 12–14.

Weisburd, D., & McElroy, J. E. (1988). Enacting the CPO role: Findings from the New York City pilot program in community policing. In J. R. Greene & S. D. Mastrofski (Eds.), *Community policing: Rhetoric of reality* (pp. 89–102). New York: Praeger.

Weisburd, D., Mastrofsky, L., McNally, A. M., & Greenspan, R. (2001). *Compstat and organizational change: Findings from a national survey*. Washington, DC: Police Foundation.

Wellins, R. S., Byham, W. C., & Wilson, J. M. (1991). *Empowered teams: Creating self-directed work groups that improve quality, productivity and participation*. San Francisco: Jossey-Bass.

Westley, W. A. (1970). *Violence and the police: A sociological study of law, custom and morality*. Cambridge, MA: MIT Press.

Wilson, J. Q. (1968). *Varieties of police behavior*. Cambridge, MA: Harvard University Press.

Wilson, J. Q., & Kelling, G. L. (1982). The police and neighborhood safety: Broken windows. *Atlantic Monthly, 127*, 29–38.

Wilson, O. W. (1950). *Police administration.* New York: McGraw-Hill.

Wilson, O. W. (1952). *Police planning.* Springfield, IL: C.C. Thomas.

Wiseman, J. P. (1970). *Stations of the lost.* Englewood Cliffs, NJ: Prentice-Hall.

Wycoff, M. A. (1988). The benefits of community policing: Evidence and conjecture. In J. R. Greene & S. D. Mastrofski (Eds.), *Community policing: Rhetoric or reality* (pp. 103–120). New York: Praeger.

Wycoff, M. A., & Skogan, W. K. (1993). *Community policing in Madison: An evaluation of implementation and impact.* Washington, DC: National Institute of Justice.

Index

About the Authors

Hans Toch, PhD, is distinguished professor at the University at Albany of the State University of New York, where he is affiliated with the School of Criminal Justice. He obtained his PhD in social psychology at Princeton University, has taught at Michigan State University and at Harvard University, and, in 1996, served as the Walker–Ames Professor at the University of Washington, Seattle. He is a fellow of both the American Psychological Association (APA) and the American Society of Criminology. In 1996, he acted as president of the American Association of Correctional Psychology. He is a recipient of the Hadley Cantril Memorial Award and, in 2001, of the August Vollmer Award of the American Society of Criminology for outstanding contributions to applied criminology.

His research interests range from mental health problems and the psychology of violence to issues of organizational reform and planned change. His books include *Violent Men* (APA, 1992), *Living in Prison* (APA, 1992), *Mosaic of Despair* (APA, 1992), *The Disturbed Violent Offender* (with Kenneth Adams, APA, 1994), *Police Violence* (with William Geller, 1996), *Corrections: A Humanistic Approach* (1997), *Crime and Punishment* (with Robert Johnson, 2000), *Acting Out* (with Kenneth Adams, APA, 2002), and *Stress in Policing* (APA, 2002).

J. Douglas Grant, PhD, was a graduate of Stanford University and the University of California, Berkeley. He was a faculty member of the Wright Institute, president of the Social Action Research Center, and director of research for the California Department of Corrections. He was project director of the New Careers Development Project and was the co-originator of the Interpersonal Maturity Level Classification Scheme for offenders.

DATE DUE

GAYLORD

PRINTED IN U.S.A.